The First Hundred Years

The First Hundred Years

MaryLou Mahan

Writers Club Press
New York Lincoln Shanghai

The First Hundred Years

Writers Club Press
an imprint of iUniverse, Inc.

For information address:
iUniverse
2021 Pine Lake Road, Suite 100
Lincoln, NE 68512
www.iuniverse.com

ISBN: 0-595-26052-7 (Pbk)
ISBN: 0-595-65509-2 (Cloth)

Printed in the United States of America

How to thank all who helped this book take form?

The Supervisor, Tom Coupart, and the Town Board who are in the process of making history.

Members of the Historical Society, the American Legion, various churches and organizations who either gave me support, gave me information, or cheered me on.

Several friends who shared their knowledge or materials—Betty Smith on the Episcopal Church, Carol Felter on the Female Seminary and so much more, John Nicklin for sharing his family letters, Judy Rappa who helped so much with getting materials to the Southern Ulster Pioneer office as well as getting some of the old newspapers available for perusal, and Craig McKinney, editor of the Southern Ulster Pioneer, who worked with me to get much of these materials out to the public. Others helped in big ways or small—thank you. Seems those who were most willing to share, have the most materials in this book.

Those who allowed an interview and shared so voluminously their experiences and insights—not only did it produce the materials found within, but set aside for each of them a soft spot in my heart that will remain always.

My Family—who suffered through: my fits of anxiety, burned dinners and piles of papers spread over tables, counters, floors, and beds—for so long I hesitate trying to remember.

To all—thank you, thank you, thank you.

CONTENTS

ILLUSTRATIONS

PREFACE

This is a collection of short articles either written by me, compiled by me, or written as a result of some research I was doing. Thus there is quite a bit of citing of others' works. To the best of my ability I gave duly deserved credit to the original authors of the materials. I tried as much as possible to cite enough to give the real flavor of what was written. This therefore becomes more of a collection of stories rather than an actual history.

Why the title, "The First Hundred Years"? I agonized over what to call this collection.

Recently a friend and former classmate of mine, Valeria Dawes Terwilliger had published a book entitled, "The Scrapings of the Pot", a collection of sayings used frequently by her family. I can remember my dad, William Hennekens, saying to me, "Mary Lou, the first hundred years are the hardest". This became the motto whenever any of us chose a task that was difficult or required a lot of time and effort.

The town of Marlborough has basically had four written histories:

1) Benzel in 1857 and only a few pages long.

2) "The History of the Town of Marlborough, Ulster County, New York: From the First Settlement in 1712 by Captain Wm. Bond to 1887", Charles H Cochrane, Poughkeepsie, 1887

3) "History of the Town of Marlborough Ulster County, New York From its Earliest Discovery", C.M. Woolsey, J.B. Lyon Company, Albany, 1908, and

4) "Town of Marlborough Celebration of 350th Hudson—Champlain Anniversary 1609-1959", Will Plank, Marlboro, 1959.

I've relied very heavily on these works as background for the pieces in this book.

"An introduction to a work on local history is apt to be a sort of apology for what the author has left undone, for all history is of necessity incomplete…." Thus begins Charles Cochrane's "History of the Town of Marlborough" published in 1887. How true this is. My original purpose in setting the following in book form was to attempt to pull together a number of articles I had written in the last few years to newspapers, organizations and local and distanced individuals. When one looks at the scope in years, people and experiences of the following materials, especially the interviews, one sees how much of recent history is captured—though, as Cochrane notes, incompletely.

I combed through the materials I had on hand in order to see what best to use. The beginnings went quite well. I picked some of my favorites and decided to include them. Then things started to get more difficult as I began to realize I had much more material than I could use in any one book. Thus it became a task of prioritizing; trying to decide which was more pertinent—the interviews or Governor Dongan; Shad fishing or Bouck White; updates on church histories or the use of the computer. I needed to do a lot of editing out. I decided, primarily to use the reports as originally written. This hopefully will give an idea of the process gone through to get this information "out to the public". There were a number of longer reports that needed a heavy hand in editing i.e. Bouck White.

I have included as many names, places and events as was possible. This is apparent especially in the interviews. In certain cases, a prior history was necessary to make the understanding of the event much clearer, or little or nothing had been written about the subject previously, or the information was not in published form and thus not readily available.

This format causes some problems. The text does not flow as it would in a more standard format. People, dates, places change rapidly from one page to another.

Also, I admit up front, I chose the materials I found most interesting. Another may have chosen differently.

MaryLou Mahan
Marlborough, NY
Oct. 30, 2002

HISTORIES

First Settlers

Of the earliest settlers of this area, not much is known. Their history primarily in the arrowheads, pottery shards, and stone tools found at various spots are our best textbooks to what their lives were like. Unfortunately, not much has been found so the history remains concealed in the mists of time.

A number of years ago, three young teen-age boys became interested in searching for arrowheads, Dennis McCourt, his brother Kevin and Jay Miller. Dennis still has some of the arrowheads they found down by the river. Dennis's prize is a quartz arrowhead which really spurred on the boys, though they never did find another quartz one.

Jay Miller followed his passion to the University of Mexico where he majored in archeology and then went on to Rudgers University where he was awarded his Ph. D. He has since written a number of books about the Native Americans and is considered an expert in the field.

I remember Liz Plank, our first town historian, telling about obsidian. Some obsidian arrowheads had been found in the area (not necessarily Marlborough). Since obsidian is not native to this area but rather the west and southwest US, it was concluded that that was proof of the range of trading that happened among and between the various tribes.

There is no evidence that the Native Americans had villages in the immediate area but they did have trails from the river to the forests to the west. It is supposed that our "Old Indian Road" in Milton was originally an Indian path. There is also the belief that there was an Indian path leading to Lattingtown from the waters' edge near Marlboro and early on there was a path from Gomez's trading post to the river, as well as to the west. It was not unusual for early white settlers to use the Indian paths and eventually wear them into roads.

The Native Americans called the Hudson River "continually flowing water". In our minds eyes, we can easily picture the hills and valleys as "the forest primeval."

Then....on September 1609 Henry Hudson in a race to find a water way to the far east first set anchor in New York Harbor. On the morning of September 12, he started his sail up river. On passing what is now Newburgh and Marlborough he wrote in his log:

> The fifteenth, in the morning, was misty until the sunne arose; then it cleered. So we weighed with the wind at South, and ran up the river twentie leagues, passing by high mountains. Wee had a very good depth, as six, seuen, eight, nine, twelue, and thirteen fathoms, and great store of salmons in the riuer.... At night we came to other mountains which lie from the riuer's side. There wee fovnd very louing people and very old men; where we were well vsed. Our boat went to fish, and caught great store of very good fish.

When Hudson finally realized the river was not a waterway through to the west, he turned around and on his return trip down the river wrote:

> The people of the Countrey came aboord vs, and brought some small skinnes with them, which we bought for kniues and trifles. This a very pleasant place to build a towne on.... The people brought a stone aboord like to emery (a stone used by glasiers to cut glasse); it would cut iron or steele. Yet being bruised small, and

water put to it, it made a colour like blacke lead glistening; it is also good for painters' colours.

Apparently the Native Americans living in the Marlborough area were generally peaceful. There are no accounts of Indian raids or Indian attacks on any white settlements in the immediate area of Marlborough. This may, in part, be due to New Paltz and Newburgh both being settled prior to Marlborough.

Of course, there are many stories of "Dans Kammer", the devil's dance chamber. Dans Kammer, just to the south of Marlborough apparently was a spot where Indians held meetings prior to setting out on a hunt or, more importantly, before going to war. It is probable it was the meeting spot for several clans if not tribes of Indians.

One can imagine with the surrounding area pitch black and the night lit only with the wildly flickering camp fires, the painted bodies of the Indians dancing and gyrating, with their shadows larger than life, being an ocean away from home and security, the early voyagers to the new world must have found it especially frightening. It is here that one finds the early diary notation about the Indians dancing in the "devil's dance chamber.

Soon you will see an overhead conveyor which extends over the railroad tracks. On occasion you will see a barge moored here to receive crushed rock from inland. The William Wade chart shows this spot to be the location of a ferry slip—probably connecting with New Hamburg and possibly Camelot to the north. In very early times before the white man, Indians had paths from here which led inland to a maze of trails. One followed a stream inland about a mile to a highway which we now call 9W. It was along this stream, called Jew's Brook", that a Spanish Jew named Moses Louis Gomez established a trading post in 1714.

(From "Boating on the Hudson", APRIL 1996, P 32 by
Norman Tardiff)
Along with the wildness, the area also has a special charm.

From the Hudson diary above, for those of us who love the Hudson
Valley, the words ring loud and true:

This a very pleasant place to build a towne on.

I love the following description of some of the magic that keeps us
bound to the beautiful Hudson.

Young Peter Kalm, sensitive Swedish naturalist, on an
American journey saw fireflies invade the dusk…and
once on a warm June night he lay on the deck of a packet
sloop anchored just above "Danskammer" to see swarms
of the little flying lamps descend upon the rigging, making each rope into a shimmering chain of light.
(From "The Hudson", Carl Carmer, 1939, p156)

There has been some concern in recent years, especially in northern
New York State, regarding the Native American claims to land long
claimed by the white man.

          *   *   *

July 17, 2000
Mr. Craig McKinney
Southern Ulster Pioneer

Dear Craig,

Apparently (as is usual), you've created quite a stir with your stories
about possible claims by Native Americans against the land owners in
Marlboro .

Please tell our folks in Marlborough not to fear—Woolsey has already covered that story. Have taken the liberty to attach some documentation as well as an article in a local newspaper of a few years ago.

It looks like it's a long stretch of the imagination to visualize a casino on Main Street in Marlborough.

Trust this clears some of the dust.

Dongan's Purchase

There is no record that any white man set foot in what is now the Town of Marlborough previous to 1684. By tradition it is claimed that previous to the time when the Twelve Patentees (New Paltz) acquired title to their lands known as the Paltz Patent, from the Indians in 1677, they had visited the country here, but had been deterred from settlement by the ruggedness and barrenness of the soil. No effort was made to obtain possession of the land at Quassaick, now Newburgh, and vicinity from the Indians until 1684, when Governor Dongan bought of Mangennett, Tsema, Keghgekapowell, alias Joghem, who claimed to be the "native proprietors and principal owners" of the lands mentioned in the deed, "with the consent of Pemeranaghin, chief sachem of Esopus Indians" and other Indians named, "all that tract and parcel of land situate, lying and being upon the west side of Hudson's River, beginning from the south side of the land called the Paltz, and extending thence southerly along the said river to the lands belonging to the Indians at the Murderer's Kill (now Moodney Creek), and extending westward to the foot of the High hills called Pit-kis-ka-ker and Aia-skawosting." This tract ran from the Paltz purchase, on the north, to Murderer's Creek (now Moodney Creek), on the south, and bounded on the northwest and west by the Shawangunk mountains until a point was reached from which a due east and west line would strike the mouth of Murder's Creek. For this immense tract Governor Dongan paid "the sum of ninety pounds and eleven shillings" in the following articles, viz.: "10 fathoms blue duffels, 10 fathoms red duffels, 200 fathoms white wampum, 10 fathoms stroudwater, (red cloth,) 10 fathoms blue cloth, 10 blankets, 10 guns, 10 kettles, 10 duffel coats, 10 drawing knives, 10 shirts, 10 tobacco boxes, 10 children's shirts, 10 pairs of hose, 10 pairs of shoes, 50 lbs. powder, 50 bars of lead, 10 cutlasses, 10 hatchets, 10 scissors, 10 tobacco tongues, 100 flints, 2 rolls tobacco, 20 gallons of rum, 2 vats of strong beer, and 1 barrel of cider." These lands were relinquished, and the Indians residing thereon united with Maringoman at his castle on Murderer's Creek, about eight miles from its confluence with the Hudson.

From Woolsey

Dongan was governor from 1672 to 1688. He is remembered for creating a colonial assembly that proclaimed religious freedom, the right to vote, trial by jury and no taxation without representation.

England's James II didn't like Dongan's "liberalism" and appointed a replacement. It was assumed for some time that the only physical presence in New York State of Dongan was a plaque in a New York City Catholic Church. It was discovered there is a statue of Dongan at the corners of Mill and North Clover streets in Poughkeepsie. Franklin Roosevelt dedicated it in 1930.

Thus we see that the area encompassing Marlborough was indeed bought from the Indians—I make no claim as to the fairness of the transaction.

The Evans Patent

This land, purchased by Gov. Dongan, was conveyed by Gov. Benjamin Fletcher, his successor, in a patent to Capt. John Evans, dated September 12, 1694, and was called the Manor of Fletcherdom. The patent, however, was in 1699, annulled by an act of the Colonial Assembly, and the land reverted to the Crown. It was claimed that while these lands were in the possession of Evans, no settlements were made, except one by a family near Murderer's Creek, but by his petition it appears that he had planted several families of Scotch and Irish on the lands and had disbursed a large sum of money in clearing and improving the same, and it is quite certain that Dennis Relje (Relyea), or as he was afterwards called "Old Dennis" was settled on the stream that is now called the Old Man's Kill at the present village of Marlborough soon after Evans got the patent. He was the first settler of the town of whom we have any knowledge; and the stream or kill there was called after him. We find it so called in the year 1697.

(Woolsey P. 18 &19)

*   *   *

From a report sent in to the Journal

To: Meg Downey, Millennium Editor
    Poughkeepsie Journal
    newsroom@poughkee.gannett.com

Name of community: <u>Marlborough</u>

Date Founded: 1694   Date incorporated as a municipality:
<u>1788</u>
Population in 1900:   <u>3978</u>   Population today   <u>7430</u>

Origin of name:

The town of Marlborough was named after John Churchill, the fighting Duke of Marlborough who won the great battle of Blenheim in 1703.

Villages, hamlets or neighborhoods:

Marlboro was once an incorporated village (1906-1922) but now with Milton and Lattingtown form the hamlets within the town of Marlborough. There is also a distinct area known as the "Bailey Gap" area of town.

Well-known residents, past and present, and their significance:

Too numerous to name them all but for starters—

(Old Man) Dennis Relyea—known as the first settler in Marlborough. His home was on a stream that still bears the name of "Old Man's Creek".

Captain William Bond—one of the first settlers—his daughter, Sukie, ran his farm when he was off to sea. Both buried on their land.

Edward Hallock—sailed with his wife and their twelve children in an open boat between Christmas and New Years' day to "Founder's Rock" in Milton. He and his family moved in with his son-in-law, John Young, and the fifteen of them spent the winter in a one room cabin.

Isaac Hill—an early advocate for the Farmers' Turnpike (Milton Turnpike) which opened more westerly sections to the river trade.

"The Fighting Quakers"—two brothers, John T and Edward Ketcham who, though Quakers, were that opposed to slavery that they both fought and died in the Civil War.

John Burroughs, the naturalist, taught in Marlborough during his early adulthood.

Dard Hunter—who was and is the world's authority on hand made paper.

Frederick W Goudy—the world famous type designer.

Father Devine—in the 1930's set up a "heaven" at Elverhoj, the art colony.

George Innis—landscape painter of the Hudson River School lived in Milton. His paintings hang in the Metropolitan Museum of Art in New York City.

Raphael A Weed—an artist in the early 1900's lived at "Java Head" in Milton.

James Scott—came to the Elverhoj Art Colony and became a well known painter, etcher and jewelry maker.

Kirsten Scott—wife of James was an accomplished pianist.

Grace Hallock—a professional writer, especially of children's books.

Mary Hallock Foote—well known writer and illustrator was born in Milton.

Lemuel Wilmarth—a teacher of well known artists and one of the founders of the Art League owned a home in Marlborough.

Alfred Maurer—known as the "Father of Modernism" in American painting used to board at Shady Brook Farm, owned by the Caywood's, just south of the hamlet of Marlboro.

Charles Bouck White—founder of "The Church of the Social Revolution" was tarred and feathered in the 1920's by some men folks in Marlboro for supposedly mistreating his young French bride. Others who knew him said they doubted the mistreating as he was an honest, peaceful man.

Margaret Sanger—of Planned Parenthood fame also spent some time in Marlboro where her husband built a small cottage in the woods.

Tony Canzonari, the World Champion Boxer, set up a training camp for himself near Lattingtown.

Famous structure or place and what it's known for:

(The Gomez Mill House is not in the town of Marlborough—though there has been a close association historically—this should be included)

Lewis DuBois—hero of the Revolutionary War mapped out the hamlet of Marlboro. In 1757 he built the house known as "Maple Grove" where Benedict Arnold was "read out" of the Masons. The house was fired upon by General Vaughan sailing up the river to burn Kingston.

Capt. Anning Smith—was another Revolutionary hero. His house is also still standing. He built and operated the sloop "Sally" from the dock he built in Milton.

James Birdsall—a simple Quaker in 1797 built the only house in the Town of Marlborough that is on the National Historic Register.

The Farmers' Hotel—"was erected by Lewis Mapes about 1827-28." The present "Raccoon Saloon" known for "The Best Burgers in the Hudson Valley" and a convivial atmosphere.

The Lattingtown School—built 1877—last of the old school houses still in use after centralization in 1935.

Businesses and industries in the past:

Thomas Powell—ship owner built a dock at Milton—his wife was Mary Powell, after whom the river's fastest and most famous steamer (often referred to as the "Queen of the Hudson") was named.

John Buckley manufactured broadcloth. He did carding and spinning and later added looms and engaged in making cloth.—Circa 1822

A Shoddy mill (made blankets) was operated by Sheard & Gibson—circa 1875.

An early paper mill was owned by David Munn.

The Whitney basket factory began in Milton in 1853. It was moved to Dock road in Marlboro in 1876. It was 160 feet long by 42 feet and three stories high. Square quart baskets were a principal product. Several millions of baskets were made each year. It was reported that logs came in in the morning and baskets were packed at night. The factory burned down in 1898.

Wright and Carpenter ran a button factory circa 1900. The buttons were made from freshwater mussel shells imported from the Mississippi.

In the 1880's and 90's a roller skating rink was operated in the "Rink Building"—present day Carmen's Kitchens.

George Badner gets the credit for providing the first electricity within the town. (Rate was $1 for residential service).

J M Hepworth, a pioneer in Cold Storage built his original plant in 1924.

Joseph Greaves—noted manufacturer of material dyes in the town. His dyes were world famous and his formula was kept a strict secret.

W Y Velie—primary organizer of the Hudson River Fruit Exchange in 1912. It marketed fresh fruits and operated cherry pitting and currant freezing plants. In 1936 the organization sold the entire grape crops from 189 farms to fill orders for jelly and juice makers and three wineries.

At one time summer boarding houses were very prevalent in the town.

Businesses and industries today:

Agriculture is still our largest business and we are proud of the many fine, family owned fruit farms in the town. A number of these farms go back several generations in the same family.

The associated business of cold storage is important as are several farm markets that dot Route 9W.

Ralph C Herman has a heavy equipment sales business.

In the village of Marlboro is Carmen's Kitchen Cabinets.

Chelsea Modular Homes has a large plant on 9W in Marlboro.

The Brooklyn Bottling Company has a large plant in Milton.

There are a number of restaurants, taverns, grocery and other stores as well as a good number of beauticians.

There are several nursery schools in the area.

Local excavators, contractors and landscapers can clear, build and enhance any property for the owners.

Fred Bilyou still fishes for Shad in the Hudson each Spring and has Shad and roe for sale during the season.

There are a number of farms selling Christmas trees.

Significant ethnic groups and when they first arrived:

The town was first settled by primarily English, though Lewis DuBois was French Huguenot from New Paltz and Michael Wygant was one of the early German Palentine settlers from Newburgh. There were a number of slaves in the town from the beginnings some of whom were manumitted at an early date. Several Marlborough Black families can trace their ancestry to Marlborough's earliest days.

During the large migrations from Ireland and Germany to the U S in the mid 1800's, Marlborough had an influx from these ethnic groups. In the late 1800's and early 1900's Italians were attracted to Marlborough by the rolling hills and farmland reminiscent of their homeland. Many bought small farms and set down their roots in Marlborough.

In the 1930's and 1940's the fruit industry in Marlborough required migrant workers especially during the harvest season. A number of these Black families joined their longer established counterparts.

Big historic moment:

Marlborough likes to celebrate!!! in 1912 during "Old Home Week" Governor Alfred E Smith and Judge Alton B. Parker, one time Democratic candidate for president, were guests of honor. Over 2000 people gathered just north of the hamlet of Marlboro and listened to speeches and enjoyed baseball games and other contests.

Lattingtown was at the start of the 1800's not only "the center of business activity, but of fun and frolic. There was frequently horse racing, often pugilistic encounters, dances and big Fourth of July celebrations when a Revolutionary cannon was fired annually."

(NB To quote a passage from Plank—he says it so well!!) "They Liked Their Liquor Then

There was a far greater degree of intemperance in the town during the first quarter of the last century than there has been since. Perhaps it was because so much of the product of local apple orchards went into hard cider or applejack, or perhaps it was the low price of whiskey—in many cases three cents a glass. There were far more taverns and many grocery stores sold liquor. Almost everybody carried a bottle, even many of the ministers, and it wasn't as a precaution for snake bites. So many drunkards created alarm among the residents and about 1825 pledges to abstain from whiskey were circulated. In 1834 a temperance institution was organized in every district of the town. It seemed to be necessary for so many taverns were liquor shops, having no other accommodations."

Marlborough also had large celebrations for 1959—the 350th Hudson—Champlain Anniversary, 1976—our national bicentennial and in 1988—our town's bicentennial.

*   *   *

Another Request for a Short History

The Town of Marlborough, Ulster County, New York, is located on the west side of the Hudson River, about mid-way between New York City and Albany. The township consists of the hamlets of Marlboro and Milton, and the neighborhoods of Lattingtown and part of Baileys' Gap, where the towns of Marlborough, Lloyd, and Plattekill meet.

Part of the Dongan Purchase, the area bought by the colonial governor Thomas Dongan from the Esopus Indians on Oct. 25, 1684, these lands were granted to Capt. Evans. This grant was later rescinded, but not before Dennis Relje (now spelled Relyea), settled on Old Man's Creek about 1695.

In 1743 the Precinct of New Marlborough, as the Town of Marlborough was originally called, was established by the Provincial Assembly of New York. The town was named after the famous British general John Churchill, First Duke of Marlborough. As originally established, the town included what are now the towns of Marlborough, Plattekill, Newburgh and New Windsor. An Act of Assembly in 1762 split away what are now Newburgh and New Windsor to form a separate precinct. The Town of Plattekill was formed from Marlborough in 1800.

During the Revolutionary War, the town had both Tories and patriots among its inhabitants. Col. Lewis DuBois led a contingent that marched with Gen. Montgomery's foray into Canada. His house is still standing on 9W just north of Marlboro village. Anning Smith, a patriot, lived in the Milton section of the town. Both his house and Lewis DuBois's house were fired upon by Vaughn on his sail up the Hudson to burn Kingston.

Earlier settlers began burying their dead in a field adjoining an old Indian burying ground on his property. His house still stands as well as the cemetery. Some two hundred and fifty men from Marlborough signed the pledge of fealty to the Continental Congress. The Lewises were patriots during the Revolutionary days, and were on the Committee of Safety. George Washington, according to an old tradition, stopped at the Lewises' Inn. Nathaniel Hallock ran a mill, on the property that is now the Cluett Schantz town park. The mill ground grain used by both the Colonials and the British.

In 1778 the precinct became a town. Several docks lined the Hudson River waterfront along an approximately eight mile stretch. The Woods conducted a boat building business at Milton. The famous "Mary Powell" docked at the Milton dock and many boats were filled with the fruit from Marlborough's productive farmland for voyage to New York City.

The area has long been noted for the excellent fruit grown on its many family owned farms. Marlborough is noted as the birthplace of the Antwerp raspberry. In the early and mid 1900's many cold storage plants were built to store and package the fruit.

Some of the Friends in the Milton section took part in the "Underground Railroad" following the passage of the Fugitive Slave Law. Frederick Douglas was a guest at one time. It is understandable that, in light of the Friends' strong feelings about slavery, and , in spite of their peaceful ways, several of the young men of the area joined in the fight to end slavery. Three are buried in the Friends' Cemetery in Milton.

Members of the community were also active in the Woman's Rights movement. Susan B. Anthony and Lucretia Mott wrote letters to or about Sarah Hull Hallock, who attended one of the early national meetings. Sarah Hull Hallock, through her will established the Library in Milton named for her.

Marlborough has also been home to a number of writers and artists. Among the writers are Tristrom Coffin ("Lost Goldmine of the Hudson"), Mary Hallock ("A Victorian Gentlewoman in the Far West"), and Grace Taber Hallock. George Innis, whose works hang in the Metropolitan Museum of Art in New York City, was a descendant of Anning Smith and had a studio in Milton. James Scott of Milton was also well known as was his wife, Kirsten Scott, a pianist. Frederick Goudy, THE name in type, lived in Marlboro and had a small printing press set up there. Dard Hunter, THE name in hand-made paper also was part of the Marlboro community. The Elverhoj Art Colony, run during the 19 teens and 20's by Anders Anderson, was at the foot of Old Indian Road in Milton. Elverhoj later became a summer resort for Father DeVine and his followers. Most outdoor scenes for the film "The Fugitive Kind", were shot in Milton with many townspeople taking minor parts in the film.

Marlborough cherishes its vibrant history and pastoral setting. While moving into the new millennium with alacrity and the influx of many new people, the town is striving to remain true to its past.

*   *   *

There have been a number of queries regarding how Marlborough got its name!

January 10, 1997
Echo Scott
1004 1/2 Third Street
Brilliant, OH 43913

Dear Echo,

What a lovely name.

You wrote recently inquiring about how our town, Marlborough, got its name.

There have been three books written on the history of Marlborough. The latest was written by Will Plank in 1959. In his book, Mr. Plank states:

> Town Named After Duke of Marlborough.
>
> Marlborough gets its name of course from John Churchill, the fighting Duke of Marlborough, who fighting for the British, allied with the Dutch, won the great battles of Blenheim, 1703, Ramillies, 1706 and Oudenarde, 1708, which broke the power of the French and Louis XIV and won the eternal gratitude of the two nations. This but a few short years after Britons and

Dutch had been at war and the latter lost New Amsterdam and all upstate New York as it became known immediately after.

In the town history written in 1908 C. M. Woolsey writes:
How the Town Derived Its Name.

Marlborough was so named after John Churchill, Duke of Marlborough, the greatest and most successful general in English history. He was born at Ashe, in Devonshire, England, in 1650.... He was commissioned as ensign in the guards at sixteen. He was at the battle of Tangier and in engagements with the Moors; on his return to England he became captain. His further advancement was promoted by his comely person and prepossessing manners, his own merit, and the influence of his sister, Arabella, mistress of the Duke of York. She was the mother of the celebrated Duke of Berwick. In the campaign from 1672 to 1677 his (Marlborough's) courage and ability gained him the praise and influence of the celebrated Tureene. His prosperity was still further secured by his marriage with Sarah Jennings, a lady of talent, imperious disposition, and beauty, and one of the Maids of Honor to the Princess Anna.... When King James came to the throne, he (Marlborough) was made a Peer, and a general in the army.... The same year he won the battle of Walcourt over the French, and became the head of the army. He had many successes, and rose to the position of the Duke of Marlborough. In 1704 the Duke led the allied armies into Germany, and with Prince Eugene of Savoy, stormed the French and Bavarian lines at Danauwörth and overthrew their armies in the great and decisive battle of Blenheim, in recognition of which the Parliament and the Queen caused Blenheim palace to be built. In 1705 Marlborough was made a Prince of the Empire. In 1708 he won the battle at Oudenorde which resulted in the total defeat of the French....It would fill a book to tell of his exploits. He brought great honor and renown to the English nation, and in recognition of his great services Blenheim castle was presented to him, and has ever since remained the estate of his descendants, the subsequent Dukes of Marlborough.

He was a great man in many ways, but all his descendants, the subsequent Dukes of Marlborough, have accomplished little but to marry rich American wives, who were fools enough to exchange great riches for empty titles...

(NB Woolsey lived and wrote before Winston Churchill came to power in England. I suspect Churchill's role in England as well as in the world would have changed Woolsey's words here—MLM)

The Iron Duke, as he was called, rose from small beginnings, with little education, to be the greatest general of his age. He died in 1722, idolized by all the English people.

The ancestors of many of our first settlers were soldiers under the Duke, and had marched with him through many of the countries of Europe, and had been participants in his great campaigns and battles and victories. In their childhood, in their native land and around the firesides of their forefathers it was told to them in song and story of the great deeds of the Iron Duke and of his men....Thus it was quite natural that our English ancestors would have named the

Presbyterian society, the precinct, and afterward the town, after him.

The oldest history of Marlborough was written in 1887 by Charles H. Cochrane. In his history he merely says, "Marlborough derives its name from John Churchill, the famous English general, Duke of Marlborough, born in 1650, died in 1722".

*   *   *

Thus one can see that Marlborough having been settled by mostly English in the early 1700's and that being the time of the Duke of Marlborough's greatest glory, it was fitting that Marlborough thusly acquired its name (along with Marlborough—MA, CT, VT, NJ etc., etc., etc.)

As was indicated above, it is most probable that Dennis Relyea was the first white inhabitant of Marlborough circa 1695. It was then a number of years before any other white man settled in the town. The census of the Precincts of Highlands (which included Newburgh, New Windsor, Marlborough and Plattekill) is as follows:

Peter Macgregory
Swerver
William Southerland
Michel Wynant
Burger Mynderts
Jacob Weaver
Peter Laros
Johannis Vischer
Andries Volck
Pieter Jansen
Allexander Griges

Isaac Lefevre
Gorge Lockstee
Michiel DeSchrynwercker
Daniel the Jermain
Henry Titso
William Elsworth
Dennis Relje
Christian Hennicke

I do not know where Dennis Relje was living at that time.

England was anxious to have the land settled and to have taxes coming in from the colonies in order to help defray the costs of protecting the colonies.

The Patent Process

It was usual for rather wealthy and politically knowledgeable men to petition the sovereign for a patent for the land. If this was looked on favorably, a surveyor was sent to survey the land. After the land was surveyed, the sovereign would award a patent indicating how many acres and the borders. If one can imagine trying to measure land completely in the wilderness with the crude instruments in their possession, one easily comes to the realization that the surveys were not always completely accurate. The ruling monarch would then issue a Patent indicating the taxes to be paid. Usually the crown kept for itself all minerals and trees over a certain girth a few feet up the trunk from the roots. Those trees were reserved for use as masts on the royal ships. England at this time didn't have the supply of timber it required for the masts.

There was also the caveat that the land had to be populated within a certain period of time, or the land would revert to the crown. England had previously taken the lands from the Dutch and was worried about the French to the north. A populated land was less likely to be overtaken by enemy troops. And…as the land was peopled, the land value increased, thus the taxes could be raised.

The original Patent owners usually acquired the land as an investment, and it was unusual for any of them to live on their patents. Indeed several (i.e. Harrison) had several patents and could not reside on all of them. The original Patentees then split their holdings and sold off portions—not unlike land developers today.

The Royal Treatment

Those of us who were born in the U. S. or in other lands without sovereigns may sometimes wonder about what life "Under the rule of Royalty" may have been like. We get a brief glimpse of this from some of the early land records of the town of Marlborough.

Some carry very brief introductions: 1709 From Queen Anne to John Barbarie 2000 Acres—"Anne by the Grace of God, of Great Britten, France and Ireland. Queene Defender of Faith, by the Governor of the Province to John Barbarie…"

Others are quite a bit more flowery: (This is a sale after the original Patent) Jun 14, 1716 (Land Papers 11/P179) From Archibald Kennedy To Lewis Gomez 1200A "This indenture made this 26th day of June in the 2nd year of the reign of our sovereign Lord George, by the grace of God, King of Great Britain, France and Ireland, defender of the faith AD 1716 between Archibald Kennedy of the city of New York Gent and Elizabeth, his wife, of the one part and Lewis Gomez of the same city, merchant of the other part. Whereas our said most gracious sovereign Lord King George by Letters Patent under the seal of the province of

New York bearing date the 11th day of August in the year of our Lord Christ 1715 did grant, ratify, and confirm unto the said Archibald Kennedy and to his heirs and assigns forever…" And then there's one of my favorites—does it seem a little curt? The &c is what appeals to me. Jun 12, 1710 From Queen Anne to Capt. William Bond 600 Acres "Anne, by the grace of God, quene of Great Britain, France and Ireland, defender of the faith &c., to all whom these presents shall come, or may in any wise concern, greeting: Whereas, our loving subject, William Bond, by his humble petition presented to our trusty and well beloved Robert Hunter, Esquire, Captain Generall and Governour-in-chief of our province of New York and territory depending thereon in America, and Vic Admirall of the same in Council hath prayed our Grant and confirmation of a certain tract of Land in the County of Ulster, being part of the Land formerly granted to Captain John Evans, now vacated and reserved:…"

However, it was not only the Royalty who got the royal treatment—see this for the governor of New York and….(This is a petition for a Patent)Jun 6, 1712 (Land Papers 5/P106) From William Bond to Robert Hunter 600A To his excellency Robert Hunter, Esq., Capt. General and Governor in chief in and over her Petition Majesty's province of New York, New Jersey and territories depending thereon in America and Vice Admiral of the same in Council The Humbly Petition of William Bond…"

And here are accolades for King George II, Governor George Clinton as well as "our beloved subject, George Harrison". 1750 From King George II To George Harrison, "George the Second, by the Grace of God, of Great Britten, France and Ireland, King and Defender of the Faith…To all to whom these presents shall come greeting: Whereas our beloved subject, George Harrison, did by his humble petition presented to our trusty and well beloved George Clinton, Captain General, Governor in Chief of our Province of New York and Territories, thereupon depending in America; Vice-admiral of the same and Admiral of the white squadron of our fleet.... Granted by patent 2000 acres to George Harrison in three tracts..."

All of these Patents happened only after "humble petitions" that in some cases spanned several years. The petition for a Patent was made, passed on to the proper authorities, an order was given to survey the land, a report and survey from the appointed surveyor was presented to the proper authorities and then, only in some cases, was a Patent granted. The original Patents carried the wax seal of the reigning patron. The original Patent for the Bond Patent is available for viewing at the Senate Museum in Kingston. Please call before visiting to insure its accessibility.

Marlborough Patents

The Patents and the year they were awarded are as follows:

Mar 24, 1709   LP7-P44   Queen Anne to John Barbarie, 2000 Acres.

> Anne by the Grace of God, of Great Britten, France and Ireland. Queene Defender of Faith, by the Governor of the Province to John Barbarie. Paying therefore yearly and every year from thence forth at our Custom House in the City of New York to our collector or receiver general, then for ye time being at or upon ye First day of St. Michael, the Archangel (commonly called Michalmas Day), the rent or sum of two shillings and six pence for every 100 acres of land and within the space of three years, clear and make improvements of three acres of

land at the least for every 50 acres, and if not done to revert back.

Beginning on ye West side of Hudson's River at the S bounde of ye Paltz Patent & runs along Hudson's River on a strait line S 100 chains; thence into ye woods N 61° W 182 chains; thence in ye rear N 22° E 120 chains to the limits of ye Paltz & so by the said limits S 55° E 184 chains to Hudson's River where it first begun—containing 2,000A

From "Biographical Sketches—Old New York Families"—p. 6

In 1709 and 1710 he obtained patents for 4,000 acres of land in Ulster County (John Barbarie)

Will dated 12/27/1727 proved 5/20/1728

It seems he had 2 sons—Peter, who died in his father's lifetime, and John.

To John, the son of Peter, he left 1/2 of a tract of land in NJ.

To his granddaughter, Frances, he left a tract of 2,000A on the Palts Creek in Ulster Co and

to his granddaughter, Elizabeth, daughter of Peter, the other tract on Juffrou's Hook, in the same county, on condition, however, that Denis Reilly and his wife were to live in the house at Juffrou's Hook, and have 100 acres of the land during their joint lives, subject to a rent of "a couple of hens."

The following advertisement of part of his real estate appeared in the NY Gazette of 3/24/1745-6 and of the 18th Feb. "Also one other tract in Ulster County of 2000A bounded on Yeafrow's Hook and extending southerly along said river to the land belonging to Mrs. Bond (NB Miss

Bond meaning Sukie—MLM) also called Barberie's Land; on this tract a good stream of water for a mill. Whoever inclines to purchase said land may apply to Mrs. Elizabeth Barberie, at the house of John Moore, of New York, merchant.

The Barbarie Patent covers the northeast corner of the town.

The bottom half of the Barbarie Patent—roughly 1000 acres eventually fell into the hands of the Smiths.

Anne (House of Stuart) was Queen of England and Great Britain from 1702 to 1714 covering the Patents granted to Barbarie (1709), Bond (1710), and Griggs & Graham (1712)

Jun 12, 1710 Queen Anne granted a patent to William Bond 600 acres. William also owned a patent in Plattekill. William granted the land to his daughter, Susanna (Sukie). Sukie granted parts of the grant to William Wygant (100 acres) , Jurie Mackey (100 acres), Jesse Hallock and the remainder to James Hunter (a mulatto).

The Griggs and Graham Patent eventually became the property of Lewis DuBois—all 600 acres. Lewis intended to split his land in half and leave half to each of his sons, Lewis Jr. and Wilhelmus. Unfortunately Wilhelmus died early. Lewis therefore left the half that would have gone to Wilhelmus to Wilhelmus's three sons (Nathaniel, Cornelius and John) and son-in-law (John W. Wygant). This patent included what is now the hamlet of Marlboro. Indeed Lewis had made up a map that pretty much defines the hamlet as it appears today. An interesting aside is that Lewis originally planned the triangle between King Street, Western Avenue and 9W to be a park.

George I (House of Hanover) was King from 1714 to 1727. The Patents granted by George I in Marlborough were the Lewis Morris & Co. Patent (called the Seven Patentees as there were seven original owners) granted in 1714 and the Kennedy Patent granted in 1715.

The Lewis Morris & Co. Patent stretched along the center of the town on both sides of Lattingtown Road. This ran from the Milton Turnpike down to the Orange County border. It totaled 3,600 acres. This land was carved into seven pieces, each of the main figures acquiring about 500 acres.

The Kennedy Patent was for 2,000 acres—but was in two pieces. The largest piece was 1200 acres on the south east corner of town. This began at what is now Bloom Street and ran south to the Orange County border. This land then was sold off to Francis Purdy and George Merritt.

The 800 acre parcel fell between the Bond Patent and the Griggs and Graham Patent on the river—between Milton and Marlboro. This was possessed at an early time by Richard Woolsey who disposed of it in four pieces. Three pieces were sold to Thomas Knowlton, Richard Harcourt, and Edward Hallock. The fourth quarter was split among his sons Benjamin, John and Henry.

George II (House of Hanover) was King from 1727 to 1760. Patents granted by George II were: the Harrison Patent (1750) and the Lake (or Leake) Patent of 1752.

The Harrison Patent was in three pieces. The first, 705 acres, was situated between the Griggs and Graham on the south, the Bond Patent on the north, the Kennedy Patent on the east and the Morris Patent on the west. This was called the Colden Ridge Patent and included both sides of Ridge Road. The second Harrison Patent, 900 acres, was on the northwest border of the town—to the west of the Barbarie Patent and ran into the Town of Lloyd. A third part is in the town of Plattekill.

I also find a Patent granted to John Lake (or Leake) for 1400 acres. This included several smaller pieces and was mostly along the western border of the town. A part (200 acres) of the Leake Patent became the land of John Mackey.

The remaining Patents were granted by New York State after the American Revolution.

I find a Patent granted to Peleg Ransom for 325 acres in 1790. This was in the northwest part of town and possibly also was included in the town of Plattekill.

A Patent for 400 acres was granted in 1793 to Solomon Fowler. This was again, partly in Plattekill and partly in Marlborough.

Another Patent (that has caused me a lot of angst) is the Daniel Graham Patent of 1793 for 1841 acres. This Patent straddled the Marlborough Mountains—is partly in Plattekill and is mostly wood lot.

In 1796 Lewis DuBois also applied for and was granted a Patent for the water lots in front of his property on the Hudson River.

As an interesting aside there were also some parcels of land that were confiscated during the Revolutionary War from known Loyalists. This land was later sold or granted by the state to various persons. One of these parcels is the Weed farm near the Baptist church in Lattingtown. This was confiscated during the Revolution and sold in 1795 to Thomas Wygant.

Another interesting aspect of the Patent process is a Patent in 1838 granted to Isa Figarrow as follows:

> The people of the state of New York by the grace of God, free and independent: to all to whom these presents shall come Greetings: Know Ye that under and in pursuance of the act entitled "An Act concerning Escheats" passed April 29, 1833. We have released and do by these presents release unto Isa Fegarrow (widow of John Frances Fegarrow, deceased) all such interest in the equal undivided half of the land herein after described

as we may have acquired by escheat on the death of the said John Francis Figarrow who died seized of the said land without making any devise thereof and having no heir capable of inheriting the same which said land is bounded and described as follows to wit: "All that certain piece or parcel of land situate lying and being in the Township of Marlborough, County of Ulster and State aforesaid and bounded as follows to wit: Beginning at a chestnut oak marked being the S corner of the lot hereby intended to be sold and conveyed and runs thence N 1° 30' W 25 chains and 12 links to a stone set in the ground marked; thence S 31° 30' W 30 chains and 50 links to a flat rock and thence N 87° 30' E as the needle pointed in 1795 about 16 chains and 75 links to the place of beginning Containing 20 acres of land more or less. In testimony whereof we have caused these our Letters to be made Patent and the great seal of our said State to be hereunto affixed. Witness William L. Marcy, Governor of our said state at our City of Albany the 18th day of June in the year of our Lord 1838 and in the 62nd year of our independence. Passed the secretary's office the 18th day of June 1838. Arch Campbell Dep Secretary have examined the preceding Letters Patent and do certify that the same are in due form of law. Saml Beardsley, Atty Gen'l

(NB—Black's Law Dictionary—Escheat—A reversion of property to the state in consequence of a want of any individual competent to inherit. Escheat at feudal law was the right of the lord of a fee to re-enter upon the same when it became vacant by the extinction of the blood of the tenant.)

HISTORICAL SOCIETY

One of my first projects upon becoming Town of Marlborough Historian was to initiate the formation of a historical society within the town. Contacted as many people as I could and publicized in the local newspaper.

(Note mail merge format)

Historian Town of Marlborough
18 Gobbler's Knob
Marlboro, NY 12542
(914)-236-7363

August 16, 1994

Dear ,

   This letter is to invite you to what is hoped to be the first meeting of the "Marlborough Historical Committee". One of our first tasks will be to clarify our "raison d'être". I see such a committee as an opportunity to tap into knowledgeable and interested members of our community to enhance, broaden, capture, preserve, document and pass on a rich communal history. One of our neighboring communities has had difficulty because members of the historical committee thought their task was to oversee the duties of the town historian. Believe me this is not what is in my mind—I already have too many bosses. We, as a community, have a very rich history. There is much that can be done to capture what has already passed, document what is happening presently, and pass on to the coming generations as we have had passed on to us.

   Indeed, one of our first tasks should be to provide a written statement of our purpose. I have already spoken to our supervisor, Kevin

Casey, and he has indicated that, should we desire it to be so, he will bring the formation of the committee to the town board to get official recognition.

There are a number of activities that come to my mind as possible tasks for the committee:

    1) working closely with the Southern Ulster County Genealogical Society (Betty Smith, President) to further their goals with respect to documenting genealogies—a genealogy is really a family story—many genealogies together begin to tell the community story.

    2) updating the "House Survey" done in 1968—this was a really fine effort—several of the buildings identified in that survey have already been lost.

    3) identifying by name those individuals in pictures in the town history picture file—each day that passes takes us further away from ever being able to identify many of these individuals

    4) the restoration of Lattingtown School

    5) the restoration, if possible, of the Hallock House

    6) collecting documents with community history.

The list goes on and on.

You have been invited because of your knowledge of or interest in local history. I see the committee as meeting perhaps three or four times a year. Much of the work of the committee can be done by sub-committees that are task specific and working under the umbrella of the main committee. Have checked with Evelyn Baumgartner and the date of Thursday September 15, 1994 is cleared for us to use the main room in the town building. Am suggesting we begin our meeting at 7:30 p.m. At our first meeting we can determine the meeting time and place most convenient for all.

Tentative Agenda:

    1) exploring reasons to form the group

2) appointing a committee (2 or 3) to write up a general purpose statement

3) New York State Archives Week (Oct. 9-15)—I would like to hold an "Open House" to display our town historical collection

4) brief discussion to focus us on one or two projects

5) setting our next meeting date

6) viewing of town historical collection (not completely inventoried or set up yet, but I'm pretty proud of what has been done).

I'll be away for two weeks between Aug. 27th and Sept. 10th. but I can be reached at home either before or after those dates should you care to discuss this further with me prior to the meeting. Shirley Anson, Town of Plattekill Historian, and Lindsey Sullivan, Town of Highland Historian and I have discussed the possibility of a Southern Ulster Historical Society. This committee for Marlborough could fit into those plans nicely.

Do hope you'll consider meeting on Sept. 15th. There is still a lot of Marlborough history to be discovered and I need your help.

*   *   *

I was quite pleased with the results of the first meeting.

Southern Ulster Pioneer
108 Vineyard Ave.
Highland, N. Y. 12528
Fax 691-8601

NEWS RELEASE

A meeting was held recently to explore the possibility of establishing a Marlborough Historical Committee. Due to a mix-up the regular meeting room was being used and thus the group had to meet in the hallway. Needless to say it was crowded but everyone took it in good spirits and refreshments were still served. Mary Lou Mahan, town of Marlborough Historian acted as chairperson pro tem with Minette Vanacore volunteering to act as secretary in the same capacity. There were close to twenty participants in the meeting and it is noteworthy that there was representation from Milton, Marlboro, West Marlboro, Mount Zion, and Lattingtown as well as a wide spread in ages and interests. Shirley Ansen, town of Plattekill Historian and several others from that area were also present which is quite fitting since Plattekill was a part of the town of Marlborough until 1800.

While not yet ready to commit itself to formal charter without further research the group did decide to start to tackle several projects:

1) Updating "House Survey" done in 1969 Margaret Billesimo, Cynthia Gervais, Minette   Vanacore,   Judy Rappa

2) The possible rescue to the Lattingtown School Joann Pagnotta, Pat Mackey, Dave Ballou, Betty Diorio

3) Interviewing some of our elder community members Anne Borchert Teter, Mary Lou Mahan, Judy Rappa

It was also decided to celebrate "State Archives Week" by having a display at the town building at a regular town meeting scheduled for Monday October 10, 1994. Working on this project are Joann Pagnotta, Mary Lou Mahan, Minette Vanacore, Judy Rappa, Betty Smith and Anne Teter.

The next meeting is scheduled for next month (date to be determined) at the Marlboro Free Library with some time scheduled to discover the treasures in the library's collection.

Anyone wishing to participate in any of the projects is urged to contact one of the committee members.

*   *   *

One of the first projects undertaken by the fledgling society was an attempt to save and restore the Lattingtown School.

Southern Ulster Pioneer
108 Vineyard Ave.
Highland, N. Y. 12528
Fax 691-8601

Lattingtown School Mugs for Sale

The Marlborough Historical Society is presently selling ceramic coffee mugs with a color picture of the Lattingtown School. The Society hopes to make a mug available yearly so this mug is dated "1995" and can be the beginning of a significant collection. The mugs cost $15 each and are available for Christmas. The mugs can be purchased by calling Pat Mackey 795-5175, Mary Lou Mahan 236-7363, Judy Rappa 236-7223 or Betty Smith 795-2252. The mugs may be picked up from the above or from the Billesimo Real Estate office in Marlboro. They would make wonderful Christmas presents for alumni of the Lattingtown School or Marlborough history buffs in general.

The Society is using this as a fund raiser to explore the possibility of restoring the school and making a community museum. The museum will be open to inhabitants of the town and available to the schools for field trips so children can capture the ambiance of an old fashioned school.

The Society is also interested in identifying alumni of the school. If you or anyone you know attended the Lattingtown school, please call Pat Mackey. The Society would like to set up a "Lattingtown School House Scrap Book". If you have any pictures, etc. they would be interested in having copies made for inclusion in the scrap book. Again, please call Pat Mackey.

The most significant writings about the school are from a PTA (Bertie Clarke) pamphlet on the history of the Marlborough Schools and from the 1968 "House Survey".

From <u>SCHOOLS of the Town of Marlborough</u> , PTA, (Bertie Clarke), 1937

THE LATTINGTOWN SCHOOL

The Lattingtown District (No. 7) in 1877 built a new school replacing what appears to have been the original building. The old school had hand-made benches. The large teacher's desk had a door in it. This made a convenient place to stow an unruly pupil, so the story goes. The original school faced the road. The New one-room school was built by Mr. Bloomer, the trustee, who was paid by the district for his labor. This school had seats to replace the old benches. A program of improvements consisting of furnace, driven well, single seats, ventilating system, and an addition, during the trusteeship of James Conklin, Leighton Craft, H. V. Mackey, and Mr. and Mrs. Edgar M. Clarke, Jr., began in 1919 with the painting of the building when Arnold A. Mackey was trustee. These improvements were labeled; "Temporary" by the Department of Education at Albany, but the glimpse of modern education it afforded was appreciated by the community.

From <u>HOUSE SURVEY</u>—1968-9

82   Lattingtown School House   Lattingtown
       When the schools were centralized, it was discovered that this building could not be sold. At the request of parents of children it was kept as a grade school until during the W.W.II when Lloyd Reese, then clerk, reports that lack of coal led to its closing and sending the chil-

dren by bus to Marlboro where they have gone ever since.

At the very beginning of centralization while Mrs. Plank was clerk and Edgar M Clarke board president and Edward L Dalby supervising principal, attempts were made to clear title so that the building could be sold.

It stands in a sort of hollow square; the building and land close to it belonged to the old Lattingtown district and now to the central district. The land surrounding the building was given by the Craft family with a legal arrangement that if it ever was used for anything but educational purposes it would revert to the heirs. In the thirties attempts were made to locate the heirs and again in the forties but they are so numerous by now and so hard to locate that nothing can be done. The Lattingtown Gun Club is allowed to use the building for a sort of headquarters; old school seats and desks are stored there; otherwise it stands unused.

The Gun Club keeps the building painted and in repair.

By purchasing a Lattingtown School House mug, you will be helping the Marlborough Historical Society "Recapture the Rapture" of an earlier, gentler period of our communal history.

The Lattingtown School in 1995

*   *   *

One of the activities undertaken by the society to raise funds for the restoration of the Lattingtown School was an art show and competition. Local artists were encouraged to make their personal renditions of the Lattingtown School for future reproduction on a commemorative plate.

Lattingtown School Project Art Show

On June 1, 1996 the Marlborough Historical Society held an Art Show and Wine & Cheese reception in the area of the Raccoon Saloon. It was a most beautiful day. Rita Trusdale had graciously permitted the use of her storefront as well as the portico in front of the buildings. She had placed tables with white tablecloths out on the portico making for festive environs. Numerous local artists had their paintings on easels all along the portico from the wine tasting room to the end of the Raccoon. The colors were dazzling.

The Riverview Wine Tasting Room permitted the Society the use of their facilities as well as furnishing wine. Ben Marl also donated wine for the tasting. Cheese was donated by Miller's and cheese and crackers by Wendel's.

A basket of wine was donated by Lou's Liquor Store and raffled. Sam Quimby was the winner of the lovely basket.

Within Rita Trusdale's store (next to the Wine Tasting) ten paintings of the Lattingtown School done by local artists were on display. The display indeed was powerful as each artist added their own charm to the paintings.

The Society intends to display the ten paintings at various areas within the community to elicit the community's reaction. Your "vote" will help to decide which painting will be used on a commemorative porcelain plate to be made available by the Society at a later date.

The Marlborough Historical Society would like to thank the local artists, the local businesses that contributed, Lou's Liquor Store, The Riverview Wine Tasting Room, those of the community who visited the display and especially Rita Trusdale and Pam for their gracious hospitality. They could not have been more cooperative.

Keep an eye open for the local displays of the paintings, we think you will be impressed—and do make your preference known.

Richard Ochs's water color rendition of the Lattingtown School was chosen as that which would be reproduced on the commemorative plates. Everyone was most pleased.

Please be aware the painting is much more vivid in water color

We were not successful in our attempt to restore the school. In my heart of hearts, I know I could have pulled it off had I had more support.

      *   *   *

The Historical Society also had a project intended to beautify the community.

Southern Ulster Pioneer
108 Vineyard Ave.
Highland, N. Y. 12528
Fax 691-8601

NEWS RELEASE
The Gauntlet is Down

Recently the Town of Marlborough Historical Committee under the leadership of member Helen Mestrov set up nine flower barrels in the village of Marlboro. This was done to enhance the attractiveness of the community both for residents and tourists. Donations of barrels were received from Cal Wygant, Alonges, Joe Dirago, Frank Troncillito and Steve Conti. Flowers were donated by Hepworth Markets, Frankie's Market, and Helen Mestrov. The Historical Committee also supplied funds. Topsoil was donated by Noto Landscapers and offered by Charles Weed. The barrels were cut in half by Helen's husband, George. Historical Committee members Sam Quimby and Girard Purdy did the heavy work of setting the planters in place and filling them with topsoil. Helen Mestrov, Minnette Vanacore, Toots Mazza, the three Mazza boys, and Mary Lou Mahan planted the barrels. Sandy Curci and Christin Woolsey lugged water to each of the barrels in order to give the plants a good start.

Local businesses were contacted to ask them to "adopt" a barrel. "Adopting" a flower barrel is to include the promise to water and feed the plants, pull off dying blossoms and leaves and in general, give them tender, loving care. Billesimo Real Estate, Key Bank, Amodeo's, Pizza Town, Frankie's, Village Variety, Cricchio Apartments and Alonge Brothers have all signified their willingness to do so. The committee has been very pleased with the good response given to the project. Several local businesses including Rusk, Wadlin, Heppner & Martuscello; Kronner's Hardware; and Pizza Town have made donations to keep the project going.

Response was so good that Amodeo's Service Station has vowed to have the healthiest and happiest flowers in town. Thus there is a challenge to see which flowers prosper the most. Everyone is invited to keep their eyes opened to see wherefrom come the most brilliant blooms. Helen would be pleased to hear from you with your opinions.

(Photo: Toots Mazza, Helen Mestrov, Sandy Curci, Christin Woolsey, Minnette Vanacore and the three Mazza boys, John, Jacob and Jack)

*   *   *

The Society also worked on saving the Joseph Carpenter stone.

The old stone reads, "In memory of Joseph Carpenter, the first settler of this place and planter of this orchard. Departed this life July 11, 1766, aged 61 years, 3 mos. and 6 days." The stone was formerly on the Joseph Dirago farm in Lattingtown leaning against an apple tree. Joe was kind enough to allow us to move the stone to the Lattingtown Baptist Church cemetery. There, thanks to the efforts of Shirley Weed and the cooperation of the Baptist Church board, it has been placed in a prominent, and hopefully, permanent spot.

In 1908 CM Woolsey in his History of Marlborough, NY wrote:

One of the oldest graveyards was at Lattingtown, on the lands now owned by T. B. Odell, about where his large barns now stand. All traces of the yard had been removed before Odell became the owner, except the grave of Joseph Carpenter, who died in 1766. The graveyard was first used as such about 1750, and was used as a burial ground from that time up to 1808, when the Baptist graveyard was opened, but some interments were made there after this. There were perhaps at one time a hundred graves or more of the oldest inhabitants of Lattingtown. Most of the stones at the graves were rude field stones, the yard was neglected and suffered to go to decay, the stones were removed, and the land used for other purposes. It was used at first as a family burial yard for the Carpenter, Caverly and Latting families, but afterward all the people about there used it; as it was on private ground there was no means of protecting it.

Woolsey gives more of the history of the Carpenter family and the Lattingtown area:

> The Carpenter family were among the first settlers, Joseph Carpenter, son of Benjamin, was born at Musketa Cove, September 15, 1705, and the marriage record of St. George's church of Hempstead shows that he was married on May 20, 1728, to Sarah Latting, who was a daughter of Richard and Mary (Wright) Latting of Lattingtown (near Musketa Cove). By inheritance and

purchase he had a large landed interest at "Red Springs" and "Oak Neck," which property he sold in 1753, and in company with his brother-in-law, John Latting, his son-in-law, John Caverly, and Benjamin Stanton, purchased through Lewis Morris and others and Euphemia Morris of Busks, England, a very large tract of land in Ulster county, near Newburgh, which they settled naming it "Lattingtown" after their Long Island home. He died there in 1766, and his widow died in 1790.

We would not have considered moving the stone except for the fact the stone no longer marked the gravesite and the cemetery has long since vanished. His stone was placed a short distance away from its original site, and since it is in a church cemetery, hopefully it will not have to be moved again.

How sad that "100 graves or more" can no longer be recognized: how wonderful that we still have a monument to the man who was one of the earliest white settlers in the area.

(Pictured: Dave Ballou, pastor of the Lattingtown Baptist Church; Shirley Weed, to be credited for having the stone moved and set up; and Cynthia (Carpenter) Gervais, a descendant of Joseph Carpenter)

*   *   *

The Society enjoyed holding meetings in various homes and businesses during the year.

Southern Ulster Pioneer
108 Vineyard Ave.
Highland, N. Y. 12528
Fax 691-8601

Attention Judy Rappa

NEWS RELEASE

The next meeting of the Town of Marlborough Historical Committee will be the Anniversary Dinner Friday evening September 15 beginning at 6 p.m. at the Ship Lantern Inn. The date is one year from that evening a number of residents met in the hall at the town building and decided to join together:

1) to promote and enhance the historical significance of the Town of Marlborough,

2) to engage in and encourage others to engage in historical research,

3) to gather, preserve and help make available for study—artifacts, relics, books, manuscripts, papers, photographs, records and other materials relating to the history of the Town of Marlborough for inclusion in the town's historic collection,

4) to encourage the suitable designation of places of historical interest within the town,

5) to pass on to our community's children an understanding of and respect for the efforts, endeavors and accomplishments of all those predecessors who have given our town its unique identity,

6) to educate adults and strive for a broad base of support,

7) to advance the significance of historical records and the importance of their proper maintenance.

The Ship Lantern Inn is an appropriate site to hold the dinner as, according to the owners:

"In the heart of the fruit and vineyard country of Ulster County is John Foglia's Ship Lantern Inn, Route

9W, Milton, N. Y., oldest restaurant in the valley serving continental food. The building dates back to Revolutionary War days. Its nautical decor features miniature sailing ships from Mr. Foglia's personal collection. It's the largest of its kind built by one person, Capt. H. Percy Ashley. These exquisitely detailed models show naval and commercial shipping as it was in the past: The Hudson River Sloop 'Abraham Lincoln' of Catskill 1960, Privateer 'General Armstrong' U.S.N., War of 1812. Historical Schooner 'Enterprise' U.S.N., 1799.

Mr. Foglia is one of the four original founders of the renowned Chef-Boy-Ar-Dee Company which was awarded the Army and Navy 'E' as a result of sample tastings supplied from the kitchen of this restaurant. Ship Lantern Inn is now enjoying its third generation of family management."

Friends from the community are invited to join the Historical Committee for this event. The cost is $26.00 per person. Reservations must be made before September 13th and can be done so by sending a check made out to The Town of Marlborough Historical Committee c/o Mrs. Patricia Mackey 491 Old Indian Road Milton, NY 12547. Please indicate your preference for Roast Sirloin of Black Angus, Broiled Fillet of Atlantic Salmon or Breast of Chicken.

We intend to have our usual sharing. If you have any interesting pictures, maps, papers, etc. please consider bringing them along to share.

Marlborough Historical Meeting at Baxter Homestead

The next meeting of the Marlborough Historical Society will be June 20th at 7 p.m. at the Baxter Homestead in Marlboro. The Home dates from the late 1700's or early 1800's and has been beautifully preserved. Lorraine Baxter will be our hostess.

The property is part of the Morris Patent of 1714. It was Wygant land in the early 1700's. The property is depicted on a map of 1805 in the possession of Cal Wygant. Mention is made in the deed of a "stone school house". The house is believed to have begun as a one room building lined with "clay and straw" plaster. There is a room in the house dubbed "the birthing and dying" room reflecting the fact that the major events in life once occurred in homes such as this. It is believed the house may have been a "way stop" in bygone days. The house has been in the Baxter family since Daniel Tooker sold it to John H. Baxter in 1846.

There will be reports from the standing committees as well as on the progress made on the Lattingtown School Project.

All those interested in Marlborough's History (or in making history themselves) are invited to attend. Dues for the Marlborough Historical Society are $5 per year which covers the mailing of the monthly newsletter which most often contains historical information of interest to historic buffs or members of the community. Dues can be sent to Dorothy Holveg, treasurer at PO Box 356 Milton, NY 12547.

Since the Baxter homestead is a private residence, space is limited. Should you desire to attend, please call Helen Mestrov at 236-7150.

*   *   *

Marlborough Historical Society

It was just over a year ago that a small but enthusiastic group met at the Marlborough Town Hall to explore the possibility of establishing a historical society in the community. One year later such a society not only has been established, but is diligently working on collecting, cataloging and sharing the history of our community. There are presently over fifty members of the group. Several of the members are former Marlborough residents who have wandered far and wide and, though settled in distant places, keep in touch with their roots through the Historical Society.

The goals of the Society as set forth in the by-laws include:

1) to promote and enhance the historical significance of the Town of Marlborough,

2) to engage in and encourage others to engage in historical research,

3) to gather, preserve and help make available for study—artifacts, relics, books, manuscripts, papers, photographs, records and other materials relating to the history of the Town of Marlborough for inclusion in the town's historic collection,

4) to encourage the suitable designation of places of historical interest within the town,

5) to pass on to our community's children an understanding of and respect for the efforts, endeavors and accomplishments of all those predecessors who have given our town its unique identity,

6) to educate adults and strive for a broad base of support,

7) to advance the significance of historical records and the importance of their proper maintenance.

To this end, three standing committees have been established.

The "House Survey Committee" is working on updating the historical house survey that was done in 1968. They are presently collecting old deeds and information about some of the older dwellings. They are at this time concentrating on King Street and have interviewed and collected personal remembrances of some of those homes. Pictures have been taken of the older homes. The committee met at the McCourt home and had a lovely tour. That home is reported to have been built in the mid 1700's and at one time housed a school. Chairperson of the "House Survey Committee" is Margaret Billesimo.

Other historic homes that have been the settings for Historical Society meetings include "The Gomez Mill House"—reportedly built circa 1714 and the "earliest extant Jewish residence in North America," the Tom Pollizzi home with its resident ghost, "George", the Kramer home on Mt. Zion, home of the patriot Joseph Morey, and the home of Frank and Freda Nicklin, long the center of farm life starting with the Hirsts.

The second standing committee is the "Interview Committee." We hope you've been following the interesting bits of history that have emerged from the interviews that have been published in The Southern Ulster Pioneer. Chairperson of the "Interview Committee" is Judy Rappa.

The third standing committee is "The Lattingtown School Committee." They have been hard at work collecting the history of the school in hopes of being able to help restore it. Recently a video tape was made starring three former students of the school. The video was shown at the Anniversary Dinner and it is hoped it can be shown to the public shortly. Chairperson of "The Lattingtown School Committee" is Patricia Mackey.

The Society has been involved in several other community projects. They had a float in the Memorial Day Parade (a replica of the Lattingtown School complete with students at the windows). They have been responsible for setting up and planting flower barrels in the village of Marlboro. With the help of the community, they intend to change these several times during the year. The next planting are thought to be Christmas trees.

The Society has also been responsible for saving the Joseph Carpenter Stone. The stone has been sitting in a corner of the Dirago farm for many years, though it was not in its original spot. With the approval of Joe Dirago and the effort of Dave Ballou, the stone has been moved to the Lattingtown Baptist Church yard. The stone is inscribed, "JOSEPH CARPENTER The first settler of this place and the planter of this orchard. Died July 1st, 1766 Aged 61 years, 3 Mo. and 6 Days." Joseph Carpenter was one of the earliest settlers in Marlborough.

The Society also made available for purchase a reprint of the 1908 CM Woolsey book, History of the Town of Marlborough thus helping to spread information about our history. The Society is now making available a reprint of the 1887 Cochrane History of the Town of Marlborough. Orders are presently being taken. Both are excellent books that tell of many residents and happenings during the past.

The Society is also trying to set up an "Over 90" database of residents or former residents who have reached the age of 90. It is believed they hold many memories that would benefit us all.

Meetings have also been held at the Marlboro Free Library, The Sarah Hull Hallock Library, The Town Park and Hicksite Cemetery, The Lattingtown Baptist Church, Manese's Bar & Grill (The old Miller Store) and the Anniversary Dinner at Ship Lantern Inn. The next meeting is set for Friday November 17th beginning at 2 p.m. at the First Presbyterian Church in Marlboro. The Reverend Alfred Williams will give a brief history of the church. A subscription was raised in 1763 to build a Presbyterian church "providing the Lewis DuBois does give 2 acres of land...." He did so and the original church was built on "Lot A" (presently the site of DiDonato's).

The meeting, as always, is open to anyone interested in attending and joining in our search for the past—to better understand the present— and best prepare for the future.

*   *   *

The Society also attempted to renew the effort made a number of years ago to make Route 9W be known as the "Golden Highway".

To: Judy Rappa
Southern Ulster Pioneer
<u>News Release</u>
April 30, 1996

Historical Society Seeks to Renew "Golden Highway"
In the 1930's there was a movement by various Garden Clubs to make plantings of forsythia all along 9W to create a "Golden Highway". Driving the highway today one can spot some of the work done during that period. Joe Canino of Highland remembers planting some of the forsythia as a young teenager. The Marlborough Historical Society is interested in reviving that project.

Now is the time when gardeners are busy pruning and clearing and getting ready for the summer season. Those interested in helping with the "Golden Highway" project are being asked to take cuttings from their forsythia plants and stick them in a pot of water. Forsythia is known to root easily. The more rootings available, the better. Later this spring, the Historical Society will be collecting the rootings and planting them along the highway.

For more information please call Helen Mestrov 236-7150 or Mary Lou Mahan 236-7363, members of the Historical Society's Beautification Committee

                 *   *   *

There was an attempt also to work with other groups within the community to further both our goals.

Southern Ulster Pioneer
108 Vineyard Ave.
Highland, N. Y. 12528
Fax 691-8601

Letters to the Editor

Attached find the words used at the recent "Marlborough Day at Mill House." We had a really good day and would like to thank everyone for their efforts.

On behalf of the Marlborough Historical Society, I, too, would like to welcome you to "Marlborough Day at Mill House" and thank you for your interest in our community and its history. Forgive me if I forget anyone,— it's certainly not intentional—we appreciate all your efforts.

Would especially like to thank:

- Kevin Casey—TOM (Town of Marlborough) Supervisor—for his cooperation. Casey is away this morning but hopes to be able to pop in later this afternoon

- Mike Canosa—TOM Deputy Supervisor—for his kind words of welcome—Mike has a long history of being involved with the community and preserving its history.

- Steve Adamshick—member of the Marlborough School Board who is here with the American Legion

- Ellen Healy—also a member of the Marlborough School Board who is here with the PTA

- Sam Quimby—VP of the MHS (Marlborough Historical Society) who is unfortunately out of town and can't be with us this afternoon

- Judy Rappa—VP of the MHS who worked on the MHS table—please look at the lovely book on her home and the people who inhabited it. Judy also worked with the Lattingtown Baptist Church

- The American Legion—and its commander, Vinnie Ianuzzi, for our Flag ceremonies along with Troop #72 of the Boy Scouts

- Audrey Lee—Interim Pastor of the First Presbyterian Church Marlboro, the oldest church in Marlboro

- Dave Ballou—pastor of the Lattingtown Baptist Church—and a member of the MHS

- The Presbyterian Woman's Association and Adele Lyons who are doing such a good job of getting us informed about the difficult topic of Spousal Abuse

- The Lattingtown Baptist Church and Margaret Faurie—one of the oldest churches in the town—Both Margaret and Paul have been very active in preserving town history—both are members of the MHS

- The PTA—and especially Ellen Healy who both for her own family and for the students in the Marlborough schools has displayed a keen interest in Marlborough's History

- Mary Osinski—music teacher and member of the MHS who helped us obtain Ardis Ketterer and Christine Mackey who will give a flute recital shortly. We look forward to hearing that and appreciate their efforts

- John Bellucci—for his help and suggestions

- Frank Troncillito—who is probably freezing his tail off right now, as he's hunting—but he did allow us to display some of the creative "artifacts" he has put together over the years and that once were on display at the Raccoon.

- The Raccoon Saloon—and Rita Truesdale and Pam Kelly—who lent us pictures of our neighbors and friends that Don had taken over the years at the Raccoon. Looking over the pictures and recognizing how many of those in the pictures have passed away, gives one food for contemplation.

- The Marlboro Library—and especially the director, Libby Manion for their display. Libby is also a member of the MHS, and

- Gundred Moon—for her spinning demonstration.

We need to give special thanks to Bill Maurer—he's been a wonderful person to work with. We made a list of things that had to be done, split it down the middle, and "voilà"—what you see today. Bill, I'll work with you anytime.

We all need to say a special "thank you" to the lady who's dream and incredible amount of effort, perseverance and strength of will have kept these grounds, these buildings and this history alive—Millie Starin

And "thank you" again, to all of you who came to share this special day.

Please don't be offended if I call you glue—each of us is a critical form of glue!

Whether your forebears settled here before the TOM was the TOM and are listed in the early censuses—some predating 1790—(see them on the MHS table) or you were born in Maine, Florida, California, Washington, or in a different nation

Whether your family has been here 200+ years, or six months—and number among those of us who made a conscious decision to call Marlborough "HOME"

Whether you're fabulously rich (there have been some), poorer than church mice (there have been more), middle class or working class

Whether you're Black or White, Hispanic, Native American, Asian or other,

Whatever your gender

Whether you're a farmer, a merchant, a housewife, an industrialist, a professional, a teacher, or a blue collar worker

Whether you belong to the Catholic Church, the Presbyterian Church, The Methodist Church, the Episcopal Church, The Baptist Church, The Quakers, a Synagogue or some other

Whether you're a Republican, a Democrat, a Conservative, a Liberal, a Socialist, a Libertarian or some other

Whether your native language is English, German, Gaelic, French, Italian, Polish, Spanish or some other

Whether you're nearing your centennial birthday celebration or are a young child

You and I are glue.

The glue that holds the sanctity of the family intact

The glue that binds neighbor to neighbor

Neighbors are the glue upon which neighborhoods are built

Neighborhoods adhere and form communities and, community is what today is all about.

We come together to celebrate Marlborough's proud history. Yet we must reflect. We can celebrate that history only because people long past—preserved the pictures, the documents, the artifacts, the buildings that we treasure today. They were the glue that has held those things together for us. We are the glue that holds our community together today—but our responsibility is more far reaching than that. We cannot celebrate and enjoy today our homes, our churches, our organizations, our community without recognizing our responsibilities to the future. What will Marlborough be like in another 50 years? another 100 or 200 years? What of our families, our churches, our organizations, our community will remain for our children, their children and their children's children to celebrate?

Glue—we need to be glue—we need to bind our heritage and our generation's endeavors to a future we cannot fully imagine. Our forebears did it—can we do less?

INTERVIEWS

Angelo Sasso

Angelo Sasso with wife Carole

He came down the steps to greet us. His step was surprisingly sprightly and seemed even more so when he told us he was born in 1906. Angelo Sasso was born in Switzerland, near Basel. Though his parents were Italian, they were in Switzerland as his father worked the night watch in a zinc factory. He grew up in Switzerland and attended school there until he was 16 years old.

Shortly thereafter his family moved back to Italy and Angelo got his first taste of the profession at which he would spend the major portion of his life: restaurateur (F. der. restaurer restore). He found work as a bus boy at a restaurant near Milano. Part of his job was to pick up produce at the market as early as 4:30 in the morning. When he decided to go to night school, his days were very long indeed. In the following few years he was able to get work as a waiter at The Excelsior in Venice and

The Royale in Rome—considering their international reputations, this was no mean feat for a young man at that time. This work tended to be seasonal so he also found himself traveling to The Palace Hotel in Bürgenstock, Switzerland and Vierwaldstätte near Luzern. He enjoyed long swims in the lake which helped develop his athletic prowess. He, during this period, also worked at The Luxor Hotel in Egypt near the tomb of King Tut and in Brussels he worked at The Savoy Restaurant.

He had been working a few years when one of his friends announced he was going to New York City. Angelo thought that sounded interesting and within the next few days, in September 1929, took the boat with his friend. He arrived in New York City but, since his plans were spur of the moment, he lacked the proper documentation and actually entered the country illegally.

Angelo was able to get a room at a small hotel on 46th Street between 8th and 9th Avenue. He remembers going back to his room to find someone asleep in the bed. Imagine his chagrin as he discovered he had gone to the wrong room and had to go up one more flight to find his room.

In New York City Angelo was fortunate enough (remember the year was 1929 and the crash of the Stock Market) to meet Mario Boiardi, a captain of waiters at The Plaza Hotel on 48th Street and 5th Avenue at the corner of Central Park. The Plaza was and is one of New York City's premier hotels. Mario offered him a job at the hotel where Paul Boiardi was Maitre D' and Hector Boiardi was chef.

While working at The Plaza, Angelo was able to attend English school at the YMCA nearby. Angelo soon was boxing for the Y and won a gold watch for one of his matches. Because of his physical abilities he also found himself sparring with some professional boxers. It was at the Y that he first met Tony Canzonari who later set up a boxing camp on Lattingtown Road in Marlboro.

It was during this time, following the path to work, that Angelo also went to Palm Beach to The Patio Hotel where he met many celebrities.

Returning to New York he found work week-ends at The Ship Lantern Inn in Milton. The Ship had been opened in 1926 by John Foglia. John Foglia was also a partner with Paul Boiardi in the Chef Boyardee Company. At The Ship, Angelo worked as an extra waiter and one of his jobs was to wheel around the hors d'oeuvre tray. Angelo remarks about the hors d'oeuvre tray that was such a touch of class at the better restaurants. Hors d'oeuvres ranged from fresh shrimp to caviar to other exotic tidbits. Angelo muses that such an extravagance is not economically feasible in this day and age.

Angelo was concerned about his status as an illegal alien and went to a lawyer to straighten out the situation. It cost him $1000 and he had to go to Cuba. Batista was in Cuba at the time. On his return to the US, he was able to enter the country legally for the first time.

In September 1942 Angelo received an invitation from the US government. He was drafted into the United States Army—even though he was not yet a US citizen. He was in Palm Beach at the time and was surprised when some FBI agents came knocking on his door. During a search of his room they found and confiscated a flashlight. Seems there was a fear of an Italian citizen (which Angelo still was) flashing a light at night to signal the enemy. Angelo had to get special permission to leave Palm Beach in order to come back to New York to join the US Army. He was drafted at 37 years of age and sent to Camp Buckner for basic training. He was still very athletic and Angelo earned the honor of being best on the obstacle course.

Having been born and raised in Switzerland, Angelo could also speak French and German. Because of these linguistic skills Angelo found himself sent to Camp Ritchie in MD where his job entailed interviewing German POWs.

It was while he was stationed at Camp Ritchie that Angelo came home to NYC to marry his sweetheart, Carole Heydt, who worked at the Plaza as cashier at the Persian Room . The "Just Married" couple were invited to the home of Chef Boyardi and spent their wedding night there.

Before he was shipped overseas, Angelo was sent to Washington, DC. Among a group of men he was told to raise his hand, he was given the oath and officially became a US citizen. He was sent to Chester, England from whence he was able to visit London. Two or three days after the Normandy invasion, he was sent to France. Again his job was to interrogate POWs at the front.

At the end of the war he was sent to 7th Army HQ. He was in charge of transportation in which capacity he met many figures who played a major role during W.W.II. One of his duties entailed transporting Hermann Goering, the infamous second in command to Adolf Hitler in Nazi Germany. At that time no one suspected that Goering, under the skin, held the poison pill by which he would later take his own life.

Goering on left, Angelo with back to us

During this period Angelo met a man named Carlo in the Bavarian Alps. Italians who had been German captive laborers had been freed. Angelo gave Carlo a ride in the jeep and gave him a cigarette. Imagine Angelo's surprise when years later he met the same Carlo in Newburgh. Carlo had been telling the story about the ride and the cigarette.

Upon returning home Angelo again worked at The Ship Lantern Inn. He learned of a Mrs. Hangst who owned Ronnie's Terrace, a boarding house on the banks of the Hudson River in Newburgh. Ronnie's Terrace was for sale: the price was $25,000, Ronnie's Terrace originated as the home of Senator John B. Rose. The Roses had started one of the first brick yards in the area and the community of Roseton took its name from the Rose family. Angelo fell in love with the beautiful, graceful building and soon he and his friend, the head waiter at The Chanticleer in Cicero bought the property and opened up the fine restaurant that was renamed The Beau Rivage.

The Beau Rivage

The work was difficult but Angelo loved it. Angelo was able to build up a clientele that included some of the best known families in the region as well as celebrities from far and wide (including Princess Juliana, presently the Queen of the Netherlands) . His restaurant was known for the quality of food and service as well as the genteel ambiance. His lifetime work in some of the world class restaurants in Italy, France, Belgium and the US prepared him to offer his guests fine dining in the classical sense.

Interestingly, Angelo indicated that other quality restaurants like The Ship, were not seen as competitors, but rather as supporting the art of the restaurateur in the area. There was cooperation between the fine restaurants and the owners often dined at each other's establishments.

After 32 years at The Beau Rivage and at age 75 Angelo retired and sold the place. He currently lives in what was the carriage house of the Rose Estate. On New Years Eve in 1982, Angelo and his wife were at The Ships Lantern Inn celebrating the dawn of a new year. On arriving home they were alarmed to learn that The Beau Rivage was in flames. They served coffee and refreshments during the entire night to the fire-fighters and spectators. Even with the superhuman efforts expended, the attempts to save the beautiful building were in vain and The Beau Rivage burned to the ground.

Today Angelo lives with his wife of 58 years across the road from his beloved Beau Rivage. At 95 years he is still very athletic; he walks almost daily. He is surrounded by pictures and momentos of his long and pro-ductive life. He and his wife are devoted to each other. Both still very much enjoy going out and dining at any one of the area's best restau-rants. Dining in aesthetic surroundings, savoring a well chosen and tastefully prepared meal, being tended by gracious servers surely feeds the body but perhaps most of all, nourishes the soul. Angelo has learned, and taught this lesson with artful finesse.

*   *   *

Austin Berkery

He was born in the nineteenth century on September 18, 1899 on the farm owned by his mother and father. He spent the major part of his life on that same farm moving in 1941 to "Dawesville," population 43. Austin Berkery married a Dawes. Since he moved only a mile or so from his original home, he feels perfectly content in his newer surroundings.

His father, Mike Berkery, and mother, Annie McManus, both were born in Ireland but were married in Marlboro and settled on the farm in west Marlboro on Burma Road. In 1885 they bought the 61 acre farm from the Kents. Austin's siblings include Andrew, at one time supervisor of the town of Marlborough, Emmet and Michael.

He attended the West Marlboro School with Fred Elgee. His teachers were Mrs. Clancey and Bertha Staples. Before his school days, there had been a school on Plattekill Road which was closer to his home—but this school was closed by the time Austin went to school. He remembers the mixed classes that each teacher coped with at the one room school house. After he completed the course at the West Marlboro school, he continued his education on the farm.

He remembers going to St. Mary's church when it was located at what had been the Methodist Church and now is Sarles' sales and repairs. On the farm they raised apples, grapes and other fruit. They used their horse to transport the fruit down to the Marlboro dock and the "Mary Powell." From there fruit commissioners would take the fruit down to market in New York City. Farmers got paid for their fruit several days later.

He remembers going over the old Idlewilde Road, past the Casey farm, to Plattekill near the Plattekill store. The social life at that time included going to square dances at the Grange in Plattekill. He claims he "picked up" his wife at one of these Grange dances.

The farms in those days were pretty self-sufficient as he remembers having horses, cows, pigs and chickens. At first there were a pair of horses for the farm work, then they went down to one horse and finally quit using horses altogether. Cal Staples lived down the road from the Berkerys, Greiners lived east, Toomeys west and Caseys to the north. Everyone helped out when there was a need, so there was a real sense of neighborliness and community. The Greiners have since purchased the Berkery farm.

He recalls hearing that the Baxter house was a road house at one time. Scuderi's corners was called Wygant's corners because a Wygant lived there in the past.

Though his parents came from Ireland more than a century ago, Austin has continued contact with his relatives there. He has visited Ireland several times in the last few years. As a matter of fact, no moss grows on this Marlboro nonagenarian, he plans another trip to Ireland this summer.

The "Luck of the Irish" to you, Austin. You've blessed our community with your hard work and good citizenship and we appreciate your endeavors.

*　　　　　　*　　　　　　*

CATHERINE DOWD

Don't be surprised if you're sitting in Dickie's Diner in Marlboro just before noon and a '70 Buick with the license plate CD 44 pulls up and parks. It's Catherine Dowd on her almost daily stop. Most people are amazed that at 90 years of age Catherine still drives so well. Indeed, she says doctors are surprised when they ask her what ailments she's had in her lifetime and all she has to report is that she's had her appendix taken out. "God has been good to me." reports Catherine. "It's all because of my children" she explains. She has more children than most people. Catherine never married. Those children of which she speaks are the students she's had in her classes over a professional lifetime that spanned forty-four years.

Catherine was born on April 16th 1905. Her father's farm was his portion of his father's farm in Lattingtown. He had 35 acres from the road right back to the woods with almost every acre productive. They lived on Barry's hill where the Porpiglia's live now. Her mother was a McManus and was born in Joe Connor's house. Her mother "could do anything."

Catherine's father gave her a gift of a calf one year that grew to be "Belle", the family cow. She remembers walking with a can of milk to be delivered to the Weeds who owned a boarding house in Lattingtown at that time. The family also had two horses. Catherine's horse was "Molly." She remembers cleaning and brushing Molly every Saturday and Molly nuzzling her for an apple. Catherine loved to ride Molly bareback.

Catherine attended the Lattingtown one-room schoolhouse. Her teachers were Miss Tierney (later Mrs. Patrick "Hicks" Manion) and Mrs. Martin from Highland. There were only three students in Catherine's class; Ed Rhoads, Bill McGowan and Catherine. After completing six years at the Lattingtown School, Catherine attended the Union Free School in Marlboro. She drove Molly to school and stabled her at a shed at the Methodist Church—one stall for Molly and one for the buggy. One of her teachers at the Union Free School was Ernestine Cole. Ernestine's married name is Ernestine Wygant and she lives on Hudson Terrace in Marlboro.

Catherine vividly recalls the day school was closed at 10:00 a.m. because of a snow storm. The children from her area were given a ride home on the road scraper. The scraper couldn't make Barry's hill and had to go round and about. It wasn't until after 10:00 p.m. that she arrived home. After a while Hubbie Gasparoli, who ran the general store in Lattingtown, began transporting the Lattingtown students to the Union Free School.

Catherine maintains that was the first school bus in Lattingtown. Parents paid Gasparoli directly for transporting their children.

Catherine then attended New Paltz Normal School and in later years Columbia University. She was very much impressed with the graduation ceremonies at Columbia. "I'll never forget; it was so beautiful, so large." she said.

Upon completing her certification, Catherine started her teaching career at the Milton Turnpike School, a one-room school house on the corner of Milton Turnpike and Clarke's Lane. Leonard Clarke was one of her first students. She taught grades one through six. She drove a horse and buggy to her teaching duties.

Shortly Catherine moved to the Marlboro Central school (present Marlborough Middle School) which at that time housed grades K-12. She taught various grades, 4th, 5th, 6th, and then took over Alfred Kingsley's class when he went into the service. She finally arrived at 3rd grade where she stayed for the remainder of her career.

Catherine retired in 1971. After retiring Catherine spent a good deal of time traveling—to all fifty states, Canada, and South America. During her travels she managed to sail on five different cruises.

When asked to identify a most interesting person she has met, Catherine quickly announced "Miss Reardon." Miss Reardon was one of Catherine's teachers at the Lattingtown school. Catherine said that while teaching all six grades, Miss Reardon had the wonderful ability of keeping each student busy and learning. There were many projects in the classroom and always a buzz of activity.

When asked how people entertained themselves during her early years, Catherine said, "visiting back and forth." "People don't make the time for that now." she lamented. It was their way of keeping in touch with each other.

When asked about some school matters at that time i.e. centralization, Catherine says she never got involved in school politics. She never counted the hours in the school day. "It was after school that so many stopped in for extra help," she said. She also never counted the days until the end of the school year. "I was hired to teach," she says, "I loved it, and that's what I did."

Catherine keeps in touch with many of her former students when she meets them at Dickie's Diner. "They've all been so good to me," she says, "I love them all and they're in my prayers every day."

She has touched so many lives she has lost count. Those who were fortunate enough to have had Catherine Dowd, in some cases more than one generation in a family, recognize the intangible gifts she has bestowed upon them. In turn, many prayers are raised appealing for her continued good health and happiness.

*   *   *

ERNESTINE WYGANT

She was born June 9, 1898. She was nicknamed "Boy." She was the 2nd child and was supposed to be a boy but was not. Named after her father Ernest Cole, a grocer in Hampton, New Hampshire, a small sea-side community, she was the apple of his eye. He took her with him everywhere, even when he had business meetings to attend. He never punished her but never smothered her with overprotectiveness either. She grew strong and independent as she matured into a lovely woman

In 1983 Renee Raimondi, after an interview with Ernestine Wygant wrote:

> "These days there are some pretty fancy bathing suits, but they can't compare to the bathing suits in the early 1900's. Mrs. Ernestine Wygant was a teenager who wore one of those bathing suits. They were full bloomers sewn at the waist, with black stockings underneath, and a skirt over it. There was only one slight problem with these

bathing suits, you would wear sneakers too and the rest
of the bathing suit is so bulky that it would be more like
bathing and splashing around than swimming."

Ernestine attended Mount Holyoke College and graduated in 1920
ready to set the world on fire. (In later years as an alumnae she became
president of her class).

Her first job was teaching English, French and music at a distant
town called Marlborough, NY. She traveled here by train on September
6, 1920, having to change trains in Boston and arriving in Marlboro in
the dark of evening. She remembers the sensation of winding up and up
and up in the taxi, wondering when she would reach the top. She stayed
with the principal, Mr. Taylor and his wife at their home (later the
Plank's house).

Mr. and Mrs. Taylor invited her to join them in attending a revival
meeting. They had also invited a neighbor, a young man named James
Calvin Wygant (his family built the present Esposito house). Only a few
people in town had cars; he had one. He would visit with the Taylors
and soon was taking Ernestine to the movies in Newburgh.

A friend, an old flame, from Hampton borrowed her father's car to
visit Ernestine. She smiles as she recounts that she managed to have the
car full of her lady friends during his visit so that he never had the
opportunity to "pop" the question.

The year 1920 was a significant one as it marked the passing of the
Women's Suffrage Amendment and the first time that women in the
United States had the right to vote. Ernestine Cole was among the first
women to vote in the town of Marlborough—she was just 22 years old.

She taught for two years. Ernestine reports that the students mainly
were easy to handle in Marlborough. The high school had an assembly
room and 2 recitation rooms on the 3rd floor of the old Union Free
School (present site of the Marlboro Fire Company). She and James

Calvin Wygant married December 11, 1923 and built a lovely home on Hudson Terrace which is still home to Ernestine.

Bertie Clark, who had graduated from Mount Holyoke in 1913, taught math in the Marlboro High School and married Edgar Clark, a farmer in Milton, invited Ernestine to her home to discuss setting up a Girl Scout troop. Ernestine wrote in her diary that day, "Walked to Milton to talk of Scouting with Bertie Clark." She and Bertie share the honors of having established the first Girl Scouting in Marlborough. The troop included all ages and, since it was formed shortly after World War I, reflected a military-like organization drilling in the school yard, hiking and studying survival skills, practicing Morse code, and wearing khaki uniforms. Ernestine has been seriously involved with the Girl Scouts ever since. She was a Neighborhood Chairman from 1925 to 1950. At that time she took a short hiatus from scouting as one daughter, Carol, was married and another daughter, Charlotte, and a son, Calvin were in college. With her absence, scouting began to wane and so in 1955 she returned and took over the chairmanship again. She recruited five young women, Casey, Paltridge, Esposito, Trautman and Graziosi and took them to New Paltz for training with Ruth Heigardt, a Girl Scout trainer. Scouting has since flourished in our community. Ernestine has been a President, on the Board of Directors, and in 1960 was presented with a "Thanks" Badge. In 1991, Ernestine celebrated her 65th year as a registered Girl Scout. She is presently a member of the Girl Scout Archives Committee and travels to Kingston to help put the archives in order.

Ernestine has also been very active in the Presbyterian Church. She has served as Sunday School teacher, President of the Presbyterian Church Women's Association, Superintendent of Sunday School, Church Elder and member of North River Presbytery. She is also remembered for her many hours as organizer of the church rummage sale. Some of the earlier rummage sales were held at the old McGowan's Hotel. For several weeks each year she sorted and priced, hung her ever-present leather purse around her waist, and was prepared to strike a good bargain with her many loyal customers. Clothing that remained after the sale had ended was packed up and sent to various charitable organizations.

Ernestine also was involved with the school board serving as the first female School Board member. She remembers how the men used to meet prior to the scheduled meeting, decide what they wanted to do, and then expected her to rubber stamp their decision. Needless to say, that did not go on for very long. She has also served as President of the Mid-Hudson Valley Mount Holyoke Club, President of the Marlboro Free Library Trustees, and has served on the Ulster County Cooperative BOCES Board. In 1995 the "Alumnae Medal of Honor" from Mount Holyoke College was bestowed upon her.

With her husband (since deceased) she has done extensive traveling to Europe, Africa and Australia, all by boat. She has 3 children, 9 grand children and 11 great grandchildren.

LET ME GROW LOVELY
Let me grow lovely, growing old—
So many fine things do;
Laces, and ivory, and gold,
And silks need not be new;
And there is healing in old trees,
Old streets a glamour hold;
Why may not I, as well as these,
Grow lovely, growing old?
Karle Wilson Baker

If such were Ernestine's wish, it has been granted. Few enjoy the love that emanates to her, from her family, her friends, and those of the community who hold her dear. Her loveliness radiates from a compassionate heart and a luminous spirit.

*   *   *

HELEN MCGUIRE

Helen McGuire was kind enough to give us an interview and tell us about her family and life in Marlboro.

1) The Manions

There were four Manion siblings—John Sr., Mary Ann, Nellie and Patrick. John Senior lived, as a boy, near what is now St. Mary's cemetery. He married Mamie Tighe from Newburgh who bore him two children, John Jr. and Marion. Helen McGuire remembers her mother talking about the wonderful craftsmanship that Mamie was able to impart to her sewing. Mamie, unfortunately, died young—John Jr. was only nine years old and his sister, Marion but twelve. Helen's mother then took over the task of helping to raise the two children.

John Sr. bought property on (the present) Manion's hill and farmed the land. Later he started the Manion's trucking business which his son, John Jr. later took over. Sam Quimby bought the business several years ago. He also built the Manion house at the curve on Manion's hill. John Sr. was also very involved in the ice business using Manion's pond. He had certain cutters for the ice and kept the ice in good condition by packing it in sawdust and storing it in the ice house on the edge of the pond. He then delivered the ice during the summer when there was a need. Helen remembers the dam on the edge of the pond as "always being there". The pond was always a popular site for ice skating in the winter as well as a source of water for spray during the fruit season.

Marion Manion was all set to attend Vassar college when she suffered a bout with appendicitis which lead to her death.

After a number of years, John Sr. married Winifred Driscol from Milton. He died in the 1940's.

Nellie Manion was Helen McGuire's mother. She was born in 1878 and was a graduate of New Paltz normal school.

Mary Ann married John Barry.

The youngest Manion, Patrick, was married to Mamie Tierney who taught in the Plutarch school. Patrick sold the original land for St. Mary's Cemetery (which was originally St. James's Cemetery). His heirs later sold the remaining parcel of his farm to Jay and Mary Miller.

2) The Gaffneys

The Gaffneys were a New Paltz family. Daniel Gaffney was born in 1871 and worked as a young man on the large family farm in Clintondale. Daniel married Nellie Manion. There were five children born to this marriage—three boys; Joe, Ed and Charles and two girls; Helen and Mary. Theresa Gaffney, an aunt to Helen McGuire, taught at the Lattingtown School. Helen was told that Theresa drove a horse and buggy to her teaching position and Barrett Wygant and J. Ed McGowan would take care of her horse for her.

The Gaffney children were born in New Paltz. The Gaffneys moved to Marlboro when Daniel, the father, bought the Betz farm in 1928. Daniel Gaffney operated the Lowe brick yard in New Paltz but wanted to get back to farming.

Helen graduated from New Paltz in 1927. She taught for nine years at the Mt. Kisco schools. In 1937 she married Joe McGuire and in December of that year bought her present home from her father, though Daniel Gaffney and son, Joseph, continued to run the farm until Daniel's death in 1958. Joe Gaffney continued with the farm.

Joe McGuire was the Superintendent of Repairs at Trap Rock for forty-four years. Helen subbed in the late 1940's along with Margaret Faurie. In 1958 she got a call from Mr. Alvut, the school principal, that there was an opening in the 5th grade. She taught in Marlboro for twelve years along with Katherine Cumisky, Chris LoBergio and Catharine Dowd.

Helen and Joe McGuire had two children, Mary Jo and J. Francis (better known as Frank).

3) The house and land

Mr. Betz was the head engineer for Ashokan Reservoir. He bought the property for his son Walter to farm. Walter married Jane Pratt whose father was involved with Pratt Lumber Company in Highland. Walter and Jane's wedding present was the present McGuire home which was built in 1919. Oley Sandstrom (of Marlboro) married another Pratt daughter. Oley Sandstrom and his wife got a home on Old Post Road in Marlboro (where young Joe Pesavento now lives). Walter was not a farmer and decided to move to Real Estate which he did in North Carolina.

When Helen McGuire's father bought the farm, Walter Betz was renting the house to Walter Patton—Patton was employed by NY Trap

Rock. According to Helen, Walter Betz was a very likable young man and a friend of her husband's. One day during a recent summer Helen had a visit from two of Walter Betz's daughters. They reported that Jane Pratt Betz was then about 95 or 96 years old. The two daughters had been born in the McGuire home. The house next to the McGuire home is one of the oldest house in Marlboro. J. Francis and Kevin McGuire and family presently reside there.

4) Range of the interview

It is always so fascinating to interview one of our elder citizens. Helen McGuire, especially, had some wonderful insights. It is interesting to note that when one does an interview of someone in their 90's, one can tap back into history even further than would seem possible. Helen remembers stories her mother told her. Her mother was born in 1878—and shared with Helen and the family her remembrances of a crate factory near the Clark's on Plattekill Rd. The smoke bushes near the McGuire home were there when Helen's mother was a girl more than 100 years ago.

When asked about why she chose to stay in Marlboro Helen replies, "I'm a country girl and I like openness and I like nice people". Fortunately Marlboro likes nice people too and that is why Helen McGuire has always been so welcome in our human collage.

*   *   *

Jim Clarke

His family history is wrapped tightly with the history of the Town of Marlborough. His forebears migrated from Orange County in 1817. Jim Clarke presently lives about half a mile from the house in which he was born. He was born in the Clarke family homestead on Clarke's Lane in Milton. At about age five he went to Charlotte Tuttle's nursery school on Willow Tree Road; walking the mile for the half day of school. He remembers Miss Tuttle had a wonderful garden that brightened the whole neighborhood. For grades 1-5 he attended the District Public School #4, a one room school on the corner of Clarke's Lane and Milton Turnpike. He was one of the early students of Mary Conroy, who taught in the Marlborough schools for many years. After that he went to Cherry Hill Academy on Sands Avenue in Milton. His teacher there was Dwight Warren, who was also principal. He remembers Dwight as a "tough old bird" who was a strict disciplinarian. Next he went to Highland High school. Since his mother's people were Quakers (she was a Birdsall which is a name that goes way back in Plattekill), he continued his education at a boarding school in Pennsylvania run by the Quakers.

Jim's grandfather; his father, Walter Clarke; and his aunt, Lula Clarke, went into partnership in the fruit growing business. Lula Clarke was a charter member of the Newburgh Garden Club which was founded in Marlborough. One of the aims of the Garden Club was to plant forsythia all along 9W in order to give it the distinction of being called "the Golden Highway."

Jim's grandfather was one of the first to specialize only in fruit. Previously, farmers were generalists. Jim's father had graduated from the Massachusetts Agricultural College at Amherst and brought new technology to the farming business. Jim spoke of the Hudson River Fruit Exchange which was set up to cooperatively market fruit and purchase supplies for the associated farmers. The Exchange was very big in the area until after W.W.II. George Hildebrand was the manager. Most of the big farms in the area were involved and were shareholders.

He recalls that the Milton Cold Storage Company also was an important business. Grover Ferguson was secretary and office manager. This company would store fruit for farmers before most of them had their own cold storage facilities. It would also market the fruit if the farmer so desired. The Kedem Winery now is the site of the old Milton Cold Storage facility.

The fruit early on was packed in barrels which held about three bushels of fruit. The barrels were too rough on the fruit as much of the fruit bruised from the weight. Also they were too heavy to handle easily as they weighed about a hundred and fifty pounds. Bushel baskets were then utilized; later bushel boxes and now, said Jim, it's almost all cardboard. Jim remembers packing fruit by kerosene lamp. "The quality requirements were not like today," he mused. Nevertheless, fruit from the Marlborough area was shipped all over including Great Britain and Europe. Jim's grandfather had a broker in Scotland. At one time the grandfather and grandmother made a transatlantic voyage and were entertained by the broker. The reputation for Mid-Hudson valley fruit was excellent. The Hudson River Steamer which stopped at the Milton dock carried passengers and also would transport fruit to the Washington Street market in New York City.

Fruit trees were sprayed from the early 1900s with a hand pump—a sprayer-gun was hand held. Part of the reason for the demise of the currant as a popular locally grown fruit is that it was labor intensive. Most farmers years ago had a mixed crop of fruit. Local farmers were extremely proud of the Macintosh which became the premier variety from the 1920s through the 1970s. In the days, when agriculture was just becoming more of a science and less of an art, grafting was used to get newer varieties on older trees. Jim said it was not efficient horticulturally—the trees were awkward to handle—but it was a way to establish new varieties quickly.

This era also brought the advent of the use of migrant laborers. During the depression, a farmer could get plenty of help locally. In the 30's the southern states were having a hard time financially. Blacks would find their way up here from South Carolina, Georgia, Florida and the other southern states. At first they would work their way up, but later they would come for the whole fruit season. Early on, they were awkward with the fruit as their experience had been with cotton. Gradually the migrant laborers became the backbone of the labor force in the area. This required the fruit grower to provide housing—which was "disreputable"—but it was shelter. Later the work force became more organized with work crews and crew leaders. The crew leader was the recruiter and acted like a "first sergeant". This was common until the 60's when the beginnings of "Off-shore" laborers began. Now the labor force is almost entirely Jamaican.

Jim remembers in the 20's his family had a cow, chickens, a team of horses and two cars. He admits he never learned to milk a cow. He remembers his grandmother had a Model T Ford. Jim learned to drive on that car when he was about twelve years old. At about fifteen years of age, Jim became interested in an old Essex that rested by a fence on his neighbor's property. He asked his neighbor, Al Jenkins, how much he wanted for the car. "How much you got?" asked Jenkins. Jim replied, "$3.50". A bargain was struck! All the money he had went into the upkeep of that car. Jim scoured farm dumps for discarded rubber tires. They had tubes in those days, and for 79¢ Jim could buy a kit for fixing punctures in tires. "I got to be quite an expert at fixing flats," Jim reports, "I had a flat about every two days."

Jim said he had tried out several sports during his high school and college days. He was very proud of the fact that his father made him a tennis court on the lawn behind the house. Every night, after supper, Jim and his friends would play a set or two of tennis.

There was also the "Infamous 4th of July." Jim and his brother found a muzzle loaded shotgun in the attic. "There were real old treasures up there," reports Jim. They took black powder from some fire crackers, carefully loaded the shotgun, stuck the wick from the fire cracker into the "touch hole", mounted it on a box, lit the fuse and then ran behind the corner of the house. Unfortunately, Jim's mother had a rug hanging from a line across the yard. The shot tore the rug to smithereens. Needless to say, that was their only experiment with fire arms.

Among Jim's memories of Milton are of the businesses. Chris Miller's grocery store in the Woolsey building—next to the present post office; the Shauness' (or Shaunessey's) dry goods and general store with its penny candy. Jim's early haircuts cost 25¢ and when he got older 50¢ at Dan Abruzzi's barber shop. Carl Hergert had a drug store. Another dry goods store was operated by Nick Miller; there were nice "Dutch" touches to the architecture of this building.

The library was built about 1923. John Maroldt, a reputable builder from Highland, built the library as well as Jim's father's cold storage, and indeed the house in which Jim presently lives. Before the present library was built the library was housed on the top floor of the Woolsey building.

The Bank was organized about 1921. Jim's father was on the original board of directors. Mr. Rownd was the first president. Jim's grandfather had had to go to Poughkeepsie to bank. This meant taking the ferry across the river, then a trolley to where the bank was located. This was an all day trip so it is understandable that the bank was welcomed by the Milton population.   Across from the bank, J.J. Kaley ran a grocery story. His sons Francis and Joe worked in the bank. On Dock Road was a factory that manufactured fruit baskets. In the 1930's it caught fire and went up like "a rocket." The Milton Engine Company was in existence then, but the fire was too fierce. "Billy the Baker" Pantusco had a bakery down on Dock Road. At 12 noon, when the bread came out of the oven, one could buy one of the still simmering round loaves for 10¢.

At this time the main highway ran through the town. In the 1930's 9W was altered to by-pass the village. With the advent of faster and more convenient family cars and the increase in large chain stores, shoppers tended to abandon going to the village. As a result many of the businesses folded and Milton's pace slowed considerably.

When asked about a most interesting personality that he knew in the area, Jim replied "Dr. Shelby Rook." Shelby was a minister of a

Presbyterian Church in Harlem. His wife, Dorothy Maynor Rook, was a celebrated concert soprano. The Rooks owned the Anning Smith house. Jim, his wife Louise, Shelby and his wife, Dorothy, enjoyed entertaining each other and exploring their different life stories. Shelby conducted the funeral services for Louise's father's funeral. An especially fond memory for Jim was Shelby's 50th birthday celebration. The gathering was held at the Anning Smith house. They toasted with champagne on a tranquil summer evening in the old colonial graveyard with a glistening full moon showering its radiance over the magnificent Hudson and the surrounding hillsides. "It's a romantic memory I'll treasure forever." Jim reflected.

We'd like to thank Jim and Louise for being so generous with their time and memories. Jim and his family have greatly contributed to the agricultural riches of the community. There is strong affinity for the community in which he has lived his full life, and the community is indeed indebted to him for his many gifts of time and talent.

*   *   *

JOE CONROY

He proudly wore his emerald green suspenders, new red flannels, checkered pants and his effervescent smile. He welcomed us into the very home in which he had been born 90 years earlier. With a snowy white mustache, physically agile and mentally spry, Joe Conroy related to us some of his fondest memories.

Joe lives on the Milton Turnpike and shares his home with a melodeon and two organs. The melodeon is from Modena, one organ is from Roseton, and the newest organ is from the Marlboro Methodist Church. When the church was sold to the Knights of Columbus, Joe couldn't bear the thought of the old organ going "on the block" and so added a porch on his house in order to give the organ a loving home. Awhile ago Joe was taking piano lessons in hopes of learning to play the organs—how's that for life-long learning? On the wall hangs a clock from the old Spratt store in Milton interesting in that around the perimeter are the days of the month. The clock marks the passage of minutes, hours, days, months—fitting for a man at ease with time.

Joe's father, Thomas Conroy, started out with a farm near the Ship's Lantern Inn. His mother was Bridget O'Conner. Both mother and father were born in Ireland. Joe revels in his Celtic heritage.

When queried regarding his early schooling Joe remembers well going to the old Cherry Hill Academy in Milton. His first teacher was Miss Marion Patten (who later married Eddie Wood), his second teacher was Miss Ida May DuBois (who later married Oliver B. Kent) and his third teacher was Mr. Dwight M. Warren who was also school principal. After consolidation and the abandonment of the school, Joe's brother purchased the old school house. The school bell was bought by the local priest who donated it to a church down south.

After his academy days, Joe continued his schooling and graduated from Highland High School. He remembers well the long trek to school. There were no buses in those days. Students walked, or rode second hand bicycles, and some even rode horses. Joe remembers freezing his ear one morning as it was 15° below zero.

His remembered visions of Milton include the Catholic church being green ("All for the Irish," he says with a twinkle in his voice and eye,) the stores owned by the Spratt's and the Kaley's, and Theill's Hotel next to the present firehouse. Joe and Fred Theil played baseball together and, before the advent of refrigeration, Fred was an iceman delivering ice to his customers.

Perhaps Joe's best loved memories are of playing ball. "I was a ball player you know; we had quite a team down here," he boasts. He played center field until Windy Spratt shifted him to third base. Their playing field was across from the Catholic church. "It wasn't too good (the field)," admits Joe. "Milton went and beat Red Hook up there. The team celebrated that time—I didn't get home, I guess, until the next day." His figure, tempered with age, still bears traces of the lithe young athlete within.

Milton Baseball Team, Milton, N. Y.
Front Row sitting—Windy Spratt, Jim Coe, Dobbie Ennist, Judd DeWitt
Standing—Al Eckert, Pinky (Charles) Thorne, ??? from Poughkeepsie, Fred Theill Jr.,
Joe Spratt, Pat McCabe, ???, Everitt Hyatt, Mike Conroy
Picture taken at McCabe's Field on Willow Tree Road
Joe Conroy ventured that his brother Mike Conroy was about 18 years old in this picture—his brother was born in 1894 and therefore the picture was taken about 1912.

*   *   *

JOE PESAVENTO

"August 5, 1993
Senior Citizen Award
for Outstanding Service to the
Marlboro-Milton Community
Presented by the Marlboro-Milton Lions"

This is but one of the signs that a community appreciates his efforts. Fire commissioner for nearly 50 years; Lion for 50 years, American Legionnaire for 50 years; Elk for nearly 50 years; member of Unico, the Marlboro Yacht Club, the Bocci club and more—he has indeed been a contributor to the quality of life in our town. Joseph Pesavento, Sr. was born 7/22/1917 in Cedar Cliff, a small community south of Marlboro which no longer exists. His father, Frederico, had come from Montoroso, Italy about 45 miles from Venice. The family had passed through Ellis Island and taken a train to the Cedar Cliff station. Joe, remembering family stories, tells how they arrived in winter; the river was iced over; and mistaking the frozen river for land, his father was amazed at how level the land was. Frederico Pesavento traveled with his wife, Valentina Moschi Pesavento; two sisters, Angela Pagantine and Teresa Ronkese, his brother-in-law; and his three eldest children, Olga, Dominick and Fred.

In the 1920's Cedar Cliff, alongside the railroad tracks, was made up of three stores and about 20-25 families. Herbie McMullen was the Post Master. There was a hotel on top of the hill across from the Goudy place. Trap Rock was just starting—that's where the work was. Donkey carts were loaded by hand with stone that brought 1/2¢ to 1¢ per pound. Work continued all year round with the stone loaded onto the railroad cars to be shipped to other destinations. The first steam shovel appeared on the scene about 1923. Mr. Batton, the first engineer, lived in the McGuire house near Manion's hill.

By 1924 four more children were born in Joe's family; Elizabeth, Joe, Mary and Sylvio. The family saved money and sent it to Italy to buy land. Frederico Pesavento then took his whole family back to Italy to farm the land located at the head of the Po valley. Joe remembers them raising wheat and vegetables and using oxen to plow. They remained in Italy for less than a year, though Joe does remember attending school there. Trap Rock wanted Frederico to return to work—which he did bringing his family back also. They bought a house on Buckley's Hill. Fred Goudy, the well known type artist, was a neighbor. Joe remembers when Goudy's press burned down. Julia was born circa 1924.

In 1929 the depression hit and in 1930 Trap Rock closed down with no notice given though some of the men were transferred across the river. Frederico Pesavento was one of the lucky ones. Joe remembers going to school in Cedar Cliff where Mr. Bond, who later owned Blossom Farm Inn, and Mrs. DuBois were teachers. Joe also attended the Marlboro Union Free School where Mr. Taylor was principal. Teachers included Miss Dowd, Miss Bewick, Miss Rosser (who later married Barney Herberich), Miss Shaeffer (music) and Miss Lowry (3rd grade).

Joe loved music as he boasts of being Miss Shaeffer's "pet" pupil. He was in a number of plays she produced. He played in "Peter Rabbit" at the Marlboro movie theater, capturing the prize roll of Mr. McGregor.

Miss Rosser directed a play on the grounds of the Presbyterian Church. Joe was "Robin Hood". He was supposed to shoot Leigh Figerio with an arrow—which he actually did, he tells with a grin. John Quimby was "Little John". Joe remembers stick wrestling with him on the bridge prop. Another production was "Alice in Wonderland" with Jeannie Herberich McCourt as Alice.

When the depression hit, Trap Rock at its peak was paying the men every two weeks on Fridays. The Marlboro bank stayed open to cash the approximately 120 checks. Mr. Fraust was president of the bank then followed by Misters Haviland, Carpenter and Robinson. During the depression, Joe's father was the only one in the family with a job. There was a little work in Newburgh at the pocketbook and clothing factories where his siblings worked, but not much. Farmers lent land to families so they could raise vegetables in a garden. Joe remembers how helpful Joe DallVechia was to the families in the area during those hard times. Joe's mother got his father's pay check—but $2 was withheld for Sam Quimby, Sr.—to buy grapes to make wine. Quimby had a car with fruit, vegetables and meats. He'd slaughter that day and bring the produce to people's homes. He had a scale—first on the car and then on a pick-up—to weight the produce. Joe remembers the housewives using their aprons to hold the eggs.

Mrs. Schramm's boarding house (later Meckes's place) was nearby and Joe vividly recalls the smell of baking bread wafting down the street. At that time the boarding house had tennis, swimming in the pond, hiking and other pastoral diversions to entertain guests.

Joe was also a baseball player of note in high school. His team mates included: Jack Tudicco, Tony Quintialliani, Cy Canzonari (Tony's brother), Joe Garcia, Buddy Frazier, Leigh Figerio, Ed Challandes and Fred Elgee. Most of the Milton lads went to Highland for high school.

Joe's team played other locals at the field behind the Presbyterian Church. Joe played catcher and 3rd base.

Farmers first utilized school kids when school was out to harvest their crops. Joe remembers working for Townsend Velie for 15¢ an hour after school. Later, during the war, "Farmerettes" from New York City were employed. They often stayed at Canzonari's or Chillura's on Lattingtown Road. The farmers, at that time, also used hobos. Joe remembers the hobo camps along the railroad and the camp fires they had. It was a "hobo haven." "Some came from rich families, took to drinking and ended up on the hobo circuit." In general, Joe recalls they had good reputations for the work they performed and rarely ran into trouble with the law. Joe does recall hearing, however, that John C. Quimby gave refuge to a hobo in his barn—a fire that night consumed the barn (the present Doug Laurie farm). (Sam Quimby adds—the date was Friday the 13th, 1913.)

During the War (WWII), Joe remembers that Auggie Tuturro and he were two of the first numbers called for the draft in New York State. Joe was deferred because he was the principal support for his family. Ed Quimby was chairman of the draft board. Auggie Tuturro was killed in the war. Joe was working at Trap Rock when he was almost thrown into the crusher. He had had two uncles killed at Trap Rock (Joseph Pesavento and Joseph Moschi) and so decided to call it quits. He then worked for Gussy Mondello (the present Raccoon Saloon). At that time Stewart airport was in the process of being built. Every Friday night Gussy would cash the construction workers' checks. They would be three deep at the bar. "Every third drink was on the house" Joe recalls. But duty called…Joe joined the Army. He was hurt during maneuvers in Texas. For awhile he was MP at Fort Custer in Detroit.

(At this point I realized we had more than enough materials for one report. Joe still is not married, nor has he started business which he ran for 39 years in Marlboro. We decided to stop here and pick up at another time. Therefore, we end this report with to be continued….")

  *   *   *

JOE PESAVENTO 2

We promised you a follow-up on the last Joe Pesavento interview as Joe had so much information to share with us. At the conclusion of the last interview we left Joe just before he was married and before he opened his grocery business in Marlboro.

Joe chuckles as he tells a story from his youth. His father was due home from Italy that evening. Joe was in the 3rd grade. He and some friends were playing "Follow the Leader" on the lake behind the bakery. He describes the ice as "rubber" ice meaning it was not completely frozen. Sure enough, he fell in. He was afraid he'd get into trouble if he went home, so he went to the shanty down by the railroad. They had a pot belly stove that was exuding tremendous heat. Within a half hour his clothes were dry; he hurried home, climbed into bed and his father never knew of his escapade.

Joe claims he was brought up playing Bocci. Cedar Cliff had five courts at one time. Joe is sad to think that Cedar Cliff is now all gone. The school house was one of the first to go. Ronkese's house was the last house torn down in 1980. The "Powder" house is still there—it's a concrete building. Fred Goudy, who had lived near Joe at Cedar Cliff, left Joe his baseball glove. Alice Goudy used to take Rose to antique stores.

Joe Dall Vechia had closed the meat market he ran due to the meat shortage during the war years. (It had been Lucy's meat market in earlier years.) Joe Dall Vechia talked Joe Pesavento into reopening the business. Joe started the Marlboro Beef Co. in 1943 after he bought the place from Joe Dall Vechia.

Joe reminisced about other businesses in the area before and since that time. Joe Toracca's office had a tenant living upstairs. Cumisky (prior to Joe) was next to the bank and DeVela had a drug store next door. Tony Ferrara had a t.v. store. Joe Colletti had a barber shop. Prior to Nicklin's electrical store, Yeaples had a coffee bar in the corner shop.

On Main Street (9W) Jones had an ice cream parlor. That burned down and was replaced with a restaurant, then Rhoda's and then DiSantis' "Fish Net". Richborn had a grocery store that was a predecessor of the modern grocery chain—they had a branch in Milton. The Italian American Club had a center there for awhile too.

Where Amodeo is now, was a small gas station—Matty McCourt. There was also a shoe store. Purdy (a Fire Co. Chief and Girard's father) had a plumbing shop. Joe Rosado had a liquor store and small gift shop. At one time Lawton Clarke and Bill Postel also had businesses there. Baxters had their feed store and a department store. That burned down circa 1945 during a terribly cold night. Next to Mondellos was Cremo's Pool hall. (Before Cremos it was Clark's A & P.)

Beyond Mondellos (which is the Raccoon at the present time) was Vinnie Fowler's t.v. shop, a gun store, Sam Filligram's carpenter shop (down stairs was Kramer's Pool Room) and Frank Troncellito's garage.

He remembers McGowan's Hotel as a general meeting place. (The present establishment on the site is Criccio's Apartment) McGowan helped many Cedar Cliff Italians get their citizenship papers. The fire company dinners were held there. Constables at that time thought nothing of having a beer at the bar while in uniform—nobody else thought anything of it either.

There were two taxi drivers in town, Toni Zambito and Sal. Warren had had the first cab. His daughter Ethel Rich was the Marlboro telephone operator. Her office was over the bank. There were party lines at that time and everyone knew Ethel as all calls went through her.

Joe married Rose who hails from Poughkeepsie. They have three children; Joe Jr., Marilyn and Dennis. Joe and Rose bought their house in 1949 from DuBois. Professor Tooker and his two unmarried sisters had built the house. It is a sister house to the Haviland house on Old Post Road.

The Marlboro Beef Co. occupied Joe's and Rose's attention until it closed in 1978. Joe bought the whole "Carpenter" building in the late

50's. (The drug store was torn down for a drive-in window for the bank.) He started as a meat market and then expanded to a full grocery store. He knocked down the inside walls of two stores and doubled his space. The walls were made of tin and insulated with saw dust, he reports. There were apartments upstairs. Joe claims he made deliveries until the last day of operation even though at the end it was a losing proposition. Joe is very proud of the services he performed for his customers.

He and Rose made a lot of friends. To this day both he and Rose are greeted in the streets by the customers who patronized their store for many years. "It's a good feeling," said Joe, "to know that people valued our business practices." Even the migrants who frequented his store recognized the honesty and returned that honesty with honesty of their own. Joe said he was never cheated out of money owed by any of the migrants.

Joe is proud of his association with the Lions Club. He and Ed Young started the Christmas light project in Marlboro and Milton. His store had the switch to turn the Marlboro lights on and off. Rose tells how Joe would get up at midnight to go to the store to turn the lights off. Joe tells how Rose made him look at other towns to see what holiday decorations they were using. Joe was President of the Lions Club as was his son. Theirs was the first father/son combination to so serve. Joe is proud of the good work the Lions Club does in raising money for the blind. They continue to expand their donations to charitable causes.

He also takes pride in the fire company. "I'm happy to see it get as far as it has," he states, "it's one of the best in the Hudson Valley." Another of his favorite organizations if the Marlboro Yacht Club. Joe is justifiably proud of the volunteer work that Rose has done in various organizations over the years.

"Marlboro is a good, safe place to live," says Joe. "The schools are good and the small size of the community helps keep people friendly." "It feels good to say, 'I'm from Marlborough.'"

Joe has a saying that what one tosses into the wind comes back. Joe has sown many cheerful thoughts, given years of honest labor, and has contributed to the welfare of the town in so many ways—what's coming back to him is respect and appreciation from the community he has served so steadfastly.

*   *   *

JOHN LYNN

His eyes burn bright with the passion he feels for our Hudson River. It has been an important element throughout his life. John Lynn shares with us some of the copies he has of some of the fantastic old river boats. He names the lines and the boats each maintained: Hudson River Dayline with the "Albany", the "Robert Fulton", the "DeWitt Clinton", the "Peter

Styverson", the "Washington Irving", the "Alexander Hamilton", the "Hendrick Hudson", and the "Chauncy M Dephew"—Central Hudson Line with the "Benjamin B. O'dell", the "Newburgh", the "Poughkeepsie", the "Homer Ramsdell" and the "Jacob Tremper"—the Hudson River Night Line with the "W C Morris", the "Fort Orange", the "Rensselaer", the "Berkshire" and the "Trojan." The pictures show these beautiful ships with their luxurious libraries, writing rooms and ballrooms and nudge us into realizing what "the good old days" really connotes.

John tells the story of the time his friend Clayton and he were boating and Clayton decided to run circles around the "Alexander Hamilton." George Carrol was the captain. Carrol got on his bullhorn and called out, "OK you two, I've got your number." Clayton ended up having to pay a fine. The "Alexander Hamilton" was the last running on the river. "They had some beauties of boats" says John. One of the most famous steamers was the dayliner "Henrick Hudson." It could hold 5,500 people and was usually chock full. It would dock at Kingston and some passengers would pick up the Delaware & Hudson train and travel up to Phoenicia. The rail are still in place and the railroad cars are now used to carry "tubers" from the end of their rides back to their cars parked at the starting point of their voyage.

The Hudson River Nightline also carried automobiles. People would often put their automobiles on the Nightline, take the train to Albany and there pick up their autos. This was circa the late 1920's and before the advent of the Thruway. Dayliners were chartered by local church groups for an exciting afternoon excursion on the river. They then would stop at the Marlboro dock to pick up and discharge passengers. John remembers quite vividly going on a "Moonlight Excursion" and the splendor of the lovely river boat with its mahogany bar, spectacular ballroom and the wonderful music of a live band. "That was some party" he muses.

Sam Roesoffs bought a number of these boats when the companies folded in hopes of being able to resell them. There were a number of them tied up on the river near Roesoff's home. Two had fires. The "Benjamin O'Dell" was badly burned but was able to be towed away. The "Trojan" was burned so badly it sank near the Van Vliets sand bank. The remains are still a short distance offshore and it is reported the hull can be visible if the conditions are right. The Marlboro Fire Company was called to that fire which occurred circa 1940.

The "fruit" boats played a most important role in Marlborough's history. John remembers when the farmers' laden, horse drawn wagons would be parked from the dock clear up Dock Road and onto 9W. The "Poughkeepsie", the "O'Dell", the "Homer Ramsdel" and the "Jacob Trumper" were mostly all fruit boats. John says he can remember a day when the "Poughkeepsie" was loading fruit at the dock and the "Jacob Trumper" was treading water in the river waiting to pull in. There was a cherry pitting factory down at the docks. It was a small operation which would wash and pit the cherries and add sugar to them. The cherries were used to make pies down in New York City. There was also a rather long building near the present Yacht club. Local farmers would rent space in the building from Ralph Young to store their fruit for short periods of time. John said the poles holding the building erect had the names of the farmers who were renting those spaces. The building stood until recent years. At the Yacht club there is also a weigh station. Large barn doors at one end allowed a horse and wagon or truck to enter. The scale where the fruit was weighed, right on the vehicle, was in the center of the building. Barn doors at the opposite end of the building permitted the vehicle to exit while another entered through the first doors. The weigh station is scheduled for demolition by the Yacht club.

John also remembers as a boy hitching a ride on an empty horse and wagon up Dock Road and hitching a ride back down the hill on a full one. Barges would also land at Marlboro, mostly at Johnson's. They brought such things as coal from Pennsylvania and manure from New York City. Local farmers used the manure for fertilizer. The unloading was all with shovel and pitch fork and took many man hours. The manure was also used for fertilizer at some local mushroom farms. Griggs, Conns and Oliver Mackey were local mushroom growers. The Griggs had caves (behind our new Wendel's) for growing the mushrooms.

The Central Hudson railroad was also located near the Marlboro dock. The station that was torn down circa late 1950's was actually the second station house in Marlboro. The first was north of where the second was built. One of the reasons for building the second was that one had to cross the track twice in order to get to the first station. There were two tracks at that time so it is easy to understand both the difficulty and the danger. New York Central also had a big freight house near the river as well as a big water tank—the railroads were steam at that time.

The advent of automobiles brought additional problems. John remembers the old Model T chain drive Fords. They had no fuel pumps and as one attempted to climb Dock Road, the gas could not reach the carburetors even if the tanks were nearly full. The cars would then stall. The local gentry found it easier to back their cars all the way up Dock Road rather than to have them stall near the crest.

Joe Smalling lived in a shack on an island in Old Man's creek near the river. He made a living fishing on the river. He fished for Shad, Herring and put "stake nets" out for carp in the creek. As far as can be determined he claimed his small plot of ground by "squatters' rights." He never drove a car. John said, "Everything was man, muscle and boat." He had a 20' rowboat which he was able to handle solo. He was also able to throw his shad nets out by himself. A shad net consisted of about 500' of net in "a shot"—usually up to four "shots" were used and would stretch almost the whole width of the river. On the end were cork floats about a foot square that held the kerosene lanterns used to mark the floats. Problems arose when a ship would come up or down the river. The fisherman had to scramble to get his nets out of the way or risk having them torn. John remembers fishing so in the river and standing up in his boat and shouting to a boat captain to go around the nets. "Do you expect me to sail this thing up on the shore?" the captain replied.

Making or repairing the nets was an arduous chore. They were made of linen and almost "knit" with spindles. "Old man" Scott and Joe Casscles made and repaired fish nets. They usually did so during the long evenings of winter.

John's blood still ebbs and flows with the river tides. Each morning he wends his way down to the Yacht club to feed his friends. There are many more gulls and ducks on the river now than there were in the recent past. "They stay as long as there is open water," he says. When the water at the Yacht club freezes John suspects they head for Danscammer where Central Hudson pumps river water in to cool their condensers and then returns warmed water to the river. They begin their quacking as his car pulls up and waddle their way towards him as he opens his trunk to bring out the bread they have come to expect. Then this pensive man sits on the banks of the river that has meant so much to him throughout his lifetime, feeds his gentle feathered friends and ponders the significance of "That Old Man River that just keeps rolling along."

*   *   *

JOHN LYNN REVISITED

At the conclusion of our last interview with John Lynn, we recognized that he still had more "Marlborough Story" to tell and so persuaded him to meet with us again.

John was born on King Street (in the present Joe McCourt House). At the time of his birth, it was a three family house—on the top floor was the Lawrence Felter family, on the main floor was John Lynn's family, and in the south wing lived "Old Man Prizzia". John Bingham owned the house at that time.

As he was growing up John remembers the following about the immediate area:

Ed McGowan's "Exchange Hotel" was in full swing and quite a substantial establishment. Ed McGowan's sister, Margaret, had the hotel in later years. (Now the site of Cricio Apartments)

Jesse Edwards built on what had been the empty lot next to the Exchange Hotel. He ran a butcher and grocery store. (Now "The Brick House" Restaurant)

Sam Filigram, a carpenter, lived in the "Casey House".

Next was an interesting small house that has since been razed.

Dr. Palmer, a very busy local physician and his family lived in the "Palmer House". The doctor had an office in a part of his home.

Next was John's home (now the McCourt home).

Jack Warren and his mother lived in the next house down. Millard Coy lived in the house at a later date.

In the Purdy "Tenant House" lived John DuBois. The house had been built by Purdy.

The last house on that block was the "Baxter House". John remembers Ethel Rich living in the north wing.

Just across DuBois Street was at that time a vacant lot. Later Frank Powell ran a Shell gas station there. Stan Sutton and then DuBois had gas stations there in later years, and now it is back to being a vacant lot.

John remembers being hit by a Model T Ford right in front of the "Flat Iron Building" (present site of Realty) when he was four or five years old.

John also talked about "Coutantville"—(near the corner of Highland and Western Avenue). There were several Coutant families living in that area and Mrs. Emma Coutant had a store there.

Ice Boating on the Hudson was quite the sport when John was a young man. Ice Boaters started out near Ralph and Adeleid Young's dock. John remembers Stanley Harcourt, John Manion and Christie Tuttle as quite the dare devil's on the ice. The boats could reach as much as 60-65 miles per hour. John DuBois had "The Cyclone" which he stored in a hayloft in his barn.

However, Marlborough's young blades were not satisfied with just ice boating. John remembers the winters of '25-'35 as being particularly cold. The young Marlboroughites would use a 2"x10"x12" to get their Model A Fords, 4 cylinder Chevies and early Buicks over the ridge of ice formed right at the shore by the freezing and thawing ice. Once on the ice there were many exciting rides on the virtually frictionless ice. Drivers would race alongside the open channel in the center of the river or brake quickly and set their cars in a wild spin. One of the fastest drivers was James Hunter from Hudson Terrace. On occasion, the ice would be frozen across the whole river, but the ice breakers "East Wind" and "West Wind" usually maintained a channel of open water.

One year "Yank" Conn had a Model A ford spinning so swiftly on the ice that it spun right into the open channel. He marked the ice where the car had gone under, went and got Schantz's white feed truck (which was equipped with a block and fall with a hook) and dropped the hook near the spot he had marked on the ice (right off Roesoff's). First time he dropped the hook, he was able to hook the car. He was then able to get the car out, took it to Shantz's (where he worked), dried it out, checked the spark plugs, changed the oil and started it up.

"Those were the days," John mused. "Wearing a derby, sporting a big cigar…Saturday nights,…say no more we made our own fun."

One of John's first jobs was with the Diamond D bus lines (1932). This was during the depression and John felt proud to be bringing in $16-$18 per week. The company had 26 or 27 buses. The big trip was the daily trip between Kingston and New York City via the old Storm King highway. He remembers one hair raising experience when the bus he was driving broke down and he ended up in a ditch, in the rain on the old, curvy Storm King Highway.

The Diamond D building was built by John AC DuBois as a car agency. He sold Model Ts and Chevies in the 1920's. The building could park seven or eight buses. There had been a barn there before that. Diamond D also had garages in Highland & Poughkeepsie. Diamond D was sold to George Carrol in the 1980's.

North of Diamond D was Lyons' Diner—in later years Jim Woodward's Diner. Where Amodeo has his garage, Mattie McCourt had a small garage "hanging over the sucker hole with a pump right on the 9W curb".

John was working two jobs at one point. He also worked part time for the Marlboro Water District. Bill Clark was the water superintendent. At that time there was only "a little dinky" reservoir. During the dry seasons, it would tend to dry up. Sometimes water had to be pumped out of the "Old Man's Creek". The water department used a civilian defense pump and Manion's truck. At Consoli's bridge there would be three shifts overseeing the pumping. Allen Purdy, Sr., Russell McConnell and several others worked on the project. The water had to be chlorinated by feeding the chlorine into the suction line of the pump. This happened for seven or eight years during the drought season. There was a fire hydrant at Consoli's. Planks would be put across the road to protect the hoses. This pumping of water from the creek sometimes went as long as Thanksgiving. John remembers one year when even the creek dried to a trickle and the crew had to go to Johnson's property and pull the water almost directly from the river. The water was pumped into a fire hydrant and another pump was used to pull the water up the hill on Dock Road.

When John Quimby was supervisor Borchert's D6 was brought up the hill to the reservoir and the reservoir was made three times larger. That year they took advantage of the dry weather to work on the expansion of the reservoir.

John eventually took over the position of water supervisor with Bob Johnson assisting him. They were responsible for putting the water meters in. To this day the reservoir serves the community but in a different capacity. With permission, local fishermen are able to fish on the reservoir and many are able to provide their families with an especially tasty meal of beautiful "Marlboro Reservoir" trout.

(To be Continued)

*   *   *

JOHN LYNN REVISITED 2

Marlboro is presently hooked up to the New York City Delaware Aqueduct via Shaft 5A which is located on Lattingtown Road just over the county line in Orange County. John Lynn indicates Marlboro is lucky to have been able to do this as New York City has the reputation of having the finest drinking water in the world. The aqueduct is a tunnel 1010 feet deep at the point of Shaft 5A. The nearest access other than Shaft 5A is Shaft 5 in Plattekill on one side and Chelsea—five miles away on the other side of the river. The aqueduct crosses under the river at Roseton. John remembers that George Cutillo's brother was killed while working in Shaft 5.

The shafts were started with jack hammers. The engineering was impressive. A number of local men worked on it. Leonard Schreiber was one. The shaft was started in 1939 and work continued through the early 40's. There were three eight hour shifts. Ted Pressler had a store near the shaft opening that has since been torn down. The building there now is the pump station where the water is chlorinated and metered.

The shaft going down to the aqueduct is 12 feet in diameter and goes down 1010 feet. At the bottom of the shaft (which is all bed rock) they built a room that was grouted with concrete. Electric locomotives were used to haul the stone while they were digging the tunnel. There was a railroad track in the tunnel and the men and stone went up and down the shaft in a bucket. The Colombo Brothers bought the shale which was used for driveways, etc.

John remembers when Joe Cutillo and he started walking along the track leading under the Hudson river—when they saw some leaking water, they became uneasy. John said whenever a leak was found, high pressure guns were used to pump a quick curing cement into the cracks. He was amazed at how effective this was—the cracks would seal right up. The pressure is incredible as witnessed by the statistic that at the pump station the valves used to turn the water on and off have 90 pounds of pressure per square inch. "That's at the top!", John emphasizes.

As indicated the job was started in 1939, continued, though curtailed to a degree, during the war and was finished in the 40's. Milton now also has the advantage of being hooked into the system. Not many years ago Milton was served by seven to nine wells at the foot of Van Orden Road near the river. They had been only getting five or six gallons per minute which was not adequate and caused concern with respect to having enough water to fight fires.

Sam Roesoff, who had gotten his start in New York City, (he was nicknamed "Subway Sam"), also had some contracts for portions of the aqueduct. John explained that contractors bid on five mile sections. Sam Roesoff got the bid for two five mile sections near Ellenville.

"Subway Sam" had previously had contracts for some of the subways in New York City. Some of the rock taken from the New York City subways was transported by barge to Marlboro and Milton and used along the railroad tracts. It is still possible to find holes in some of the rock where drill holes were made for blasting. Sam also had some sand banks in Marlboro (Roesoff's Hill). Cinders were brought by gondola (trains) to the Marlboro docks and made into "cinder blocks". Frank DeGeorge, Sr. worked for Sam as well as numerous other local citizens. John remembers Sam saying, "I can't read or write, but I have enough money to hire others to do it for me."

Roesoff built a beautiful home on "Roesoff's Hill". The house later became the "Harbor Lights" restaurant. Unfortunately, the restaurant burned in the late 50's or early 60's during a cold, snowy period.

John was also instrumental in founding the Marlborough Yacht Club. Some of the original members included Fran Johnson, Jim Paltridge, Christie Tuttle, John Manion, Harry Lyons and Cluett Schantz. They were able to purchase the Traphagen/Young property of about four acres at the Marlboro dock circa 1943. John served as Commodore from 1950 to 1955.

John Hedeman was the last to live in the old "weigh station" on the Yacht Club property. He built a boat in the long building. Originally he conceived of constructing the boat out of concrete. All told he made three boats in Yonkers bringing one to the Marlboro Yacht Club. He sold one to someone in the Newburgh Yacht Club—that eventually sank off Roseton.

Dick and Flo Barcia ran the small restaurant down at the Yacht Club for a number of years giving non-members an opportunity to partake of the ambiance of the Marlboro River front.

John was married to Erma Spencer and has three children: John Edward (Marlboro), Lorraine and Gary Richard. John is also a proud grandfather.

How fortunate for John Lynn that his life has included so many interesting experiences. How fortunate for us that John is able to so vividly recall the people and places that made those experiences so interesting.

*   *   *

JOSEPHINE TRUNCALI

They came to Marlboro in 1920. The father moved them from New York City—lock, stock and barrel—father, mother, 2 children, maternal grandmother and uncle. They had bought the place from the Reverend Williams, a minister affiliated with Amity Chapel. Josephine Truncale tells us her mother wanted to stay in New York City, because she enjoyed city life. Her mother was a seamstress and Josephine shines with pride as she recalls that her mother's superior craftsmanship was evidenced by the fact that she sewed the "sample" dresses.

They lived on a self contained farm. Josephine reports they had cows (only two at a time), pigs, chickens, ducks and goats as well as a variety of fruit. On her way to school Josephine would drop a full milkcan at her neighbor's house and pick up an empty can on the way home. Her father took the produce from the farm to the Marlboro dock for shipping. The carting was done by horse and wagon. The family transportation was also horse and wagon—the fancier family conveyance had a "fringe" on the top reports Josephine. In 1926 they purchased their first truck which gave the family easier transportation. At that time they were able to do more traveling to shops and church.

The house, a beautiful, big edifice with many rooms sits on the edge of Bingham Road and dates back at least to the early 1850's. There had been a gate for horse and buggy convenience near a porch at the end of the house. The rooms on the top floor at one time were numbered. Josephine ventured they were used by recuperating patients of Dr. Taylor, a former owner.

Dr. Taylor and his family inhabited the house in the 1850's. Josephine produced several interesting artifacts found in a walled off space. One pink silk ballet slipper led to many romantic guesses as to its owner. That she was well loved was obvious. The slipper exuded an essence of love and beauty and style. Also found was a "Reward of Merit" presented to James M. Taylor in 1859 by Miss D. B. Starbird, his teacher. A notebook filled with the likes of "This is a fair specimen of my handwriting, June 25, 1862" was another discovered treasure. Josephine reports that in the 1950's a son of the Taylors, a man in his sixties and a minister, came to revisit the house.

Josephine's family at one time ran a boarding house for visitors mostly from New York City. The large, spacious house easily lent itself to this usage. Many other Marlborough families provided similar refuge from the city's heat to "summer boarders."

Memories of school—at the West Marlboro two room schoolhouse were still alive in Josephine's memory. The West Marlboro school is near the intersection of Bingham and Lattingtown roads and is the present home of the Cumuglias. Miss Crispell, was Josephine's teacher for the first four grades. Mrs. McCarthy taught her for the last four grades at the school. The rhythm of the hickory stick did not take place until after a 6 a.m. berry picking session at home and then a mile long walk to school. There was no gym at the school. The community fathers apparently thought recess activities along with a mile walk to school and then a mile walk back home (part of the way carrying the milkcan) was enough physical exercise. Josephine, without a moment's hesitation named Clarence Reynolds, Fred Elgee, Jack McCarthy, Jacob Alonge and herself as the 1931 graduates of the school.

With respect to memories of town, Josephine recalled Baxter's Feed store which often extended credit when needed until the crops were harvested and hard money was more available. Lucy ran a meat market and Cumisky had a grocery store where the Rusk law office is now. Herbrich bakery sold a luscious Washington Pie (a spice cake) for 2¢. From the look in her eye, one could sense Josephine savoring the cake again in her memory. The candy store across from the school (later to be Costello's which was across from the Union Free school—now the Marlboro Hose Company) was the source of candy for the students. Getting a pink candy brought with it an additional prize. Father Hanley and the Catholic church held turkey dinners in the recreation building which was where the present church parking lot is now.

On Saturdays and Sundays it was possible to catch a bus into Newburgh and go to the Strand movie theater on Liberty Street, or out to the Orange Lake Amusement Park.

Other families living in the area of Bingham Road at that time were Meehan, Williams, Reynolds, Scott (2), Westmore, Magliato, Rhoads (2), Burroughs and Elgee.

Josephine gave us a short tour of the house with its beautiful marble fireplaces, high ceilings, intricate moldings and air of elegance. She is justifiable proud of the lovely and loving home and the place it and the Truncale family have played in the community's history.

*   *   *

MARY DUBOIS

"I was mad, I wanted to move back to Cold Spring." That was her reaction in 1931. Now, Mary DuBois wouldn't leave Marlborough—this is her home. Her family came from Cold Spring when her brother and step-father got work on helping to construct 9W—they were cement finishers (there was more money in construction than in farming). They first lived in a stucco house in Marlboro and then her father bought a farm on Bingham Road. The thought though, of leaving her family was too much. She agreed to stay on one condition, "I get to drive the horse and wagon." She loved the horse and that decision to stay was perhaps one of the most significant she has ever made. "Now, you couldn't get me out of Marlborough", she says.

As a young woman she walked from Bingham Road down Rosebank Road to 9W to catch the bus into Newburgh where she worked in an underwear factory on Liberty Street. She had to catch the bus at 7 a.m. Often she and Josephine Troncali would wait for the bus in Panzella's (now Bobby Diorio's on 9W, only in the winter though when the traveling was the most difficult due to the deep snow. The nice weather was spent working on the farm. She learned from her family the lesson of the satisfaction gained from one's own labor. She points with pride to the fact that her family were all workers. At first she brought in six or seven dollars a week. That was a big help at that time to her family. Younger members of the family were still going to school and "paper and pencils were not free then." She also helped to provide the meat for Sunday dinners as well as a treat of some tobacco for her brother and father—they spent nights rolling their own cigarettes.

Prices were better then—"You could get this much groceries" she says placing her arms in an expansive gesture, "for $5.00. Now you can carry $5.00 worth of stuff in the palm of your hand". "You could get 3 pounds of hamburger for 25¢."

In 1947 she married Carlyle DuBois, a direct descendent of Colonel Lewis DuBois of Revolutionary and early Marlboro fame. Carlyle's grandfather was James L. DuBois who married Sophia Masten after his first wife, Sophia's sister, died. Sophia was Carlyle's grandmother. To this union were born Apheous, Dimmick, James, George, Lyman, Alice and Oscar B. (Carlyle's father). Dimmick was a carpenter with Mr. Kohl in Marlboro and Middlehope. Alice married a Bloomer and became a midwife in town.

Carlyle's uncle, George DuBois, was custodian for many years in the school district. He started at the Union Free School (site of the present

Fire House in Marlboro). The Union Free School was heated by coal and had to be carefully watched during the long, cold winter evenings. George was given a lovely plaque at his retirement a number of years ago demonstrating the respect he had earned from the community.

Carlyle's grandmother would build a house and then, if someone wanted it, would sell and build a new one. As a result, there are many deeds that carry her name.

Among the many things Carlyle shared with her was his love for the town and its history. She is aware on her own account of things that transpired in town since the early '30s, but from listening to Carlyle, she is also well informed on the earlier history of the town. She has an extensive library of photos of the town that have been handed down through the DuBois family. She had added her own "finds" to the collection also. "I never throw anything away" she chortles. She treasures them and has a deep appreciation of their worth.

Mary has pictures of the Advance Lodge #490 which was instituted in Marlborough January 18, 1882. Some of her papers indicate that at one time there was a YMCA in Marlboro. Right behind Mary's house on Western Avenue stands the tall brick chimney of the "shoddy mill." The mill was used to manufacture felt boots and horse blankets when Carlyle was a youngster. A man named Knaust bought it and wanted to raise mushrooms "but couldn't get enough horse manure and therefore did carpentry work." The present owner of the property is Mark Tolman; it was once the home of Mr. and Mrs. Alvut. Mr. Alvut, during the '50s was high school principal.

The American Legion building in around 1931 housed the Kindergarten and 1st grade due to overcrowding at other schools. Mary chortles as she recalls how Joey Noto cried so hard on his first days of school, that his mother had to sneak away so he didn't know she was leaving. At one time the building was also a button sorting factory. Buttons from the factory on Dock Road would be brought here to be sorted. Buttons can still be found on the property.

She has pictures of Decker's blacksmith shop (present site Amodeo's Garage). She indicated that at one time the fire house was just north of the present Raccoon Saloon. George Young, Carlyle's grandfather on his mother's side, ran the mill before Schantz (just north of Kroner's Hardware). Part of Schantz's mill has since burned. Mary has pictures of the mill.

Mary recalls Carlyle "scapping for herring" in the Hudson River. He went down to the river through where Hermans is now located. He used the herring to fertilize crops much as the Native Americans did centuries ago. Mary also remembers swimming in the Hudson down by the Marlboro Yacht Club.

Though past the time when most folks "retire" (she's 80 years old), Mary still brims with energy. For many years she supervised the nursery at the Presbyterian Church so parents could attend services. This July she celebrates 25 years of service as custodian at the Marlboro Free Library and, if that and her volunteer activities aren't enough, she can be seen early mornings mowing her lawn or tending the lovely flowers that surround her home.

Marlborough indeed has been fortunate that Mary was given the opportunity to "drive the horse and wagon" those many years ago. She has over the years, and still does contribute much to our community. She does us proud.

       *   *   *

MILLIE WEAVER

Her grandfather graduated from New York Medical School February 15, 1876. With great pride Millicent Weaver shares her remembrances, pictures and news stories of her grandfather—the beloved Dr. Palmer. After his graduation, he promptly moved to Marlboro in order to help the older Dr. Knapp. His name appears on a great numbers of birth certificates registered with the Town of Marlborough Clerk.

In April of 1879 he married Sarah Matilda Burnside from Plattekill. Their wedding certificate is a small pink slip of paper. One story from the Marlborough newspaper reports, "Dr. A.H. Palmer and his bride have returned from their wedding tour. The brass band turned out and serenaded the bride and groom on their arrival at their residence". His residence was on King Street. He bought the house and property from Augustus Clark for $2975.

The house was a small house, and as the family grew, Dr. Palmer added a wing for an office with a bath and bedroom above. Dr. and Mrs. Palmer had four children: Mamie, Emogene, Clara and John. John Palmer married Irene Rosencrantz and had four daughters. Clara Louise was Millie Weaver's mom; Millie's father was Clarence Selden. Clarence was an electrical engineer and a graduate of Cooper Union. Clarence and Clara met at a Catholic church dance held in the building that was behind the church. The Seldens had three children; Donald, Janet and Millicent. Millie and her cousin Patty are the only grandchildren of Dr. Palmer still living.

Millie remembers the daybook that Dr. Palmer used to register the births. She also remembers him using a fish scale—he'd wrap the babies in a diaper, put it on the scale and weigh the babies. Millie said that Dr. Palmer, "went to every medical convention". She remembers his Van Dyke beard as he got older—it was always meticulously trimmed. Dr. Palmer was Vice President of the Marlboro Bank in 1911. Dr. Palmer died in 1925 after forty-nine years of faithfully serving his community.

Dr. Palmer was survived by his wife who in 1942 was the oldest member of the Methodist Church with seventy four years of membership. She was born in 1853 and died in 1950 at 97 years of age.

That the Palmers lived, not only long, but with passion and joie d' vivre is demonstrated by the following newspaper story of their family life:

"The residence of Dr. A.H. Palmer presented a fine appearance on the evening of July 4. The yard was brightly illuminated with Japanese lanterns and a display of fireworks added beauty to the scene. Not only were the doctor and family celebrating the glorious Day of Independence, it was also the birthday of his oldest daughter Miss Mamie who had invited a number of her young friends to celebrate with her. Candies and ice cream were in abundance. The young people spent an enjoyable evening. When they left for home, all felt that

as a host and hostess Dr. and Mrs. Palmer were all that
could be desired."

Millie's mother was born in the house on King Street, was married
from the house in 1909 and returned to the house in 1920 with her
three children after her husband passed away. She spent the remainder
of her life in the very house into which she was born.

Millie doesn't exactly remember it, but remembers hearing of the
burning of the Methodist church in 1915—that was the year Millie was
born. In 1929 Millie's sister, Janet received a letter from Thomas Edison.
This has been a family treasure ever since. Millie attended the Union
Free School and graduated in 1932. The graduation ceremonies were
held in the (new) Methodist Church as the school had no gym or audi-
torium. There were seven who graduated in 1932—Salvadore Dragotta,
Clifton Casscles, Nat Clarke, Alton Sarles, Connie Ferguson, Doris
Lowery and Millie Selden. Of the seven only Nat Clarke, Alton Sarles
and Millie are still living. When Millie married Joe Weaver, Bert
Kniffen, then town clerk, signed the certificate—he ran the meat market
(beyond the old post office on Western Avenue) and Millie is still
impressed with the neatness of the penmanship.

Millie has some interesting memories of the house on King Street.
Her mother slept in the NE corner room—there were 2 single beds on 2
sides—her brother slept with her grandmother and grandfather. They
had an out house until the attic of the old house was converted to a
bath. There were stairs from the attic to the back of the kitchen as well
as in the living room. The children would love to circle the inside of the
house going up one set of stairs and down the other. Millie remembers
the back steps as being quite steep with very narrow treads. There was a
small kitchen with a big old coal stove—that and a three burner
kerosene stove heated the house. The house had large closets. Towards
the McCourt house, under a window, was a big table her grandmother
and mother used as a work table. Millie remembers her grand mother
had a parrot—"beautiful colors"—but it would take the buttons off any

shirt it came near. There was a carriage house toward the rear of the house—Harrison Lockwood drove the car for Dr. Palmer to make his house calls.

In 1959 Millie and her husband, Joe, returned to the house. In 1976 Millie's mother died. In 1986 Millie sold the house. When she speaks of selling the house that had served her family so well for 107 years, the misting around the eyes gives evidence of how difficult it was to do so.

Millie has other memories of Marlboro as she was growing up. The jail was behind Pesavento and Torraco. Lucy had a meat market there also. Mondello's was always a "man's bar". Rickborn's was on Main Street with Mattie McCourt's drug store across the street. Froemels (who lived on King Street) had a restaurant on Western Ave., Rudolph Froemel had a candy store also. Herbriches had the best tasting coffee cake. In Carlton Merritt's grocery store, merchandise was stuffed into barrels (now Frank's Deli). The movie theater on Main Street had two shows, 7 p.m. and 9 p.m. Millie sold tickets for a while and loved it because after the newsreel was done, there were usually no other customers coming in and she could watch the feature film with no disturbance. Clifford Stant owned the theater which was also used for high school plays. Rosanos had a little gift shop and lived over the store. The Odd Fellows met in their building. Bill Clarke ran an A & P and Millie's brother worked for him for a while. Millie remembers loving to play in the back of the Baxter's feed store—the smells were wonderful and the windows gave a beautiful panorama of the Hudson.

Millie followed in her grandfather's medical footsteps and became a School Nurse Teacher. Millie has one son, Paul, two grand children and three great-grandchildren. She is retired after serving many years in the Newburgh Schools.

Millie takes pride in the pictures, scrap books, newspaper clippings and documents that she has preserved for so many years. She has a wonderful picture of Dr. Palmer with his horse drawn wagon in front of the King Street home. She has been a true historian—preserving some of the wonderful memorabilia that allows us to create mental snapshots of life and legends of a bygone era.

*   *   *

PAUL FAURIE

He was born October 5, 1911, a Tuesday at 8:30 at Union City, NJ. "I was supposed to be a girl," he reports with an engaging grin. He graduated from Fordham University June 4, 1934 and on June 5 moved finally and totally to Marlboro. "I couldn't get here fast enough," he declares. From these and other gleanings from his fantastic memory, one begins to expect that Paul Faurie's memory predates his birth.

Paul's father bought his place in 1910 from LaGross. LaGross cut timber and supplied the railroad between Highland and Newburgh with ties. Horses were used to skid the logs out of the woods. When the horses got too old to work, LaGross would take them "up in the back" and shoot them. That area became known as "the horse cemetery." Paul remembers as a boy, lining up the bones trying to re configure a horse's skeleton.

Paul went to school at Union City but remembers spending all of his vacations and week-ends in Marlboro. He came whenever he could and thus was born his enduring love for the area. On top of the Lattingtown hill lived the Fauries, the Trautmans and the Pat McGowans (now Hart Schoonmaker). Paul remembers walking to get the mail at the Moscas because the mailman's horse couldn't make the hill. The mailman was Ted Covert.

Further down the hill were the Moscas, Kaleys and the Weeds. Where the Lattingtown garage is presently was a store. Emil Gasparoli built the garage at a more recent date. The store itself was divided into a house and a store—the store entrance was on the east side. For a few pennies one could buy candy. On the corner—a little west of the garage was a bunk house owned by Leighton Craft. Ed Matthews had another store nearby. Near the corners stood the Lattingtown Baptist church, for many years unused.

On the corner on Lattingtown road, was the Craft house. The Craft building had been a stop for the stage coaches many, many years ago—it had been a hotel. Another store, next to the Lattingtown school, was owned by Anthony Albano. At one time there was a tavern there also. Going south down the road were William Mackey, then Oliver Mackey and then the Chillura place which at one time was quite a popular summer resort.

Further south on Lattingtown road was Barret Wygant, Sam Vanacore, and Benjamin Harcourt. Harcourts owned the last stand of virgin white oak in the area. Then came the dairy farm of Dan Hannigan—the present Troncillito farm. Paul advised that the large wheels in front of Frank Troncellito's house came from the old steam roller that was used to pave the Lattingtown road. Paul remembers playing on the roller when it was parked at the Weeds.

Canzonaries was a training camp for professional boxers. Tony Canzonarie at one time was light weight and then middle weight champion of the world. This later became the San Catri. Just before hitting Mt. Zion road, Ralph Kramer (of superb sweet corn fame) was on the left with John Kramer and brothers on the right.

Going north from Lattingtown where Frank Williams now lives, Gus Wygant ran a farm. Gus Wygant had the last yoke of oxen in the area. Paul remembers, as a boy, sitting on a stone wall watching Wygant plow a field with the team. Up from there, Joe Porpiglia's used to be Mike Dowd. Conklin's Hill was named for Jim Conklin.

Going east from Lattingtown were Bill and Etta Wooley—"That farm goes way back." They owned quite a bit of property. Fritz Vail also had a big farm—about 90 some acres.

When Paul was young, he remembers they filled a rowboat on their pond with water in the mornings. They let the sun heat it all day, and in the evenings would take their baths right in the warm water in the rowboat.

Shopping trips to Marlboro took almost all day. The family also brought produce to the docks in Marlboro. The wagons would be packed early in the morning and Paul would spend about two or two and a half hours on the trip to town. The "Mary Powell" picked up the produce. There would then be another two or two and a half hour trip back to Lattingtown. Paul remembers the day one of the horses (not his) was hit by the train just as it arrived in Marlboro.

Sam Hewitt ran a hardware store (presently Kronner's). Sam dealt in horses and would "try them out" right on 9W—before it was paved. Paul remembers also racing the horses on the "flats" right in front of his red barn in Lattingtown.

Mackey's Road was a short-cut to Plattekill and Paul remembers many a buggy ride along that road.

Other fascinating memories evoked were of "One Ear", the moonshiner who lived on Mt. Zion Road. "One Ear" was so named because, in a fight he had had his ear chewed off. With ear in hand, he went to Doc Harris hoping to have it sewn back on. When Paul worked for Cluett Schantz at the mill, "One Ear" would come and sweep up all the grain spilled on the floor and take it to his home on Mt. Zion to distill it.

Paul indicated that Cluett Schantz ground grain at his mill (by the bridge just North of Kronners) until about 1935 or 36. He didn't grind too much as most of the grain was ground by Schantz's uncle, Phil Schantz, in Highland. Cluett had a feed store. Paul worked for him, as did Al Trautman. "Everyone worked for him," said Paul.

Paul has been on the Marlborough Planning Board since 1963. His love for his community rings loudly and clearly. With so many wonderful visions in his memory bank, it is no wonder that the community profits from this one man who, by so clearly remembering the past, insures the quality of Marlborough's future.

       *   *   *

ALTON SARLES

On that cold blustery evening it was wonderful to be welcomed into the lovely, warm and cozy home of Alton and Helen Sarles. The house was bought by the Sarleses in 1870 from Hudson DuBois explained Alton. Helen, with a wife's pride, added that a unique feature of the house is that it is octagonal. "It gives assessors and surveyors fits," Alton grinned. There is a challenge to finding out the square footage contained within. Local high school teachers have brought their geometry students to the house to tackle the problem. Indeed, it is a beautiful example of geometry put to practice.

The Sarles name first appeared in Marlboro when Alton's father was a young boy. The family moved up from Westchester County. The family was amused by the fact that his grandfather's will was published in the local newspaper. During this interview, Alton is aided by his gracious wife, Helen. Though not born in Marlboro, Helen was very close to Alton's mother and often listened to the elder Mrs. Sarles's descriptions, filing them away in her memory as beloved treasures of family history.

Alton recalls that the Memorial Day parades used to pass his house on Grand Street and take his lane to 9W. He remembers the sidewalks that passed in front of his house to the Union Free School.

The Sarles's business is on 9W and that building itself has quite a colorful story. The building was originally built by the Marlborough Methodist Church. According to a history of the church, the building was dedicated October 20, 1830 by the Reverend Benjamin Griffin. In 1867, the Methodists built a new church on Grand and Church Street and the building was sold to the Catholic Church. The Catholics met at this building for many years before building their church on 9W and selling the property which eventually ended up in the Sarles family.

Across Bloom street from the Sarles's business is the Marlboro Free library. On that site on 9W once stood a school house. John Burroughs, the naturalist, taught at that school when he was nineteen years old. After the school was abandoned, it served as a residence. Alton remembers the religiously zealous Billy Treys living there as well as the Van Buskirk brothers. The building was torn down sometime after 1957.

Alton went to the Union Free School (present site of the Marlboro Hose Company). The school, as he recalls with a slight smile, had eight rooms and "attic stairs" to get to the top floor where the high school was housed. The students played basketball at the Methodist Church. D.D. Taylor was the first principal that Alton remembered. He recalled good humoredly how, when he was a boy, the youngsters would pull hot tar from the roof and chew on it like licorice.

Many of those who traveled long distances to the Presbyterian Church services would keep their horses in a long shed on the side of the Church.

As Alton shared with us some of his remembrances of Marlboro, he cautioned that he was in the Navy from 1932 to 1936. "There were many changes in the town during that period," he said. Using a tracing from a map of Marlboro drawn by Henry Schlesinger (courtesy of the Rusk Agency), Alton identified many of the families and businesses in town during his formative years. This was done from memory and is not expected to be complete, therefore we trust the reader will treat gently any possible inconsistencies.

We finished the interview much fortified with enthusiasm and facts and figures of the Marlboro of years gone by, and most appreciative of the generous sharing of their memories by Alton and Helen Sarles.

*　　　　　　　*　　　　　　　*

STELLA MACKEY

Stella Mackey Palmer was born in Lattingtown in 1903. March 6, 1919 at the age of 16 she left to work in a factory in Poughkeepsie. She has not lived in Lattingtown since though she has been back to visit family. Her memories of Lattingtown are not befuddled by knowledge of the day to day activities of the community since 1919. Thus it is as if we had a living snapshot of the Lattingtown of the early 1900's frozen in time.

Stella's great grandfather was William Mackey who is buried in the Lattingtown cemetery. William's wife was Elisabeth Anderson, the daughter of Elija who was a corporal during the Revolutionary War. William and Elisabeth had three children; one son who died young, a daughter Dolly who married a Shorter from Milton, and William Wesley, Stella's grandfather. William Wes had five sons and three daughters. One of William Wes's sons, named Osmar Hollister Mackey, was Stella's father. Stella was born in the Mackey house near the bridge.

She remembers when Hattie and Eli Reynolds had the Lattingtown store—the very "heart" of the community—the penny candies, the canned goods, bread, etc. Eli was also the school custodian and Stella realizes it was he who went to the school to fire up the furnace so the building would be warm when the students arrived. Leighton Craft had the first car in Lattingtown. Leighton married the daughter of a sea captain named Smith. The Lattingtown church was opened sporadically. Edith Mackey restarted the Sunday school. Ms. Etta Wooley played the organ. The Lattingtown Road was dirt.

Some of the families in the area were: the Fallons who lived next to the Crafts, the Halls who lived across from Arnold Mackey, the DeWitts who lived across from Stella, the Guernseys who lived in a big house nearby. Milton O'Dell made vinegar in his cellar and sold it. Sam Wygant (Barrett's father) had a wagon with a high seat. He had an unfortunate accident, fell off the seat and broke his neck. Some of the early "cold storage" was when Barrett Wygant put his produce on the dirt floor in his barn where it stayed cool for several days. Barrett married a "farmerette". Barrett's farm had a sand bank—the sand was used for roads. Stella remembers making "sand castles" using the sand in the road.

Just before the outbreak of World War I, flu broke out in the community. Milton O'Dell lost his pregnant wife. He moved away from the area shortly thereafter. Other families also suffered losses.

As a child Stella remembers playing with leaves as money. "The bigger Lilac leaves were dollars, smaller leaves were coins." There were three or four swings strung on a pole between two trees. The children enjoyed "tight-rope walking" across the pole. At a later age there were barn dances.

Her memories of the Lattingtown school were wonderful. The students attending included: the McGowans, John, Maynard, Bart, James and William; Joe O'Brien and his sisters; Josephine and Marion Barry; John, Bill and Margaret Kaley, Catherine and Mary Dowd, and the St. Johns amongst others. The school at that time had only one room. There was a fence between the paths leading to the boys' room and the girls' room (an old fashioned outhouse on the corner of the school property near the Crafts). Upon exiting the building, boys turned one way, the girls the other. The teacher could watch out the window as the students made their treks. Near the center of the room was a large stove that provided heat during the inclement weather. There was a pail with a dipper situated in the classroom that served as the communal "water jug". Her first teacher was Mrs. Martin who drove a horse and wagon from Highland. She would keep her horse in Reynold's barn during the school day. At noon all of the students went home for lunch. Stella thought they used McGuffy's readers but was sure her parents had to pay for her books. It was usual for school books to be passed down to younger brothers or sisters.

Parents also had to buy paper and pencils. A 5¢ pad could be purchased in Poughkeepsie. Stella could both read and write before she started school as her older brothers and sisters helped her to learn how. There were shelves on the desks to store books not in use at the time. The seat from one student formed the front of the desk for the student behind. The desks also had ink wells and, yes, the boys did enjoy dipping the girls' braids. Stella's good friends were Helen Rhodes and her sisters and Margaret Kaley (who later married Charlie Weed). Margaret further endeared herself by announcing that Stella was "the smartest kid that ever went to the Lattingtown school." Miss Reardon was a "wonderful teacher who taught us how to knit". Miss Reardon later married Hicks Manion who lived next to St. Mary's cemetery.

During recess the students played tag, baseball and other familiar sports. The ground around the school was worn bare by their constant activities. Stella remembers fondly the learning of poetry. The school had kerosene lanterns hanging from the walls and the biggest thrill was being able to hang the lanterns. Stella also remembers having to "clap" the erasers outside the school to remove the chalk-dust. It was noted that Stella wrote with her left hand. We queried whether she was permitted to write with her left hand in school. She learned to write with her right hand and ever since has been ambidextrous.

Stella's father, Osmar Mackey, claimed the trees on the school property were planted when he was a student at the school. Osmar was born in 1865. It's a special treat to stand today under those beautiful, sprawling trees.

Stella had to take regents' exams even that long ago. She remembers that often teachers of the younger students were young girls who had completed the prescribed grammar school curriculum. Her folks had to pay for her to attend the Union Free School in Marlboro. She walked from Lattingtown to the Union Free School (the site of the present Fire house). Stella's aunt, Althea Mackey, had previously followed that route and later was in the first graduating class of Vassar Hospital nurses.

Stella's grandfather William W. Mackey had very strong political views. He took to the trail and campaigned for Grover Cleveland in Pennsylvania and New York. He was made post master (Stella remembers playing with the postmaster's letter file). During Cleveland's second campaign, William W. vowed not to shave until Cleveland won the election. Cleveland lost and William W. wore a long flowing beard that reached to his midsection to the day he died.

We very much appreciate Stella's sharing her memories with us. She has given us insights into the Lattingtown of the early 1900's and a better understanding of that community as seen through the eyes of a youngster. She has introduced us to people of that time and has made our "snapshot in time" breathe life.

RECORDS FILES

The records from the town of Marlborough provide mental pictures for a productive glimpse into the Marlborough of our forebears. There are a number of different records available; Town Minutes, Deeds, Wills, business journals, diaries, pictures, etc.

*   *   *

TOWN MINUTES

These are the minutes from when Marlborough was still a part of the precinct of Newburgh.

April 1763. Then this book was presented by Capt. Jonathan Hasbrouck to the precinct of Newburgh.

At a precinct meeting held at the house of Capt. Jonathan Hasbrouck for the precinct of Newburgh. The first Tuesday in April in the year of our Lord one thousand seven hundred and sixty-three according to an act of the Assembly for that purpose.

Samuel Sands	Clerk
Capt. Jonathan Hasbrouck	Supervisor
Richard Harker	
John Windfield	Assessors
Samuel Wiatt	
David Gedney	Constable
Henry Smith	Collector
Joseph Gedney	
Benjamin Woolsey	Poor Masters

John McCrary
John Wandal
Burras Holms
Isaac Fowler   Path Masters
Umphrey Merrit
Thomas Woolsey
Nathan Purdy
Isaac Fowler   Fence Viewers and
                                         Appraisers of Damage

Leonard Smith chose to collect the quit rent the patten he now lives on. Then adjourned to the house of Capt. Jonathan Hasbrouck.
(The house of Capt. Jonathan Hasbrouck where the meeting was held is the present Washington Headquarters at Newburgh.)

        *   *   *

At a precinct meeting held at the house of Capt. Jonathan Hasbrouck for the precinct of Newburgh the first Tuesday in April in the year of our Lord one thousand seven hundred and sixty-four according to an act of Assembly.

Samuel Sands   Clerk
Louis DuBois   Supervisor
Nehemiah Denton
Henry Terbush   Assessors
Peter Ostrander
Samuel Winslow   Constable and Collector

Nehemiah Denton security for Samuel Windslow for collecting and paying and the tax that laid on the precinct of Newburgh for the year 1764.

Danniel Thurstone
Michael Dermott   Poor Masters
Covnelius Wood
Martin Wygant
Lenard Smith
Henry Smith, Senior   Path Masters
Gilber Denton
Edward Halleck
Benjamin Carpenter
Samuel Sprage   Fence Viewers &
                                   Appraisers of Dammage

Henry Smith
Jehiel Clark
David Purdy
Isaac Fowler   Pounder
Then adjourned to the house of Capt. Jonathan Hasbrouck.

*   *   *

At a precinct meeting held at the house of Capt. Jonathan Hasbrouck for the precinct of Newburgh the first Tuesday in April 1765 and in the year of our Lord one thousand seven hundred and sixty-five according to an act of Assembly.

Samuel Sands   Clerk
John Wandal   Supervisor
Nehemiah Denton
Henry Terbush   Assessors
William Thomson
Henry Smith, Senior   Collector
        Markas Ostrander and Danniel Rodgers Overseers of
the Poor

Samuel Sands, Path Master from Cornelius Woods to the Wallkill precinct

John Wandal, Path Master for Newburgh to work to the westward as far as Cornelius Woods.

Nehemiah Denton, Path Master from Albertson's gate northward as far as the German patent extends and also the New Wallkill Road to William's meadow.

John Terpeny from Williams road to the New Paltz road.

Arthur Smith from the German patent east to David Purdy's patent.

Isiah Purdy from David Purdys for Purdys Patent.

Joshua Conklin for David Purdys Patent as far as the Jews Creek

Lewis DuBois, Path Master from the Jews Creek as far as Woolsey Patent.

Samuel Merrit, Path Master on the new road from Lewis DuBoises mill to the Walter DuBois land.

Lattin Carpenter, Path Master on the new road from Walter DuBois land to the Ten Stone meadow.

John Belfield, Path Master from the above mentioned road to Bonds.

Micheal Wygant, Path Master on that road by Urian Wygants

Voted that there be a public town pound erected for the use of the German Patent or precinct near the house of Martin Wygant.

Joshua Conklin and Arthur Smith	Fence Viewer
Isaac Fowler	Pounder

Then the meeting adjourned to the house of Capt. Jonathan Hasbrouck.

*   *   *

PLATTEKILL'S 200TH

In the year 2000 Plattekill celebrated its 200th birthday having been a part of Marlborough until 1800. On behalf of the Town of Marlborough, presented a copy of the early records to Shirley Anson who was Town of Plattekill Historian at that time. Here they are—

NEW MARLBOROUGH 1772

The precinct of New Marlborough was set off from Newburgh March 12, 1772, and the precinct became a town by act of the legislature March 7, 1788. The meetings, therefore, were called precinct meetings between those dates and since then town meetings. Plattekill was represented at these meetings prior to 1800. The first precinct meeting was held at the house of Henry Deyo, April 7, 1772. At this meeting Abijah Perkins was chosen clerk; supervisor, Lewis DuBois; assessors, John Yonge, Jacob Wood, Marcus Ostrander; poormasters, Robert Merritt, Joseph Mory; commissioners, Richard Woolsey, Durmee Relyea; pounder, Silas Purdy; fence viewers, Caleb Merritt, Richard Carpenter; pathmasters, Gabriel Merritt, James Quimby, Jacob Wood, Samuel Merritt, Henry Deyo, constable, William Martin.

To the Town of Plattekill
on the 200th Anniversary of the Founding

At a Town meeting held at Henry Deyos on April ye 7, 1772 for the precinct of New Marlborough according to the Act of Assembly for the province of New York.

In Meeting Assembled
    Chosen Clark   Abijah Perkins

	for precinct & poor
Supervisor	Lewis Dubois
Assessors	John Yonge
	Jacob Wood
	Marcus Ostrander
Poor Masters	Robert Meritt
	Joseph Mory
Commissioners	Lewis Dubois
	Richard Woolsey
	Durnee Relyee
Pounder	Silas Purdy
Fence Viewers	Caleb Merritt
	Richard Carpenter
Path Masters	Gabriel Merritt
	James Quimby
	Jacob Wood
	Samuel Merritt
	Henry Dayo
Constable	William Martin
Security	Jeremiah Mackey

At a Special Town Meeting held at the House of Robert Gilmores in the Town of Marlborough the Eighth day of March One Thousand Eight Hundred; agreeable to Publick Notice for that Purpose given The following Votes was by a majority Entered into vis

Voted,—That the Town of Marlborough be divided into Two Towns as Follows (Provided the Assent of the Legislature Can be Obtained for that Purpose)

Beginning on the Line Between the Town of Newburgh and the Town of Marlborough Two Chains and Seventy five links East of the North West Corner of the five Pattentees from Thence Northward on a

Strait line to the Most Eastermost Line of Robert Tiffts land where it Joines the Line of the Town of New Paltz

Voted,   Also that the New Town on the West Side of the Mountains, be Called the Town of Patterkiln And the First Town Metting be held at the House of Robert Gilmores. And the Remainder of the Town on the East Side of the Mountains Retain its Present Name of Marlborough; and the first Town Meeting be held at the House of David Meritts in Latting Town

Voted,   That Joseph Morey Esq and Cornelius Drake be appointed to Carry a Petition and the proceedings of this Meeting to the Legislature; And to have Twenty four Dollars for their Services to be paid by the Town
        Attest   Benjamin Townsend Town Clerk

*   *   *

What Road is This?

Can you guess to which road the following refers?

From Historical Records—Ulster Co. Archives
    By virtu of an Act of the General Assembly of the Provinsce of New York passed the sixth Year of our present Majesty's Reign entitled an Act for the better clearing menting and further laying out Publick High Roads and others in the County of Ulster—We the Commisioners of the Precinct of New Marlborough for puting in Execution the good purposes of the said Act and by a Petition of the Inhabitents being Freeholders, have laid out an open publick Road three Rods wide Beguining on the West side of the Road that leads from Latting Tound to Silus Purdees Mil and on the Line that runs between Richard

Woolsey & Joseph Mor and so along the line thereof West two Rods on the South side of the Line and one on the North side to the Northwest corner of said Woolseys Land thense on the line between said Mory and Nathanil Husons to a Swamp thense turning Southerly on said Husons Land and again Westerly by marked Trees to said Mory's South Line thense along the Line thereof on said Husons Land to the North West corner of said Husons Land thence Southerly on said Husons Land by marked trees unto John Lesters Land thense Westerly by a line of marked Trees until it cums to said Mory's South line again thense West along said Morys Line to the Foot of a hy hill thense Northerly alon'd the Foot of said Hill a croast said Morys Land thense by a line of marked Trees a croast the Mountn to a bog meado thense on the Northside thereof by marked trees to Edmond Turners House from thense on a line Southerly between said Turner and Joseph Darby a croast an out let that leads from the aforesaid meado thense Westerly by marked Trees to a Swamp near Daniel Meguins poot Ash Works to said Meguins line thense along the line thereof untill it cums into the Road that leads from the Palts Road to the Nuborough Road. We do order the Road above mentioned to be open and publick and that the same may be Recorded among the publick Records of the County of Ulster and that the same Record may be and remain an open and publick Road. In testimony whereof we have hereunto set our Hands this 17th Day of August and in the Yar of our Lord Christ 1773.

> Richard Woolsy
> Joseph Mory
> Caleb Merritt

If you guessed Mt. Zion Road, you are right!

*   *   *

HISTORY'S MYSTERIES—I LOVE THEM

From the records of Nehemiah Smith, Justice of the Peace for the Town of Marlborough (living in Lattingtown)—have left the original spelling.

Tuesday 24 March partes met
Jury called and swarn—Elisa Mackey 12-5, Abraham Young 12-5, David Staples Jr. 12-5, Valentine Lewis 12-5, John Caverly 12-5, Barnard Wygant 12-5

Witness names—John Duffield 12-5, Joseph Rhoads 12-5, Peleg Ransom 12-5, Daniel Chrawford 12-5, Benjamin Hasbrouck 12-5, Peter R Johnsun 12-5, Hendrick Deyo 12-5, Griffin Ransom 12-5, Peter Johnsun 12-5, Simon Dayo 12-5, Michael Leroye 12-5, John Buckhout 12-5, Zachariah Hasbrouck 12-5, Andres Dubois 12-5, Henry Woolsey 12-5, Josiah Deyo 12-5, Barnebus Benton 12-5

Debt—issue jined—the plantiff demands the sum of twenty five dollars for detaining his slave an prentis (prentice is the colloquial for apprentice MLM)—the defendant denise the charg and pleads that he is nither slave nor prentice—

Adjurned to tuesday the 24th instant to be tried by jury—

March the 24th 1807 this day Calep Church obtained judgment aganst Henry Chrawford before me on the verdic of the jury

	D	C	M
Debt	0	6	0
Justices fees	3	46	5
Constable Rhoads fees	0	79	0
Jurers fees	0	75	0

(in the above the D stands for dollars, the C for cents (the hundredth part of the U.S. dollar—short for centesimus , "hundredth") and the M stands for the Roman numeral for 1000 or thousandth part of a US dollar or a tenth of a cent—yes, there was a tenth of a cent used in the early 1800's—MLM)

Plantiff paid the jury (NB note the jurors and the witnesses each got 12 1/2 cents)

May the 29th 1809 then receved of the
    plantiff on the above judgment   4   25   5

It's difficult to ascertain exactly what is happening here. It appears to me as though Henry Crawford was suing Caleb Church for non performance of duties. Was Caleb apprenticed to Crawford as was the practice of the day? Was Caleb an indentured servant as was also the practice of the day. Or, was Caleb a black slave?

Checking Woolsey, Cochrane, Poucher and Terwilliger, and the censuses of 1790, 1800 and 1810, one finds the following:

Woolsey makes no mention of either a Church or a Crawford,

Cochrane (pg 149) lists Henry Crawford and a John Church as being residents in 1816,

Poucher and Terwilliger have many listings for both Church and Crawford. The only C. Church is buried in Plattekill Jan 13, 1845, a possibility. The only Henry Crawfords are a Henry buried in 1855, but only 17 years old—not the above Henry; and a Henry buried in the Crawford Cemetery in Shawangunk—he was less than a year old—again, not the Henry from above.

There are no Caleb Churches in the 1790, 1800 or 1810 censuses.

A Henry Crawford shows up in the 1790 census, in the 1800 census as owning one slave, in the 1810 census as owning one slave (obviously not referring to Caleb) and there is no Henry Crawford in the 1820 census.

Suspect Caleb Church was not a black slave, but possibly a loose form of indentured servant.

WILL THE REAL HENRY CRAWFORD STAND UP???

Was quite excited when I found the following:

Will dated March 27, 1816

Unto my loving wife, Abagail £1000 the use whereof she shall have while she remains my widow or does not marry any other man during her life she shall then have the entire Priveledge of desposing of the £1000 among her Connextion as she seet fit but if she Chuses or does Marry an other man then the £1000 shall be devided among her own Akin and among those whom my Executors may Judge will stand in the most real want of it of her akin and executors to see that it is not squandered but put to the best use. Also the entire use of all my Property both personal and real as long as she remains my widow except $2000 (as beqieathed).

Unto my nephew Absalum Crawford son of Absalum Crawford and Phebe Crawford $1000 at age of 21 years and the interest of the same for bringing him up,—Unto Selah Tuthill Martin $1000 at age of 21 and the interest for bringing him up—he is a son of James Martin and Phebe Martin.

To my Nephew Henry Crawford son of Charles Crawford and Louise Crawford $500.—To my nephew Henry Crawford son of Daniel Crawford and Nelly Crawford $300 and my $200 in the Farmers turnpike stock.—To my nephew Henry Crawford son of David Crawford and Jane Crawford $500—To my brother John Crawford $200 six months after my decease. To Henry C. Griggs son of Verdinant Griggs and Elizabeth Griggs $500. To Henry Fosdick son of Samuel Fosdick and Elizabeth Fosdick $250.

Residue of estate to be equally divided among the heirs of all my brothers.

I give my two blacks Tom and his wife Yanna free at my decease if they should Choose it if not to remain with my wife. My two blacks if my place or farm should be sold shall be free and may and I do give and bequeath them and James York blackman against whose property I have a Mortgage of $3000 the use of which I give the three blacks during their lives and shall not be disturbed by the mortgage during their lives and after their decease my Executors to foreclose the mortgage, and divide it among the nephews.

Wife and my trusty and well beloved friends Verdinent Griggs and Nathaniel Chittenden appointed executors.

Henry Crawford

(his mark)

Note in the above there are references to no less than four Henry Crawfords—the Henry Crawford I believe from the Church suit above and three nephews—each named Henry Crawford. Also note the reference to the $200 in the Farmers turnpike stock. The Farmers Turnpike was set up as a corporation to run a road from Milton to the lands to the west of Marlborough. It was meant as an outlet from the interior of the state to the Hudson River at Milton. At Milton, produce could be loaded onto boats for shipment to far and wide. Individuals bought shares, just as one would buy a share in a corporation today. The Farmers Turnpike was what is now the Milton Turnpike. For many years there was a toll booth set up (near O'Hara Road) to collect tolls from those using the road.

Don't know if we've solved the mystery of what exactly was happening in the above suit, but we sure did learn quite a bit about some other town history!

*   *   *

ANNING SMITH WILL

(NB this is a quick abstraction)

Will Anning Smith—WC/P356

son Anning—S half of land—River W until it makes 100A, Grist mill, 10 rods in width of the meadow land N of the Post road adj Wm Holister

son Lewis—other equal N half—meadow land given to
    Anning together with a piece beginning at NW corner of
    my land adj Nath Kelsey and running E along line of
    Zopher Perkins, then S sufficient width to contain 15A
    then W to Nath Kelsey
and land W of above 200A to SE corner of buttonwood bridge then N to line of Zopher Perkins—be divided into 5 equal parts—division lines running N&S
    1 son Eliphalet
    1 son Lewis
    1 son Anning
    1 heirs of son Nathan
    1 heirs of son Clark
son Anning—rest of land W of button wood bridge except 6A on SW corner adj Nath Kelsey to grandson Nathan & Harvey Smith
    Eliphalet & Anning to get saw mill

*   *   *

FEMALE SEMINARY IN MARLBORO

MRS. WILLIAM WYGANT HAS COPIES OF MINUTES OF EARLY MEETINGS

Did you know that Marlborough once had a "Female seminary?" Mrs. William Wygant who is especially well versed in the history of the town. brings us interesting excerpts from the minutes of meetings of its directors. They tell their own story.

January, 17th 1825

Pursuant to previous public notice a number of the inhabitants of the Village of Marlborough, and vicinity, County of Ulster, State of New York, met at the factory, of Messrs Buckley & Thorn for the purpose of taking into consideration the establishment of a female seminary in said place. Mr. Cornelius DuBois offered a sufficient quantity of ground for a house. etc. on Lot No. 2. opposite the Presbyterian meeting house in said village.

Resolved that this offer be accepted that a female academy be established and that measures be immediately taken for erecting a house on said lot, 28 by 18 with ten foot posts.

Resolved that a cupola be made on the house sufficient to receive and sustain a suitable bell and that, if possible the house be finished by the first of April next.

Messrs Lewis DuBois, Cornelius DuBois and James I Ostrom were appointed trustees of this seminary for the ensuing year.

Mssers John W. Wygant. and James Thorn, were appointed to receive and hold in trust for this seminary a title for the land, on which the house is to be built.

Resolved that no males shall at any time be admitted as scholars into this school.

Mr. James Thorn was appointed to wait on Miss Hughes and engage her to teach the school, the ensuing season.

Nov 1826

Society met.

James Ostrom was chosen chairman and C B Presaluer.

That it be a standing rule of this institution that the trustees employ the teachers, regulate the prices of tuition and visit the shool,

2ndly that the contingent expenses for fuel, repairs, etc., be collected from this tax apportioned on the scholars equally.

Adjourned

(NB—this would today be the Library Lot—Thanks to Carol Felter for this material)

*   *   *

ELIZABETH DUBOIS WILL

Can you imagine?

Can you imagine being a black woman living in the town of Marlborough in 1827? Can you imagine you're a free black woman? Not only that, you own real estate, and…a set of silver spoons! Now comes the hard part. Can you imagine all that and imagine that you could only leave your real estate to your husband "whenever his freedom shall be clearly established." Such is the story told by the Will of Elizabeth DuBois:

In the name of God, Amen. I, Elizabeth DuBois, of the Town of Marlborough in the County of Ulster and State of New York, a Colored Woman, being weak in body but of sound mind and memory do make and publish this my last Will and Testament in Manner and form following—

First—it is my Will that my Debts be paid out of my real and personal Estate excepting the articles of personal property hereinafter bequeathed. The said Debts are mostly due to my sons; Ceaser, Thomas and Abraham and to Abraham D Soper.

Secondly—I give and devise to my beloved Husband, Ceaser, *whenever his freedom shall be clearly established*, the use of all my real estate and such of my household goods as are not hereinafter bequeathed, for and during his natural life—and until his freedom shall be established, it is my Will that my Executors hereinafter named furnish him with use of said Estate. It is further my Will that my daughter, Lucy, live with my said husband in the same manner that we now live together.

Thirdly I give and bequeath to my granddaughter, Loisa, daughter of my said daughter, Lucy, one set of silver spoons, one Britainia metal tea pot and the bed, bedding and bedsted in which my said daughter, Lucy, now sleeps—the use of said articles to belong to my said daughter, Lucy, during her natural life, unless her husband shall attempt to take possession or dispose of said articles, in which case they are to belong to said Loisa whenever said attempt shall be made.

Fourthly I give and devise to my sons, Henry, Ceaser, Thomas and Abraham, four fifths of all my real and personal estate as tenants in common subject to the things above mentioned to them and their heirs and assigns forever. The remaining one fifth of all my real and personal Estate, subject to what I have before directed, I give and devise to my said Granddaughter, Loisa, and my Grandson, Abraham, son of my said daughter, Lucy, after the death of my said daughter, Lucy. And during her life, my said executors are to give to her the use of said one fifth part of said Estate and not to her husband—And to take her receipt in full discharge of the same as if it shall be paid.

Sixthly I hereby authorize and empower my Executors hereinafter named to sell and convey a part of said real Estate with the consent of my said Husband, Ceaser, and daughter, Lucy, and then to make division of the moneys arising from said sale in the same proportions, way and manner in which I have above directed to be done with such estates.

Lastly I do hereby nominate and appoint my said sons, Henry, Ceaser, Thomas and Abraham, Executors of this my last Will and Testament.

In witness whereof I have hereunto set my hand and seal the twenty fourth day of March in the year One Thousand eight hundred and twenty seven.

Can you imagine?

Somehow reading this Will brought the past and the people involved closer to me. The pathos contained within reached across the years and touched a responsive chord. Trust readers will share an interest in this document and appreciate the view given of life in early Marlborough.

*   *   *

Horse Manure

T Craig McKinny
SUP

Dear Craig,

Thought your readers might enjoy the following—

Separating the wheat from the chaff—

Sometimes it's good to look at old records and reflect on those things that were important to our forebears. We, today, take for granted so many of the things that at one time were absolute necessities to the livelihood of the family, especially in a farming community such as Marlborough.

Separating the wheat from the chaff—don't say they didn't know how to do it "back then"…In a deed from 1913 from Carl Rueger & Margaret, his wife to Catherine Weed we find the following notation:

Being a part of the farm known as the Thomas D. Bloomer Farm upon which he resided at the time of his death and being a part of the premises described in a release of legacy given to the said Wm. Bloomer by Mary Bloomer 10/1/1887 and being a portion of the premises conveyed to parties of the first part 1/2/1911

The said Carl G Rueger excepts for a term of 10 years—three horse stalls in the horse stable, and the use of the carriage house for the use of his wagons and harnesses—the use of a part of said barn to store hay and grain, which may be necessary for the feeding of his horses.

The three horse stalls are to be kept in repair by party of the first part

All manure made from said horses is to be the property of the party of the second part."

PEOPLE

Kate's Back in Town

KAY MAURER

"The Girls" had a pleasant surprise. They learned that Kate Maurer would be back in town, if only for a short visit. Mary Miller took charge and made arrangements for lunch. On the appointed day there were sixteen of Kate's long time friends anxious to catch up on the news. Kate and George Maurer and their family lived for many years in Marlboro—making many friends and becoming quite involved in town activities.

Kate is now living in Colorado near one of her children, but takes the opportunity every year to renew and keep strong the Marlboro ties.

The Maurer family lived on the corner of Plattekill Road and Hampton Road in a lovely big house complete with swimming pool. I had hoped the house was an old one as my land records indicate that the property was sold in 1848 by Nathaniel Wygant to Daniel Wygant. The property consisted of more than 90 acres at that time. Daniel died and his wife, Harriet and children, Cecelia C Carpenter (Wygant), Nathaniel S Wygant, Anna M Kniffin (Wygant), Charles Reynolds (probably married to a Wygant), Sarah C Wygant and Frank Reynolds (either son or husband of a Wygant daughter). sold the property to Abraham Smith in 1884. In 1891 Smith sold two acres—"being a part of the farm on which the said parties of the first part now reside". However, Kate told us the house only dates from the 1930's. The original house had burned just prior to the erection of the present house.

The lunch held at Casey's was delightful, as is the case with lunch at Casey's. The chatter from "the girls" verged, at times, on a roar, but everyone enjoyed. Those attending were Kate Maurer, Jeanne (her daughter), Stella Canosa, Jackie Canosa, Ann Yeaple, Rose Nolen, Rose Gilberti, Bernie

Polizzi, Marie Renaud, Virginia McCourt, Marry Miller, Clara Healy, Doris Hennekens, Frances Walters, Ruth Baxter and Mary Lou Mahan.

*   *   *

FATHER DEVINE IN MILTON

FATHER DIVINE'S Peace Missions in "The Promised Land," was in Ulster County, New York from the mid 1930s to the early 1960s

FATHER DIVINE

Milton-on-the-Hudson

Elverhoj, the Artist Colony in Milton-on-the-Hudson, purchased in 1939 by followers of FATHER DIVINE was enjoyed and maintained for about 10 years before being sold to the Northeastern Conference of Seventh Day Adventists in 1952.

FATHER DIVINE spoke at 326 Mulberry Street, Newark, N.J. July 25-26, 1938 A.D.F.D. re: The opening of The Artist Colony Extension. Excerpt: "You have the privilege to go to the great, the famous, Artist Colony in Milton, New York, widely known throughout the country and in other countries. This Colony has been purchased by the followers of FATHER DIVINE; it is owned and operated by them. It has been renovated in a great measure. There we expect to have a real demonstration and Dedication of that particular Extension assembly, for the purpose of the Peace Mission Movement and for the benefit of all who may be interested. The dock is just about finished. It is right on the Hudson and the dock has been finished to accommodate any boat— any size boat going up the Hudson. This is accomplished by the cooperative system of the FATHER DIVINE PEACE MISSION MOVEMENT. Followers purchased and renovated the Colony and have made all improvements.
Note: Two Day round trip—Adults 1.00 Children up to 18 years—Free.

The purchasers of the property were: Anderson, Esther NYC & Rooman, L Irvington & Faithful Love (Pauline Mesmer)—NYC & Johnson, Irene—NYC & Cassandra Rylander—NYC & Golden Love

(Genevieve Hoffman)—NYC & Agnes Hammans—New Paltz & Bliss Love—Krumville & Peace Harmony (Orlandoe H Mathews)—Olive Bridge & Mayme Walker—Newark & Vida Victoria—Krumville & Thankful Daylight—New Paltz & Henri Stephe—NYC & Marjorie I Burns—High Falls.

They purchased 25A that was originally the homestead of Sherbourne Sears, a sea captain, who bought the property (35 acres) in 1839. Prior to Sears the property was owned by Moses Quimby before 1824, and Noah Jenkins and Jacob Townsend. It was in 1912 that Anders Anderson bought the land from Grace Silverman and started the Elverhoj Art Colony. Unfortunately, Anderson lost the land in 1934 when the bank foreclosed the mortgage.

It did flourish until that time as an Art Colony with one of the first dinner theaters in the Hudson Valley. There were some very well known Broadway stars who deigned to perform in Milton. The colony was also noted for their jewelry and their pottery.

"To Bring an End to All Divisibility We must Unite Together Individually, Severally, Collectively, Nationally, and thence Internationally."

Excerpt from FATHER DIVINE'S Remarks Given October 10, 1951 A.D.F.D. "I do not feel that we are in our right places segregated and isolated, but, to the extreme reverse, when we are amalgamated and unified together, as was by the Creator in the creation, according to the historians—GOD formed all nations of men to dwell upon the face of the whole earth out of the one blood—and according to same, I see that we must bring all peoples back together and bring an abolition to all division and segregation among the nations!

Some of the above information from—
"http://www.libertynet.org/fdipmm/"

Will Plank—<u>The Fifty-Niner</u>

First Summer Theatre Was at Elverhoj

Few people realize that one of the first summer theatres that have since become so popular was established at the Elverhoj Art Colony on the river, near the old Sears dock, between Marlborough and Milton. The rustic theatre was built and actors appeared behind the footlights for the first time soon after the end of the first war. Although good, the first attractions did not draw well and the theatre was closed a few years. In the mid-twenties Hubert Osborne, famous Broadway producer of "Shore Leave" operated the theatre with a good cast and patronage through the summer. Other producers put on plays there year after year, importing many stars from Broadway, including Dorothy Gish, Glenn Hunter and others. Edith Barrett and Norman Foster played as amateurs at Elverhoj before going on to fame in the metropolis. The theatre was finally given up when others were started in the Mid Hudson region. This was before the bridge was built and it was difficult for patrons across the river to come here by ferry, but the theatre operated long enough to demonstrate there was a definite field for legitimate entertainment in the country.

Originally designed as a summer retreat and workshop for the arts and crafts, Elverhoj later had a beautiful Moorish terrace overlooking the river which became a popular restaurant and night club. When the property was sold to Father Divine in the thirties it became one of his most popular "heavens" and colored people flocked there every summer. A new dock was built and some of his chartered excursion boats docked there to disgorge hundreds of dusky visitors on a holiday. A good restaurant was maintained there until Divine gave up possession. The property has recently been sold to plastic manufacturers of New Jersey. At present they use the buildings for storage but later plan to operate a plant here. p. 16-17

                    *   *   *

Eight-year-old Girl Enters Sixth Grade In Public School

From The Marlborough Record 9/8/1933
Betty Meckes Has Gone Three Years To Mrs. Eckerson's School

Betty Meckes, eight-and-a-half-year old daughter of Mr. and Mrs. Lou Meckes of Marlborough, Mrs. Meckes was formerly Edith Caywood, has been entered as a fully accredited pupil in the sixth grade of the Marlborough School. Betty has spent three years in the little private school conducted by Mrs. Cornelius Eckerson; this included her kindergarten work.

Mrs. Eckerson follows the Calvert School method and uses its supplies. Each pupil progresses as rapidly as individually practical; there is no pushing ahead, nor, on the other hand, are pupils held back by others or by required schedules. This system, of course, would not be feasible in a large public school where each pupil cannot get much of the teacher's attention, but can be managed where there are only a few pupils.

Betty took a long and inclusive test at the local school this week, to learn her standing. She could have entered eighth grade, but her parents thought the sixth was advanced enough for one of her years.

*   *   *

A baby son was born Tuesday afternoon to Mr. and Mrs. Paul Affuso. He has been named Dominick.
From The Marlborough Record 9/8/1933

*   *   *

CHARLES BOUCK WHITE

Indulge me on this one. Have written quite a bit about Bouck White and Camp Chambers. I find Bouck White such an intriguing character. Camp Chambers was my first introduction to Marlborough at less than 1 year old and was such an important aspect of our family life through my early years.

The Saga of a Research Project

Had gotten a letter from Patricia Edwards (Circleville, NY) regarding her interest in doing research on Charles Bouck White for an article she would like to publish. We spoke over the phone and agreed to set up a meeting at "Camp Chambers" the former Bouck White homestead. The present owners are Cindy and Alphonso Lanzetta and they agreed to host a meeting at their home. Frank Nicklin had known Bouck White when he lived in Marlboro and thus he and his wife Freda were invited to the meeting. My brother, Bob Hennekens, had vivid memories of Camp Chambers as a boy and thus he as well at Pat Clyne's husband attended.

Pat Clyne and I both agreed to do some research and share at the meeting.

Checked through some land records that had researched previously and came up with:

Apr 13, 1918   Nicklin, Wm T to White, Bouck   7A
                Bounded on the N by lands of Richard Norton, formerly James Norton; S by lands of James Barry; E by J Foster Wygant; W by heirs of John DuBois, dec'd Being a part of the premises that were conveyed to party of the first part by John Collins

Jul 20, 1918   Wygant, J Foster to White, Bouck   24.1A
                Being the same premises that were conveyed to Clemence Wygant by John Curran 4/18/1899 (L375-P84)

Aug 13, 1920   White, Bouck to Sanger, Wm 4.5A
                Off the N front of my farm from E to W. Beginning at a pile of stones at the NE corner of the lands herein conveyed and being on the E side of lands of Griener and S side of land of RB Norton; thence along the S side of lands of said Norton and John Quimby to and along a stone wall S 87° 10' E 978' to the W side of a public lane; thence along W side of said lane S 39° 30' W 130'; thence also along said lane S 27° 30' W 116' to other lands of party of the first part; thence along the lands of said party of the first part N 87° 10' W 906.9' (?); to lands of Greiner; thence along the lands of said Greiner N 17° 30' E 216.8' to a point or place of beginning. Containing 4.5A

My next goal was to get the newspaper reports of the tar and feather incident. Frank Nicklin assured me the story had made the New York City papers. At the Newburgh Free Library was able to find the Index to the New York Times. Interestingly, had trouble finding the materials as was looking under "Bouck White", and found the materials only after checking "White". Pat Clyne had the opposite experience. She had tried looking up under "White", and did not find the material she desired until she had checked under "Bouck White".

The above land records gave the dates between which to search.

The Study Group—Frank Clyne, Al Lanzeta, MaryLou Mahan,
Bob Hennekens, Frank & Freda Nicklin (Photo by Pat Clyne)

The New York Times
May 29, 1921

BOUCK WHITE SUED BY FRENCH BRIDE

Wife, 19, Whom He Met in Paris, Says Husband Concealed Radical Ideas From Her Parents.

WANTS MARRIAGE ANNULLED

Guardian Ad Litem Appointed for Her Pending Action Filed in Poughkeepsie.

(Special to the New York Times.)

Annulment of her marriage to C. Bouck White, self-styled pastor of the Church of the Social Revolution, on the ground of fraud in that he concealed his radical ideas from her parents, is asked by Andree Emilie Simon White, a French girl, 19-year-old, in an action filed in the Supreme Court here today. White, who lives near Marlboro, Ulster County, has not been served, but Justice A. H. F. Seeger of Newburgh appointed Harry G. Harper of Poughkeepsie guardian ad litem for Mrs. White.

In the complaint filed with the Court by her attorney, Bernard F. Cecire, Mrs. White says she met White at a bazaar in Paris in February of this year, that he spoke French fluently and entertainingly and made a good impression upon both her parents and herself.

May 30, 1921

Bouck White Tarred And Feathered on Wife's Complaint

Dragged From Bed by Twelve Autoists,
Taken 13 Miles From Home, Stripped and Lashed.

WIFE TELLS OF CRUELTIES
Hotel Proprietor With Whom She Took Refuge
Says He Ordered Radical from Place.

PREACHER DENIES WHIPPING
Found with William Sanger, He Asserts
Blisters on His Neck Are Merely "Sunburn."

(Special to The New York Times.)

Marlboro, N. Y., May 29.—Twelve men in three automobiles stopped in front of the mountainside shack of Charles Bouck White, self-styled pastor of the "Church of the Social Revolution," on Monday night last. They took the unfrocked preacher of social disorder from his bed, tied a rope around his waist, and hauled him, vehemently protesting, to the road.

Then they stripped, horsewhipped him, applied tar, carbolic acid and feathers, shanghaied him in his scorching covering and whirled down through the sleeping countryside to a desolate spot in the outskirts of Newburgh. The former clergyman was dumped out and two of his captors took him aside.

"Will you promise to treat your wife right?" they asked.

"Yes, I'll take care of her," he answered.

"All right," was the reply; "get along the road home."

The men then climbed into their machines and sped away, and White turned around and hiked back along the thirteen dark, dismal miles to what he calls his "monastic retreat."

Back of the rough handling accorded the advocate of radical doctrines, and only spurred by his wife's charges of fraud, cruelty and subnormal matrimonial ideas, was the desire of the Marlboro section of Ulster County to rid itself of a decidedly unpopular figure.

The former pastor's preachings against the Government, his flagburning record and a recent attempt to win followers here have stirred the community to deep anger. Several months ago, it was said, White advertised a meeting to discuss social problems. He began his usual outbursts against the Government and several girls—apparently they were there just for that purpose—arose "and shut him up."

Before White left the meeting place, it was disclosed today, he had declared this country a pretty good sort of place, had said time and again that he was "for it," and had quaveringly sung "the Star Spangled Banner."

Supplementing the cut-and-dried legal phraseology of the complaint in the annulment proceedings, which Bernard F. Cecire, Poughkeepsie attorney, handed up to Supreme Court Justice A. F. H. Seeger, there came this afternoon from four sources other facts concerning White and his bride of five weeks.

According to Mr. Cecire the complaint related how Miss Simon had married White in Paris on April 21 after a swift courtship. She, the daughter of Marcel Simon, once wealthy resident of Rheims and now a chemist and superintendent of the Panhard-Levassuor motor works in Paris, was introduced to White at a bazaar in Paris. After relating how they had come to this country, arriving nine days after the marriage ceremony in a Protestant chapel in Paris, the complaint set forth how White had attempted to inculcate the cultured French girl with the germs of radicalism.

...(At McElrath's Hotel on Mountain Road)

But just then McElrath himself came out of the door. He is about 45 years old, more than six feet tall, bearded, and of massive build—a combination of hard-working farmer and mountaineer, his jobs when the hotel business is not good.

"Yes," he said taking up the narrative, "that's the fact, but don't forget that Andree properly scratched White's face. I took her in and I told her that she could live here, providing she liked the place and the folks, for the rest of her life and that if White came around here trying to bother her—I'd—" McElrath doubled up a fist that Andree's countryman, Carpentier, might be proud of, and added: "Knock his head off his shoulders."

The big mountaineer, farmer and, now and then Boniface paused to let his anger cool and went on:

"Along about 2 o'clock the next day after Andree came here to us, White came loafing down the road. He had a couple of written notices that his wife had left his bed and board and that he would not be responsible for her. I listened to him tell me all about it—we was standing over there by the barn—and then I told him what the girl had told me and Mrs. Swifle."

"'Oh,' he says, 'I can explain that,' but I didn't let him explain any. I just looked right at him and I says:

"Get the hell off the place. He went on up the road. He didn't say anything."

May 31, 1921

War Veterans Pelt White Out Of Town

Vegetables and Stones Thrown at ex-Preacher
When He Goes to Marlboro in Auto.

Citizens Hoot And Jeer

His French Bride, Through an Interpreter,
Tells of Her Five Weeks of Married Life.

(Special to the New York Times.)

MARLBORO, N. Y., May 30.—C. Bouck White, champion of social unrest, chose Memorial Day to drive down to this town. When he arrived the tree-lined streets were just filling with veterans of American wars preparing to do honor to the men who had died for the flag, and White was hooted out of the village.

Fleeing in his flivver at top speed the pastor of the "Church of the Social Revolution" was pelted with decayed vegetables, tin cans and stones, thrown to the accompaniment of catcalls and yells from ex-soldiers and civilians alike.

At 9 o'clock this morning, having driven the three miles from his shack on the mountainside, White put on the brakes in front of the village cobbler's. On his way down he had passed the Marlboro Mountain House where William McElrath, the proprietor, is sheltering Mrs. Andree Emilie Simon White, the radical preacher's 20-year-old French bride, who has sued for annulment of her marriage.

The cobbler's shop is on the main street. Up and down blue-coated soldiers of Antietam and Gettysburg were sauntering, awaiting the signal to fall in back of those who fought in Flanders or in Cuba.

Groups Form as White Arrives.

The arrival of the man accused of beating his young wife, whom the whole countryside seems to hate because he is rated "not a real American" was noted at once.

Groups formed, and as White went into the shop a party of small boys became possessed of New York newspapers telling of the tar and feathering episode and of the girl wife's story of cruelty.

When White emerged with his usual self-confident smile and a pair of mended shoes, he found his car plastered with the newspapers, the headlines out. He threw the shoes into the machine and laughingly removed the posters. While he was doing this a Civil War veteran shouted something at him—something about the flag.

Then from all angles came a barrage. Potatoes and even bunches of asparagus whistled around the disciple of revolt. He disregarded the attack until one well-directed tuber took his hat off. Then he hastily climbed into his machine and went off as speedily as his antique conveyance would permit.

With his departure, however, the resentment against him increased rather than diminished. Tonight the residents of Marlboro, judging from their conversation, are not sure that "enough has been done to him," and there appeared to be reason to expect that the solitary man on the mountainside might be the target for further punishment....

Ordered to Arise at 6 A. M.

"I sat down on the one chair and cried. I cried most of the night, and at 6 o'clock in the morning Mr. White said to me:

'Get up.' It was an order, but I thought he was jesting. I could not think any one got up with the dawn. But he insisted. I laughed and then he was very angry. He finally dragged me out and ordered me to clean up the place."

"'You are my servant,' he said, 'and when you don't do as I wish I'll use you as a cow.'"

For two days, the girl continued, she endured "this animal life," and then came the alleged beating and her escape to the home of McElrath.

"As for my future," she added as a last word, "I like America. I want to stay here. Perhaps I can support myself here—for a time at least, for my mother must be grieving for me. Perhaps I can tutor in French or be a governess. I don't know what—but I like America and some Americans."

White, who was busy today cementing the walls of a fieldstone pump house he is adding to his estate, again attributed all his troubles to the incompatibility of the French and American temperaments. Also to overalls. He was wearing a pair and as he glanced down at them he said:

"It was these overalls that were largely responsible for the separation. She didn't want me to do any manual labor, I tried to tell her that I was a working man and that I had to, but she insisted that I had to wear city clothes and a white collar all the time."

White indulged in further exposition of his views on large topics, and announced that he "shunned" Bolshevism, socialism and the Lenin brand of communism. He said he was now a 'municipalist." This he defined as a person who was endeavoring to awaken the civic conscience of the cities. He again denied the story of his tar and feathering, and also declared that he never had mistreated his wife.

It was learned today that on May 9, the day Mrs. White fled from him, Justice Doyly Hutchins of Marlboro issued a warrant for his arrest on a charge of assault, after his wife had told her story to the Justice.

The next day Mrs. White and Deputy Sheriff William McConnell went to White's house, but the warrant was not served, because after a talk Mrs. White agreed to withdraw her charge. Then Bernard F. Cecire, a Poughkeepsie attorney, entered the case and White agreed to pay $400 to his wife as passage money back to France. He paid $3 in cash and gave her a check for $21, said McConnell, and since then has paid nothing.

June 8, 1921

Movies Seek Mrs. White

Several Producers Make Her Offers—
She Also Gets Marriage Proposals.

(Special to the New York Times.)
POUGHKEEPSIE, N. Y., June 7.—Andree Emilie Simon White, wife of Bouck White, will probably blossom forth soon as a film star, as she has had many offers to enter the pictures. Her attorney, Barnard F. Cecire, admits that she has already refused several offers, but says that representatives of well-known concerns have been here to see her and had even taken pictures of her to test whether her picture on the screen would show up the beauty which is hers.

June 19, 1921

Bouck White Silent

Makes No Answer to Court in Wife's Annulment Suit.

(Special to the New York Times.)
POUGHKEEPSIE, N. Y., June 18.—Charles Bouck White, Socialist and communist, of Marlborough, has lost his last chance to fight the suit for

annulment brought by his three-months French bride, Emilie Andree Simon White.

This became known today, when the time for the filing of an answer expired.

Having found The New York Times articles, my next chore was to locate the articles printed in the local newspaper, "The Marlboro Record". This was made easier because I now had the exact dates. The newspapers were located at the office of The Southern Ulster Pioneer. During my search, I also was made aware of "The Newspaper Project", a federal project to locate, inventory and list all of the newspapers still in existence—my thanks to Jim Hayes at the Marlboro Free Library for his help here.

The newspapers are located in a back closet. "Charlie" Martin indicated there were requests two or three times in the last 10 years to see the papers. They are bound by year, but in very fragile condition. This necessitated my taking the information by longhand—an arduous process that took the better part of a day. It was then possible to put it into the computer.

THE MARLBOROUGH RECORD—May 13, 1921

"Brings Back French Bride"

J. Bouck White, the well known writer, who has spent much of his time during the past year in Paris, returned to New York a week ago Friday, bringing with him a young and charming French bride. After spending a week in New York Mr. and Mrs. White reached Marlboro and will spend the summer at Mr. White's home in this place.

THE MARLBOROUGH RECORD—May 27, 1921

An article on **"A Strange Rumor from Snake Hallow"**

—no names given

THE MARLBOROUGH RECORD—June 3, 1921

"Story Welcomed by New York Newspapers"
Droves of reporters make Newspaper Mecca of Marlborough

Marlboro has been a Mecca for the sensational story hunters from the New York City Newspapers the past several days. They spared neither time nor expense to get all the material they could for lurid stories of the Bouck White case, and failing in their attempt to tap the right wires to get the real truth of the tar and feather incident The Record mentioned last week, they went to White to get his version of the affair or drew on their own fertile imagination until they got out some greatly distorted stories of the affair. The first reporters came in Sunday and were followed by car loads coming up with photographers and special story writers next day. Tuesday brought even more reporters for by this time, just one week after the tar and feather party, every leading daily in New York City was telling of it. Some of the reporters fairly camped at the White and McElrath farm, interviewing White and his wife, who is staying at the latter place. They drank in every word that White had to say, and he was in the midst of his story, talking freely telling them his views on social welfare, condemning Franco-American marriage alliances, and giving some of them a flat denial that he was tarred and feathered at all, and others that he was brutally treated but bore it stoically in a true martyr fashion, becoming the hero he pretended to be. It was a good chance to get himself well advertised and it cannot be said that he let it go to waste.

...Among the newspapers who had reporters and photographers on the job at Marlboro, were "The Tribune", "The Times", "Daily News", "Evening Journal", "The Telegram", "Examiner", "Sun", "World", and "Herald" and perhaps others. Two young French girls who were up to converse with Mrs. White, got the best story from her. Reporters, photographers and feature writers who were up Tuesday included Don Clark, of "The World"; James Sullivan and Miss Dorothy Craigie of "The Telegram"; John Flynn of "The Herald"; and Locke of "The Newburgh News".

And now it's the "movin" pitchr' men. Wednesday a party of five, including the director and cameramen came in from NY and went out to the McElrath farm, where they "shot" Mrs. White, McElrath, and the surroundings. They then went to White's home where they took more pictures of him, his house, livestock and the country about the place. This latter should look well in pictures for the view is described as wonderful. Before leaving they went to Mrs. White with an offer to go into pictures. This together with several offers of marriage from sympathizing distant admirers, have been refused. The men were from the Selznick Studios, it is said, and were after a short feature film.

THE MARLBOROUGH RECORD—July 29, 1921

Bouck White Leaves for Greener Pastures

Best Known Resident of Marlboro Departs for Vermont and now the bashful state may get more bashful than ever.

...Sunday Mr. White departed for parts unknown. Adieu, Bouck, and if the sad tears of parting so blinded our eyes that we were unable to see you off, think not that we are uninterested in your departure and that you have any other than very best wishes for you in your new abode.

THE MARLBOROUGH RECORD—October 14, 1921

Mrs. White is now a tutor in NYC. Bouck making pottery in Malden, Mass.

Our "Bouck White" Interest group met at the Lanzetta's home on Sunday April 30, 1995.

From my notes:
Frank Nicklin—
Bouck White had once told Frank that he was a full blooded Mohigan Indian. He had an old Model T that he used to bring stone up the hill. This was a story going around at that time—
Bouck White was staying at a small hotel in Paris—the landlady's daughter ran through the halls naked—Bouck White ended up marrying her. He brought her to Marlboro, pointed at his cow and chickens and said—the cows are for milking and the chickens for eggs. Apparently she was upset as she thought she had gotten quite a catch with a rich American. She ran away. Locals believing her to be mistreated decided to use old fashioned justice.
Frank indicated that Bouck White was a good neighbor and a scrupulously honest man—his word was his bond. Frank was pretty adamant that there was no physical abuse present. Frank's father sold some property to Bouck White. Frank thinks Camp was part of the Collins "Shady Pines." Frank also thought Henry Weber worked on the Collins place before coming to camp.

The Henry Weber Connection

Bob Hennekens—Henry Weber lived at Camp Chambers for many, many years. Henry had told the story of a "pacifist" meeting he had attended in New York City. The idea was that the brotherhood of man was superior and more important than artificial barriers caused by nationalism. Individuals were chosen to burn their national flags as a symbol of bridging the gaps caused by nationalism. Henry was chosen to burn the German flag. According to Henry there were no problems until someone burned the American flag—"then the cops came". Henry had to hide out and thus came to Marlboro. Henry was an exquisite gardener, usually went barefooted or cut the toes out of his shoes, and always had a long flowing white beard.

The Camp Chambers Connection

Our family came to Camp Chambers through the church which we attended in New York City. My mother, Freda Hennekens, and my aunt, Victoria Fridl, were the cooks at the camp. This made for the least expensive way for our family to enjoy country life during the summers.

From the Directory of Mount Morris (Harlem) and
Harlem Baptist Church; February 1930—Pg. 13-17

Camp Chambers Invitation Song
Tune: "Our Director"

> Come into the mountains
> Breathe mountain air
> Swim mountain waters
> Pack your sack and swing along the ranges
> Sing around our hearth-fire
> True friends and dear
> Come to Camp Chambers
> And share our cheer.

THE SUMMER AT OUR COOPERATIVE CAMP AN INFORMAL REPORT

The key note of the life at Camp Chambers this summer has been the cooperative development of our mountain camps as an opportunity for pleasant and profitable vacations for all who care to share in its activities. Each member of the staff has his own responsibilities and has sought to execute them successfully. But the success of the Camp has been dependent on all the persons who have shared in its privileges. The staff feels that taking share in the responsibility of the Camp not only serves the purpose of making possible fine vacations at a minimum cost, but that conjoint responsibility makes life normal and sweet and is in a true and fundamental way a process of character building....

In order to make concrete the idea of cooperation at the camp let me cite some of the various contributions of one kind or another which have gone into the life here this summer. First of all, of course, there is the work of the Camp Committee and Pastor Lorimer and the donations of money from the Gould Foundation and from individual friends. Then come the contributions of Henry Weber, the faithful; care-taker of the property throughout the year—the spading up of land, the provision of fresh vegetables, the provision of wood, all without charge, and the example of an unselfish life. The V. I. V. I. members, especially Marie, Freda Hennekens and Assunta, with Miss Dederick's support, renovated the inner aspect of the building. Mrs. Bartell contributed clouds of washing dust and a pavement of soap. One guest arrived with a ham and another with a strudel cake, and the friends of "Pop" Hennekens (my Grandfather), Singna and Joyce contributed birthday cakes. Teddy Kutschera and "Dickey Dear" served as color-sergeants. At the call "Water Boy" some loyal Gunga Din fetched pails from the pump. The "labor gang" performed all sorts of convict labor. Faith Lorimer organized a sewing class. Bill Hennekens, Frank Vasti, Loretta

Donovan and Faith Lorimer tried to bring the woods near home, transplanting some of the local flora....Three visitors in the neighborhood, Helen, Mary, and Peggy, joined in the activities of the Camp and shared its spirit. Among other things they participated in the July Saturday Night production, "Lost Lamb Island." In this play Philip Lavora, Mary Bachraty and Victoria Fridl (my Aunt Vic) starred. Bill Hennekens, Harry, Jimmy and others worked repairing the car. Henry Lutz and "Pop" Hennekens contributed their happy spirit playing with all, infants and adults. Those who came to prepare the meals, Freda Jones Hennekens, and Victoria Fridl, not only did this work efficiently and delectably, but they also added to the whole congenial atmosphere in a sincere and effective way....All participated in kitchen and dormitory duties....Life there has been happy and worthwhile for all of us.

Special activities included overnight hikes for the older young people and picnic for the children. Every afternoon anywhere from twenty to fifty people enjoyed the swimming and diving at the lake. Some interesting and valuable services have been held at the camp on Sunday mornings. Treasure hunts, volley ball, quoits, hare and hounds, show nights, stories, song-fests, and charades have been popular events.

Personally, I have profited greatly through the experiences of the summer, and although the days have been strenuous I feel rested and refreshed at the end of the season.

Frank Lorimer, Director

A SIDELIGHT FROM THE MATRONS

On reaching Camp the first week-end, we were surprised to find that the Camp and the locality were even more beautiful than we had expected. While painting the furniture little Victoria Fridl (my Cousin Vicki), asked her mother, "Mother, why are you painting everything green where there is so much green outside?" The children loved the place so much that they did not want to go home.

The above has been added to the narrative on Bouck White to show that what the French bride found a "shack" and what The New York Times derisively called an "estate" was charming in the eyes of others.

In an article in Hudson Valley Newspapers—Sept 10, 1986 on Christ Episcopal Church, Marlboro written by Betty Smith, it says:

"Gert's Kitchen (dedicated to Gertrude Boyd) was made beneath the chancel. Among its equipment is a large cookstove that was used at Camp Chambers which no longer exists in Marlboro."

Pat Clyne:

Pat indicated she thought Bouck White had gotten the Bouck because he was related to a Bouck who was a governor of New York State.

Bouck White—after leaving Marlboro went to Slingerland where he built a stone building that is quite impressive—SW of Albany. Bouck White had been arrested in New York City prior to World War I for supporting women workers. She also provided us with the following Chronology of Charles Bouck White:

Charles Bouck White

1874—Oct. 20—Charles Bouck White born in Middleburgh, Schoharie Co., NY

1891—Graduates from Middleburgh High School and goes to Harvard; University later attends Union Seminary

1910—Publishes "The Book of Daniel Drew"; aligns himself with Socialist Party

1913—Publishes "The Mixing"

1914—Forms Church of the Revolution; is imprisoned several times for various acts of social agitation

1917-1919—Allegedly serves as war correspondent

1921—Moves to Marlboro, UC—brief marriage to a French woman is annulled; CBW moves to Vermont, then Massachusetts; studies pottery-making

1928—Living in Paris; then French Riviera; develops ceramic known as Bouckware

1934—Moves to Albany; then to Helderberg area where he builds a castle-like complex of limestone

1943—Suffers a stroke; enters home for aged men

1951—June 7—CBW dies

(Pat also has a good resource for information on Dorothy Day which she later sends to me)

The Pottery Connection

Freda Nicklin is nice enough to brave the storms and return home and to her daughter's house in order to bring two pieces of Bouck White's pottery. Pat Clyne has her camera and takes pictures.

The Sanger Connection

Sanger; is mentioned above in the deeds—he buys some land from Bouck White—as well as in the newspaper reports. Frank Nicklin indicates that when things got "too hot" in New York City for Margaret, i.e. there was a lot of controversy stirred up, Margaret spent some time at the Sanger cabin next to Bouck White's. Frank thought that eventually Margaret split from her husband and spent time in France.

Cindy Lanzetta shared a book that the family had found when they took over the property. Eugenics—Natures Secrets Revealed—Scientific Knowledge of the Laws of Sex Life and Heredity—Prof. T. W. Shannon, Mullekin Co., 1914.

Al Lanzetta said the Sanger fireplace was still standing though the building was long gone. Frank Nicklin indicated at one time he and his brothers had discovered letters in the abandoned building but they too are gone.

We agreed to meet again and visit the Sanger fireplace. Pat Clyne took numerous pictures. Al Lanzetta took us through the "pump" house mentioned in the newspaper articles as well as in the Church Directory—on the wall is inscribed in the concrete:

"FOR
A UNITED STATES
CONSTITUTIONAL
CONVENTION THAT
SHALL RESTORE
LOCAL SELF-
DETERMINATION
1921"

We commented on the currentness of that sentiment.

Bob Hennekens remembered the fire place in the main house at Camp Chambers as being quite a structure—there again was a motto with some fancy scribe work—the fireplace was made of native stone.

May 21, 1995

The Bouck White interest group met again on Sunday May 21, 1995. This time the weather was with us and we trekked to the Sanger fireplace. Pat Clyne brought all sorts of photos from the last meeting which she shared with each of us.

Bouck White the Writer Philosopher

Since Pat Clyne had given us several citations for Bouck White's work, went to the Marlboro Free Library and checked on the availability. We were able to order three books from the US Military Academy Library at West Point. The books were:

"The Call of the Carpenter", Bouck White, Doubleday, Garden City, 1911

"The Book of Daniel Drew", Bouck White, Doubleday, New York, 1910

"The Carpenter and the Rich Man", Bouck White, Doubleday, Garden City 1914

I did some scanning but Bob Hennekens read all three. These are some of his gleanings (sorry no page citations)

"His (Jesus')two parables, the Wine Skin and the Patched Garment had for their purpose to sink home into the minds of the people the irrepressible revolution that was upon the world, and the need of new thought-molds. Said he: 'Tis imputed unto me as a fault, that I depart so widely from the traditions of men; that I am an introducer of new thoughts and new institutions. I deny not the charge. I am an innovator. A fresh-born day is upon us. And new times demand new notions. No man puts young wine into old bottles; else the young wine will burst the bottles and be spilled. No man puts a piece of a new garment upon an old, for it agrees not with the old. Fresh bottles for the fresh wine; new cloth for new garments.'"

"Capital (i.e. property) should be confiscated every fifty years and redistributed."

"Inflated fortunes are sinful irrespective of how they are accumulated."

"The ballot box is the greatest spiritual contribution to humankind."

"Labour finds its greatest requital, not in the thing done, but in the doing of it."

"Where fences are the fewest, the country is the happiest."

"Charity is twice curst—it hardens him that gives and softens him that takes. It does more harm to the poor than exploitation because it makes them willing to be exploited."

"There are three destroyers of the human spirit: fear of death, fear of poverty, and fear of public opinion. Of these the last is chief."

"Money has never established republican institutions in the world—it has neither soul nor sentiment."

"Popular forms of government are possible only when individual men can govern their own lives on moral principles, and when duty is of more importance than pleasure, and justice than material expediency."

Have wandered far afield in these notes—my reason has been to bring as much of the tangential information together as possible. I haven't printed all of the reports. There is still more research to be done—just not now!

*   *   *

From The Marlborough Record 9/8/1933

RETURNS TO ROME

Vito Giametta who has been spending the summer vacation at the home of his parents, Mr. and Mrs. Charles Giametta of Marlborough, sails for Rome, Italy, on the French Liner 'Paris" Saturday, September the 9th.

Vito Giametta has returned to the university of Rome where he is continuing his studies of Medicine. He was a member of the 1932 graduating class at Fordham University. He has also attended and graduated from the Marlborough High School.

CANZONERI HOPES TO REGAIN LIGHTWEIGHT TITLE

Tony Canzoneri, former lightweight title-holder, will give the best that's in him next Tuesday evening in an effort to regain for himself the crown which he lost last June to Barney Ross.

The match, a fifteen-round bout, will be staged in the Polo-grounds in New York City. A large crowd is expected to witness the match which should definitely determine which is the real champion.

There was some doubt concerning the outcome of the match last June when the title was awarded to Ross. Some thought Tony should retain the title while others considered the bout a draw. Even the judges had considerable dispute over the matter but the decision was finally given to Ross.

*   *   *

ROBERT RUSSELL Where lie Your Bones?

The phone call came from Brian Toal, Municipal Historian for the town of Clark, NJ. Brian was looking for the final resting place of Robert A Russell who in 1864 was the founding father and first mayor of Clark. Brian has been searching for Robert's final resting place for many years. Brian discovered that Robert wasn't buried in Clark, his body had been shipped to "New York". Since the family had had contacts in Green Point, Brian had checked there. Still no luck. Knowing Robert had married Caroline Ward whose family had lived in Marlborough, his friend, Christianna, suggested he call me, which he did.

A quick check in Poucher & Terwilliger showed that Robert R Russell was buried in Riverside Cemetery in 1882 having died Nov. 11, 1882. Brian was very interested in visiting the final resting place of Robert and so a date was made to meet at the Raccoon on Saturday for lunch. Since Robert was married to Caroline Ward I gave a quick call to Carol Felter, who also agreed to meet us for lunch.

We all came to the table laden with papers and charts—each bringing a piece of the puzzle. Brian brought Christianna, who had first suggested he give me a call.

Brian Toal, Christianna, Carol Felter

From Brian we learned that Russell, Founding father of Clark had served as Mayor from 1864 to 1867 and then again from 1870 to 1873. He was active in politics for many years and was instrumental in setting into action the events necessary to make Clark an independent township. Brian brought census records, pictures of the Russell house in Clark, newspaper articles, etc.

I was able to bring some census records for the Russells and Wards in Marlborough, the Poucher book, a copy of the "infamous" window shade from Riverside Cemetery, and some land records. I had also contacted Edna Baker regarding visiting her house. I was pleased to be able to prove that the Baker house from 1845 to 1854 was the property of the Wards, family of Caroline, wife of Robert Russell.

Carol Felter brought family work sheets, her information on the Lt. John Waring Wygant family, letters from Charlotte Ward (mother of Caroline) to her (Charlotte's) father (John Waring Wygant), and information on the Rev. John Wm. Ward, father of Caroline.

We had a delightful lunch (as is usual at the Raccoon). Our guests were duly impressed with the natural beauty of our river and valley, and we then headed out to do some cemetery searching. Brian and Christianna had been to the cemetery in the morning, but had had no luck. From my records we knew Robert was buried next to the Ward plot. The cemetery map does not show direction and so it was a little difficult at first to get oriented. We were disappointed when we found the Ward stone, but, after much effort were unable to find the stone reported by Poucher for Robert A Russell.

The Ward and Wygant Families

Though it has been difficult to find too much information on the Russell family, the field is rich with information regarding the Wards. The Rev. John Wm. Ward was born in 1801 in New York City. His father was "Gen. Jasper Ward from whom Ward's Island in the East River takes its name, it having been his property for a time, before it was acquired by the City of New York". John was a Presbyterian Minister having been the first Presbyterian pastor of Union which before that time, (since 1794) was attached to the Dutch Church.

John Wm. Ward bought the Baker House on Lattingtown Road from Cornelius Wygant in 1845 and sold it to Clemence Wygant in 1854. It would seem that the Wards used the Baker House as a summer home as the Rev. Ward was, during the time he owned the Baker House, pastor of the Greenpoint church.

It is not unusual that he bought the house from Cornelius Wygant as, indeed, he was married to Charlotte Wygant, the sister of Cornelius. The parents of Charlotte and Cornelius were Lt. John Waring Wygant and Elizabeth DuBois Wygant. Elizabeth was the granddaughter of our Lewis DuBois (The Rusk House on 9W).

Another child born to John Wm. Ward and Charlotte Wygant Ward was John Wm. Ward, Jr. who also was mayor of the township of Clark, New Jersey from March 12, 1887 until November 3, 1887 when he gave up the position due to the sudden death of his daughter.

The Rev. John Wm. Ward (Sr.) died at Rahway, NJ Sept. 4, 1859 and it seems that Charlotte, his wife, shortly thereafter went to live with Robert Russell and Caroline, his wife, (and the daughter of Charlotte and the Rev. John Wm. Ward).

Carol Felter had brought several letters written by Charlotte Wygant Ward to her father, John Waring Wygant and other family dated between 1830 and 1850. In the letters Charlotte, the wife of a prominent pastor, implores her father to mend his relationship with God. In a letter to her mother in 1850 she writes, "Caroline left Fishkill in the cars at half past 12 o'clock—left them in Canal Street, walked one block, took a stage to Grand Street ferry, crossed over, took a Green Point Stage and was at home at half past 3 o'clock". One wonders if one could make the trip as quickly today!

In the cemetery we found there are a good number of stones that are broken, difficult or impossible to read, and piled and stacked together. We did stop at DiDonato's to see if his records go back that far—unfortunately they don't. Brian was going to check on newspapers to see if there was an Obit. Carol Felter offered to check out the Newburgh Library next time she was there.

*   *   *

From The Marlborough Record 9/8/1933

Milton Lad Ellected to State OFFICE
Fred Woolsey is Chosen President of F. F. A.
at Syracuse

SPOKE last Saturday over WABC will Go To
Kansas City

Fred Woolsey returned from Syracuse Tuesday night bearing the greatest honor that it is possible for the Young Farmer Association of New York State to bestow. He has been elected president of the entire state. The election was held Saturday and the nominating committee quickly chose three candidates and the voters quickly selected Fred for the president.

Woolsey was a graduate of last year's class at Highland High School, where he was a popular member and played first base on Coach Clearwater's baseball team. He was Secretary of the Highland Tillers and vice president of the Eastern Group of the F.F.A.

He and Leonard Gunsch Were given the Empire Farmers Degree while at Syracuse. This was necessary before one could be a candidate for president.

His first official duty was to go on the air over station WABC at four-fifteen Saturday afternoon, where he introduced several of the young speakers

In November he will make a trip to Kansas City attend a meeting of the F.F.A. All expenses will be paid for this journey. Milo Winchester, instructor of agriculture at the high school, hopes to make the trip also.

Those who attended the fair in the group were Mr. Winchester, Leonard Gunsch, Fred Woolsey, Thomas Shay and Niel Wilklow.

*   *   *

Lesson for 4th Graders at Schantz Park

1. I am a Native American—I lived on the banks of the great river that the Mohegans called "Ma ha ke negh tue" which means "continually flowing water." There were many fish in the river, salmon and shad—we often used the fish or fish heads to fertilize the soil where we planted our crops.

2. I am Henry Hudson. I am English but I sailed for the Dutch. In 1609 I was the first white man to sail up the river that was later named after me. I passed the place where many years later there would be a town called Marlborough. I wrote in my ship's log—"This is a very pleasant place to build a town on."

3. I am Peter Stuyvesant. After Henry Hudson's trip up the Hudson River the Dutch claimed all of New York state which they called New Amsterdam. I was the Dutch governor of New Amsterdam. In 1664 the English sent a fleet of ships to seize New Netherlands and I was forced to give it up.

4. There is no record that any white man set foot in what is now Marlborough before 1684. I am Governor Dongan. The King of England sent me to the Native Americans to buy a large tract of land— from the Northern part of Marlborough to New Windsor in the south and to the far mountains on the west. There is a statue of me in Poughkeepsie.

5. I am Captain John Evans. In 1694 the King of England gave me the land that Governor Dongan had bought for him. I had to promise to get men to settle the land. I only was able to get a few men to settle on the large piece of land so the King took it back from me.

6. I am Dennis Relyea. I am one of the people that Captain Evans got to settle on the land shortly after 1694. I am known as the first white man to ever live in Marlborough. I settled on a piece of property next to a small stream. They called me "Old Dennis" and they called the small stream "Old Man's Kill."

7. I am Luis Gomez. I am Jewish and a merchant. In the early 1700's I built a trading post just south of the hamlet of Marlboro. I traded with the Native Americans. A little later a mill was built here. The stream that goes past my house and mill is called "Jew's Creek."

8. I am Anne, Queen of England. I learned a lesson from the deal with John Evans. I would never give anyone such a large piece of land again. When I gave someone land, I gave them an official paper called "Letters Patent." It was like a deed. I always made sure my official seal was on the deed. The original Bond Patent complete with my seal is at the Senate House in Kingston.

9. I am Captain William Bond. Queen Anne gave me "Letters Patent" in 1710 for 600 acres. The official papers say that any gold or silver on the land belongs to the Queen. The Queen also owns any tree that is 24 inches in diameter 12 inches up from the root. I also must make sure I get people on the land to settle it, or the land will be taken from me. And—I have to pay taxes every year to the Queen.

10. I am Susanna (or Sukey) Bond. I am William's daughter. Soon after the Queen gave my father the "Letters Patent" in 1712, my father and I moved to Marlborough. I kept house for my father and looked after the property and our slaves when my father was away at sea. I never married and lived to an old age. Schantz Park is part of the Bond Patent.

11. I am Edward Hallock. In 1760 between Christmas and New Year I moved my family (by a little open schooner) from Long Island to Milton. We landed at Milton at what is known as "Forefather's Rock." With me were my wife, our ten daughters and two sons. We moved in with our Son-in-law, John Young. He had a little stone house about a half-mile from the river. In this little house, one story and attic high, not more than fifteen or twenty feet square, fifteen of us spent that first winter in an almost unbroken forest.

12. I am Phebe Hallock, Edward's wife. Our many descendants made many contributions to Marlborough history. Some of our descendants built a little water mill at the end of Long Pond.

13. I am Thomas Woolsey. In 1763 Marlborough was only a part of the larger town of Newburgh. At the annual meeting held at Capt. Jonathan Hasbrouck's house (Washington's Headquarters in Newburgh) I was elected a path master. We didn't have highway departments back then. Each person living on a road was expected to help maintain it. The Path Master was in charge of one road and made sure everyone did their job. The main road in Marlborough was "The Post Road".

14. I am Lewis DuBois. I owned a whole patent where the hamlet of Marlboro is now. My house was built in the 1750's and is across the road from Dickie's Diner. I was a hero of the Revolutionary War. The English fired cannon balls at my house from their ships as they went up the Hudson River to burn Kingston. One of the cannon balls is in the display case in the Town Hall. I am buried in the cemetery across from the library in Marlboro.

15. I am Lewis DuBois, Jr. In 1763 my father gave a small plot of land to "The Marlborough Society" for the purpose of building a church. This was the oldest religious organization in the town. They built the

Presbyterian Church near where DiDonato's Funeral Home is now. The building was burned in 1869. There is a plaque telling the story near DiDonato's garage.

16. I am Joseph Carpenter. My wife was Sarah Latting. Lattingtown was named after my wife's family. I was one of the first settlers in the area. My tombstone is at the Lattingtown Church. It says, "In memory of Joseph Carpenter, the first settler of the place and planter of this orchard. Departed this life July 11, 1766, aged 61 years, 3 months and 6 days."

17. The precinct of New Marlborough was set off from Newburgh in 1772. The precinct became a town in 1788. I am Henry Deyo. The first precinct meeting was held in 1772 at my house. At this meeting Lewis DuBois was chosen supervisor of the precinct.

18. I am Robert Gilmore. In 1800 a meeting was held at my house. It was voted : That the Town of Marlborough be divided into two Towns...the new Town on the west side of the mountains to be called the Town of Plattekill...the remainder of the town on the east side of the mountains retain its present name of Marlborough...

19. I am Henry Crawford. My will is dated March 27, 1816. In it I name all my family and what I want them to inherit. And—"I give my two blacks, Tom and his wife, Yanna free at my decease if they should choose it; if not to remain with my wife."

20. I am Elizah Lewis. In Colonial and Revolutionary times Micajah Lewis and I ran an Inn. Our property is on the original Bond Patent. Our inn began to be called "Washington's Headquarters." Our connec-

tion with Washington is that it is believed he was one of our visitors. In fact, it is believed that he stopped here on three occasions.

*   *   *

August 17, 1994
Mr. Bernie Vinzani
PO Box 70
Whiting, Maine 04691

Dear Bernie,

I am glad you called last night. It's such amusement to get pieces of the puzzle and have to work on putting them together. I am pleased to hear of "The Friends of Dard Hunter". You mentioned you were particularly interested in Elverhöj and the friendship between Dard Hunter and Ralph Pearson.

Enclosed please find:

1) Brochure from Mill House—mentions Dard Hunter, has a picture of the mill house he rebuilt, and a picture of the bed in which Dard Hunter's son was born.

2) News clipping re Mill House—mentions Dard Hunter

3) Copies of a reprint of a brochure Dard Hunter had done when he was selling Mill House
(Didn't know whether you had these or not).

4) Brief article on Elverhöj—primarily as summer theater done by a previous town historian,

5) Another brief mention done by former town historian,

6) My notes from a meeting held with Bruce Weiss, present owner of Elverhöj, when he gave Mark Murray and I a tour of the place on Oct. 20, 1993. Mark Murray had originally contacted me as he had picked up

a brass dish marked "Elverhöj" and had done some research on the colony,

7) Some pictures I took during the above tour given by Bruce Weiss.

(Now we're getting into some things of interest to you).

8) Copy of copy of article given to me by Mark Murray listing both "The Dard Hunter School of Handicraft (1909)" and "Elverhöj Colony". Listed as a key figure at Elverhöj is Ralph Pearson. There are a number of citations listed that might be worth tracking down.

(And now the real goody).

9) Copy of copy of article given to me by Mark Murray regarding the Elverhöj Colony stating "Dard Hunter, an acquaintance of Elverhöj member Ralph M. Pearson, designed the letterhead for the Colony."

As I indicated over the phone, Bruce Weiss has some other materials from Elverhöj—pamphlets, posters, etc. I don't have Bruce's address but his phone number is (914) 795-xxxx. It is an unlisted phone number so please handle it with care. If you do call Bruce, please tell him I said to call. He was wonderful in showing us every nook and cranny on the place.

Mark Murray had done quite a bit of research on Elverhöj and, as I said, has a brass dish imprinted "Elverhöj". Again, I don't have his address, but his phone number is (914) 473-xxxx. He's a delight.

As I said over the phone, I would very much appreciate getting information about your organization, about how to contact Ralph Pearson's and Dard Hunter's sons, and any other information you might deem appropriate for us to add to our local historical collection.

Should you need any further information, please feel free to give me a call. Presently our historical collection doesn't have much more than I've sent you on Dard Hunter but I'm willing to cooperate in any way possible.

         *   *   *

A Gal after my own Heart
Sarah Hull Hallock

The Sarah Hull Hallock Library has an interesting history.

The Sarah Hull Hallock Library dates back to 1886 and at this point is over 115 years old. It was started when Sarah Hull Hallock died in 1884 and left an endowment to maintain a free library in Milton.

Sarah Hull Hallock named her sister, Dorcus Hull, and several other citizens to the board of trustees. In 1886 the library was fully incorporated as the Sarah Hull Hallock Library Association of Milton and in the same year the Articles of Incorporation were adopted.

Until 1896 it was necessary to house the Library's books in various homes in the community. At that point the more than 3,000 volumes were moved to the Woolsey building until a permanent building was erected in 1927.

Volunteers fulfilled the tasks of running the library.

Local residents who have served as librarians include Caroline Sears, Helen Bell, Elizabeth Warren, Madeleine Card, Janet Rhoades and Patricia Russo.

In the 1980s it was decided that the library needed to expand. A new addition was to be added. This was accomplished in part at the behest of Roy L. Featherstone who donated money in-memory of his wife, Hope. Hope Featherstone was along-time board member and supporter of the library. Ground was broken in 1989.

Frank Taylor, a local architect, donated his services and designed an addition replicating the original facility and more than doubling the size of the original building. The opening ceremony was held in the fall of 1990.

(From recent article written by Friends of the Library)

SARAH HULL HALLOCK

In "Our Quaker Forbears" edited by Theodora M Carrell (in the Milton Library) it states:

> In a gabled house overlooking the river, surrounded by trees through which the placid Hudson was seen, lived Aunt Sarah Hallock, worker for the suffrage for women, and her sister Cousin Dorcas Hull. Aunt Sarah was aunt by virtue of her marriage to Uncle Edward, Uncle Nathaniel's brother. Her face, too, was framed in white curls, and she was a charming, gifted and well known woman. She was living in 1884 but not in 1889, when Sue and I went to spend a day with Cousin Dorcas, who carried on several years, so that I came to know her very pleasantly. My diary speaks of the lovely views of the river and of guests in the house, Mrs. Inness, wife of George Inness, the landscape painter, who was shut in his room that day because of illness.

In another description, she is depicted thusly:

> The women were for the most part silent, but not Aunt Sarah! She was Uncle Edward Hallock's second wife, a comparatively young woman when he died. She had no children and her stepsons were married men. With half her life's energies unspent she gave herself to books and gardening and friendship and reform. At intervals, between 1856 and the Civil War, we were visited by missionary lecturers sent forth by the New York

Anti-slavery Society. (The New York Anti Slavery society was organized at a convention held in Utica in 1835, with Mary Hallock Foote's uncle, Townsend Hallock, as one of its vice-presidents. The object was the "entire Abolition of Slavery in the United States."—MLM) Aunt Sarah, who belonged to the society, invited them, and the Republicans, those weary voters, got up meetings for them and met their trains, and they were the guests of the Hallocks at large.

(A Victorian Gentlewoman in the Far West by Mary Hallock Foote, Henry E. Huntington Library and Art Gallery, 1972)

Another interesting article is written on "National Woman Suffrage Association" stationery

Rochester, NY
June 25, 1887
My Dear Miss Hull,

On this lovely June morning in a pile of old envelopes—addressed and stamped, I came to this ??? to your dear sister and my most excellent friend, Sarah H Hallock. The date of the envelope shows that the thought of her was several years ago!

It seems impossible to see your lovely home among the vines there without dear Sarah in it, though it is many years since I saw her there. My last glimpse of her was in the press of a Washington Convention 3 or 4 years ago.

When I first heard of her passage to the beyond I fully intended to write you of my love and admiration of the one gone and my sympathy for the lonely one left in that beautiful hillside home, but alas the days are not long enough for me to do the half of the needful things I am prompted to do—so to very many of my best friends I seem to be forgetful if not ungrateful. But I shall not forget your bright, beautiful, clear-sighted sister, Sarah, nor your own dear self, while memory lasts. I wish she could have remained over to be with us in the celebration of the fortieth anniversary of the first Woman's Right's Convention.

She was at the third one at Worcester two years later, while I was at home on my dear father's Rochester farm reading the report of it in the "New York Daily Tribune".

Very few of those who stood for the grand principle two score of years ago are now left. I hope you will be able to attend the Council.

With Love & Sympathy
Yours as ever,

Susan B. Anthony

This letter may be viewed at the Marlboro Library. It was given to the library by Carla Lesh, granddaughter of Liz Plank, Marlborough's first Town Historian. I think this letter is interesting as it is proof that Susan B. Anthony was in Milton and it proves that our own Sarah Hull Hallock was a moving force during her lifetime. By the way, in November 1872, suffragist Susan B. Anthony was fined $100 for attempting to vote for President Grant. It is believed she never paid the fine.

CHURCHES

CHRIST CHURCH EPISCOPAL

Rectors:

Robert Shaw	1837-1838
Samual Hawkley	1845-1855
James Richmond (supplied)	1856-1858
Samuel W. Akerley	1858-1875
George Waters	1875-1876
John Buckmaster	1876-1892
H. P. Hobson	1892-1898
Charles Tibballs	1899-1904
Harold Moore	1904-1905
G. H. Reckeicker	1906-1908
Henry M. Kirby	1908-1914
Thomas Davies	1915-1918
Lee M. Dean	1918-1920
John Harding	1921-1921
Leighton Williams	1921-1932
A. Van de Beek Vos	1932-1945
Allen Grayson	1945-1949
John Phillips	1949-1954
Arthur Brown	1954-1955
Leonel E. W. Mitchell	1956-1966
David Eylers	1966-1970
Ralph E. Smith	1971-1987
Nancy Baillie Strong	1990-Pastor

CHRIST EPISCOPAL CHURCH, MARLBORO
by Elizabeth F. Smith

Christ Episcopal Church will celebrate its 150th anniversary next year, it was organized in 1837 by the Rev. Robert Shaw of St. Andrew's Church, Walden. With mission support from St. George's, Newburgh, Rev. Shaw removed to Marlborough in 1858.

A small wooden church, with a tower and belfry, was consecrated in 1839. Until then services were held in the school house at Hampton or at the Marlboro Methodist meeting-house....

On the Sunday following the Christmas of 1857 the church was destroyed by fire. A beautiful new brick building with brownstone trim was built on the same site (land given by Dennis Doyle). Designed by Richard Upjohn and Sons, a striped slate roof and narrow buttresses adorned the church. The "semi-octagonal" chancel faced the river. It was adjoined by a "robin room" on the north side of the building. The interior had a high-ceilinged "open finished roof" and a tower broke the roof-line in the southwest corner. Altar, pulpit, seats and bishop's chair were "black walnut;" the floors and doors of "Georgia Pine." In the basement was a Sunday school room and a cellar at the west end held a furnace in 1887.

The Rev. Samuel M. Ackerly first served that church, continuing care of the Milton church consecrated in 1859.

The parsonage was built in 1863 on land donated by Mrs. Hester Doyle. Stairs were built to connect the main church with the basement. More recently, the stairway from the "robing room" was changed to connect both floors; a cover was built to protect hall entry and stairs from the weather.

The church has known periods of much religious activity and lean years when it was in danger of closing. "Today, however," one parishioner told me, "it is the fastest growing church in our diocese."

On June 20, 1981 the Church Hall in the basement of the church was dedicated. Many years of work went into the project, most of it done by church members themselves. Mr. Jack Boyd recounts hours, men and shovels that moved yards of dirt and gravel from the sides of the walled "walkway" that extended the full length of the building. Bricks and cement were used to give extra support of the thick walls of the main church. Above these, closets were made. Plastered/cement walls were added to make a large "coffee" and "fellowship" room. Gert's Kitchen (dedicated to Gertrude Boyd) was made beneath the chancel. Among its equipment is a large cookstove that was used at Camp Chambers which no longer exists in Marlboro. The reception room is dedicated to Ralph McMullen (a relation of Mr. McMullen who earlier owned Pleasant View Hotel.)

Some of the windows are apparently the original "windows filled with enameled glass with stained glass borders;" others are clearly marked, "Helen Maitland Armstrong 1926." The windows are all of exceptional beauty....

The wooden cross that hangs above the altar was Marlboro made by Barney Cunningham. It is suspended by chains, pulleys and ropes that allow it to be raised and lowered when required.

The baptismal font at the back of the church is from All Saints Church in Milton (closed several years) and the baptismal "pitcher" is the one donated to St. Agnes Chapel in Balmville (closed—was located by the Balmville Tree).

The pews are now missing some of their original numbering and have been moved around to accommodate needs. The tan kneelers were a craft project of one of the members; the red ones have been there "as long as remembered."

The present vicar is the Rev. Ralph E. Smith.

The Brotherhood of the Kingdom
"Thy Kingdom come,
Thy will be done on earth"

Preliminary Announcement of the Fifteenth Annual Conference, Marlborough-on-Hudson, N. Y. August 2-6, 1909

...Each evening, except Thursday, open air twilight meetings will be held, as usual. Arrangements will be made to hold a public meeting in the village of Marlborough on Thursday evening, August 5....

Marlborough is located on the line of the West Shore Railroad, sixty-four miles from New York and eighty-six miles from Albany, in the midst of vine-clad hills and charming scenery. The Conference is held on a hill-top a mile and a half back from the village and five hundred feet above the river; with a panoramic view in all directions. It is easily reached by West Shore trains, of which there are six each way daily. Fare from New York, $1.44. Or, by Day Boat to Newburgh, sixty miles, and thence by train to Marlborough. During the Conference stages run from the station to the Conference ground.

Arrangements are being made to supply accommodations in tents on the Conference ground as needed. Mr. Robert Clack whose residence has been the stopping place for many of our Brotherhood and its guests, has sold his property and it will not be available for our use hereafter. Ample accommodations, however, will be provided on the Conference ground in cottages or tents and meals served at a total cost of $1.00 per day....

We earnestly hope that you will arrange to be present with us at this Conference.

LEIGHTON WILLIAMS
Chairman of Executive Committee,
312 West 54th Street, New York City

*   *   *

SAMUEL HAWKSLEY

Oct. 1, 1996
Mrs. Cindy Lanzetta
Mountain Road
Marlboro, NY 12542

Dear Cindy,

Here's information gathered on our friend, the Reverend Samuel Hawksley. What an interesting life! What dedication and service! What a wonderful story to study!

With some of the older church records (being able to at least see his name if not more in the official records), with his monument so close to the church, with the history that has been retained, he really is an interesting story to search out.

Trust this is as you requested. Have included all that I've found. Don't get your hopes up, there's a lot of duplication. Woolsey wrote the chapter on "Marlborough" in Clearwater (though not the chapter on The Episcopal Church in the county which was written by Rev. Charles Mercer Hall, M.A.). It appears that was the practice and once someone wrote on a topic, they reused it in their own text. There probably was a lot of plagiarism too, unfortunately. I don't know of other sources that are readily available. As you know, church records and vital records for this period are scarce or non-existent.

Have included some information on the Rev. Brown of Newburgh. They were contemporaries with the same occupations in close vicinity, and I would assume, since Brown was the older man, Hawksley probably found him a good model. Brown is so fascinating as his story begins with taps into the Revolution, proceeds to the Civil War and continues through my grandmother's period. Such links to the past are priceless.

Thank you for the opportunity to search out information on Rev. Hawksley as I found him incredibly fascinating.

FROM CHRIST CHURCH PAPERS

1844—Samuel Hawksley started to serve church as a Lay-Reader, continued to study theology and April 14, 1846 was asked to serve Christ Church as Rev. Samuel Hawksley. It was at a vestry meeting at this time that the cemetery was planned; family plots were organized. Rev. Hawksley served Christ Church 1844-1855, and organized All Saints Church, Milton—1850. His monument is at the entrance to cemetery. Also—check early church books—my notes indicate there are notations about some fundings for Rev. Hawksley. Especially if you're working with kids taking them back to original sources can be fascinating.

HISTORY OF THE TOWN OF MARLBOROUGH

by Will Plank in The Fifty-Niner No. 2 (no page marked)

EPISCOPAL CHURCHES

All Saints Church was organized in Milton in 1850 by the Rev. Samuel Hawksley of Christ Church....

(NB much of the following has been deleted here as there is a lot of repetition)

HISTORY OF MARLBOROUGH NEW YORK

C.M. Woolsey, 1908 (P 420—421)

Services were continued by the neighboring clergy until the spring of 1844, when Rev. Samuel Hawksley became the rector. He was born in England, and came to this country when a child. Friends afterward sent him to Trinity College, Hartford, from which he graduated in 1839. He then entered a theological seminary....

The older people of the town well remember him, not only as traveling on foot Sunday after Sunday from one charge to another, but as passing from house to house, calling upon people of all denominations, making a pleasant and friendly call with all, saying kind words, giving friendly instruction and advice, and leaving pleasant memories and remembrance in the homes of all. I think all will remember him as a zealous worker in the cause, and a true, consistent and faithful minister. I well remember his pleasant calls at my father's house, and how all the family liked him.

THE HISTORY OF ULSTER COUNTY NEW YORK
edited by Alphonso T. Clearwater, LL.D., 1907 (p. 467)
Christ Church, Marlborough....The rectors of this parish have been:...Rev. Samuel Hawksley, 1847....

NEWBURGH HER INSTITUTIONS, INDUSTRIES AND LEADING CITIZENS
compiled by John J. Nutt, 1891
There is no mention of Rev. Hawksley but, (p 126) gives a report on Rev. John Brown, D. D. who would have been the minister who served at St. George's in Newburgh in 1847 when Rev. Hawksley was ordained. His history also is fascinating and since, in a way, he would have been a mentor for Rev. Hawksley, it might be interesting to note:
Dr. Brown was born 1791 in New York City.
He graduated from Colombia College in 1811 as valedictorian.
He was for many years the only minister of his church on the west side of the Hudson River between New York and Catskill.
He organized the churches at Monticello, Middletown, Cornwall and Marlborough.
He received the degree of Master of Arts from Columbia College in 1815 and the degree of D.D. from Hobart College in 1841. He declined the proffer of the Presidency of Hobart College at its organization.
During his ministry Dr. Brown preached special sermons on the occasion of the death of ten Presidents of the United States.
January 14, 1856, he presided at the obsequies of Uzal Knapp, the last of the Life Guards of Washington.

He was chaplain of the Nineteenth Regiment and delivered a sermon to its members one Sunday afternoon in April, 1864, in St. George's Church, a few days before the regiment left for the front.

At the reception of Lafayette in Newburgh in 1824 he delivered an address of welcome.

He was the oldest minister of his denomination in the State. Old residents say of his preaching that it was remarkably thoughtful, logical, impressive, reverent and imbued with the spirit of religion.

He died August 15, 1884, after a residence of sixty-nine years in the parish. He is buried at St. George's Cemetery.

THE HISTORY OF THE TOWN OF MARLBOROUGH
by Charles H. Cochrane, 1887 (p 127-129)
(See Below)

1855 NEW YORK CENSUS

Dist.	1
Number	34
last Name	Hawksly
first name	Samuel
age	39
born	Eng.
occupation	EP Clergyman
yrs resident	12
other	boarder

1850 FEDERAL CENSUS

Family number	460
(living with)	Cecelia Carpenter (35) and Mercy Carpenter (74)
Name	Samuel Hawksly

Age   30
occupation   PE Clergyman

There was no 1845 New York Census and he is not on the 1840 Federal
Census

To Craig—
    <u>Note</u>—Christ Church will be holding a celebration on Nov. 2 regard-
ing the Reverend Samuel Hawksley and I thought you'd appreciate the
following information in anticipation of that.

HISTORY OF ULSTER COUNTY, NEW YORK
Nathaniel Bartlett Sylvester—1880
(note—Sylvester used local people to do much of the writing of this
text. Unfortunately he doesn't seem to credit the person who did the
writing for Marlborough)
    Rev. Samuel Hawksley—Christ Episcopal Church Marlboro
    He was succeeded by Mr. Samuel Hawksley, who was born in
England, and came to this country while quite young, with an elder sister and her husband, landing in Philadelphia, where they remained a
short time. Leaving him there, they went to the West. Young Hawksley
was aided by the Rev. William Cooper Mead, D. D., rector of Trinity
Church, who placed him at school, and afterwards sent him to Trinity
College, Hartford, where he graduated A.B. in 1839. He entered the
General Theological Seminary in New York in 1840. His close applica-
tion to study so severely affected his sight that he was obliged to ask for
an extended leave of absence, during which time he visited England. On
his return, his sight being improved, he asked for a dismissal from the
seminary. Soon after he was employed as a tutor in the family of a gentleman living near Marlborough. He volunteered his services as a lay

reader, and was gladly accepted. Bishop Brownell, of Connecticut, admitted him to deacon's orders in Christ Church, Hartford, in 1845. Soon after he was appointed missionary to Marlborough. He then relinquished teaching, and devoted himself to the duties of the ministry. After two years of incessant labor, holding service at different places, baptizing the children, and by his kind and sympathizing disposition gaining the confidence and esteem of the working-people, he gathered in the church a congregation respectable in numbers and regular in their attendance. On Sunday, the 2d of May, 1847, he was advanced to priest's orders by Bishop De Lancey, of Western New York, in St. George's church, Newburgh. Soon after he was made rector of the church in Marlborough. His missionary labors extended to Milton and Lloyd, afterwards to Stone Ridge and Ellenville, frequently journeying on foot from village to village. In 1850 he organized All Saints' Church, Milton, in 1853, St. Paul's Church, Ellenville, and had charge of St. Peter's Church, Stone Ridge, preaching in each place one Sunday in the month, and on the other Sundays procuring lay readers for them.

These arduous labors gradually undermined his constitution. His health was so much impaired that he was obliged to relinquish his duties and seek a change of air. He visited the sea-shore, and after a short rest returned home somewhat improved in health, but without that buoyancy of spirits for which he was noted. On resuming his duties before he fully recovered his strength, he was assisted by a member of the congregation, who read the prayers for him, he reading his sermons seated on a chair in the chancel. The following summer he was again confined to his bed. At the urgent request of his friends he consented to have a physician called; it was then too late. It might not be irreverent to say that he was prematurely worn out in the service of his Master. After lingering a few days, he died on Sunday morning, the 2d of September. A very appropriate monument marks his grave, bearing the following inscriptions:

Rev. Samuel Hawksley, Presbyter.

Rector of Christ Church, Marlborough.

Departed this life 2d September, 1855, aged 41 years.

"Even so, saith the Spirit, for they rest from their labors."

After Mr. Hawksley's death the services were suspended for two weeks,....

*   *   *

ST. JAMES RC CHURCH

(excerpts from Centennial Anniversary Celebration St. James Church 1874-1974)

It all began in 1874 when Father James Francis Mee came to Milton as the first resident pastor of the Parish of St. James.

Prior to Father Mee's pastorate, Milton was supplied by Father O'Toole and Father Brady from Rosendale of which parish Milton was a mission. Mass was celebrated every two or three weeks in the old village hall.

Father Mee did the pioneering work from a parochial residence that had been secured by the parishioners. He completed the church in 1876 and when Archbishop McCloskey came to administer the Sacrament of Confirmation in 1877 it was officially dedicated.

Father Mee was in charge of the Milton parish, with missions at Marlborough and Ireland Corners. About 1882 he purchased grounds for the catholic cemetery at Lattingtown which was duly consecrated. In 1888, he was transferred to the village of Rye, New York.

Father J. L. Hoey 1888-1894

Father Hoey prior to his Milton assignment saw Ireland Corners become a separate parish and he also built a church in New Paltz. When he became pastor of St. James he had St. Mary's Church in Marlborough and the Roseton church in his charge.

Father Edward J. Kenney 1896-1900

Father Edward Kenney founded the church of St. Augustine in Highland when he was pastor of St. James and it was at that time St. Mary's Church in Marlborough was legally incorporated as a separate parish on January 3, 1900.

Father James Dooley 1900-1908

It was during this period that Highland began as a mission to St. James Parish. The St. James Parish role as "the Mother Church" was now sustaining and ministering to the needs of a new mission.

Father Richard Cushion 1908-1913

When he died in 1948 he willed his chalice be given to St. James because of his love for his first pastorate.

Father Thomas Prendergast 1918-1923

Father Prendergast built the parish hall and made many improvements in the church and rectory.

Father Michael J. Tighe 1923-1929

He gave the church a center aisle and extended the building to accommodate more at Mass and other church services.

Father Gregory Mullin 1934-1941

Father Mullin is responsible for the brick front which enhanced the beauty of the church. He also installed the bell....

Father John T. Halpin 1947-1950

Father Halpin was pastor of Saint James at the time the Diamond Jubilee Celebration was organized and held and it was through his pastorate that St. Augustine was established as a separate parish in Highland.

Monsignor James J. Lynch 1969-1973

Father Lynch coming from Cathedral College in 1969 instituted the Parish Council and began proceedings for refurbishing the church for the Centennial celebration.

Construction on the church hall was begun by Father Prendergast and completed in Father Tighe's pastorate.

Woolsey's History of Marlborough states that the church had been enlarged and renovated several times between the time the church was built and 1908.

Somewhere along the line, a family by the name of Gould (summer boarders from New York City) donated an altar and large Sacred Heart statue.

Music was provided by melodeon until about 1919 or so. A single key-board pipe organ was donated to the Church at that time. An electronic Wurlitzer organ was purchased in 1950's.

Church lengthened in 1928.

A fire in the Church sacristy in late April, 1923, was stopped before getting into the Church. However, there was much heat and water damage in the Church.

When construction was first started on the Church building, the frame was blown down during a big wind storm.

The Church had a tin roof for many years. At one time the rear of the main building had a large hallway—partition was torn down to make larger area.

Brick front added in 1935—belfry built, steeple raised and bell installed at the same time. The old Sacred Heart statue was coated, and put in park on cobble stone pedestal built by Jack Santora.

Father Crew donated new outdoor statue of Sacred Heart after the old one disintegrated. Father Crew also donated electric contrivance for ringing the angelus.

*   *   *

THE BAPTIST CHURCH SOCIETY

From Woolsey

    For several years prior to 1782 the pastor of the Baptist church at the old village of Fishkill, situated some miles back from the river, performed missionary labors at different places in Dutchess and Ulster counties. In 1782 he succeeded in organizing a branch of the society in the precinct of New Marlborough, then recently a part of the precinct of Newburgh. At a regular meeting of this branch church, held on the 24th day of May, 1785, at the house of Reuben Drake, (Elder Philips presiding), a petition was presented by Nathan Ellet and William Purdy on behalf of themselves and others that the society be constituted a separate church, and that Jonathan Atherton be ordained pastor....

The organization thus formed was called "The Baptist Church of Pleasant Valley." It will be seen that this was the Plattekill part of the precinct of New Marlborough. In 1789 a branch was established at Lattintown and one at New Paltz.

After 1789 meetings were held at Lattintown at the schoolhouse and at the houses of Nehemiah L. Smith, Noah Woolsey, Mathew Benedict and others. In 1807 steps were taken to organize a church and build a church edifice. The oldest record I find is as follows:

Record of the Trustees of the Meeting-House Belonging to the Baptist Church of Latintown, in Marlborough

Laten Town, January 25th, 1807.

Church met according to appointment and elected Nehemiah L. Smith, Noah Woolsey, and Mathew Benedoct Trustees of said Church, to manage the affairs of the meeting-house in Latentown.

(NB these church records are not now in the possession of the church—MLM)

The form and shape of the church has never been changed. The following is mainly from a sketch, which was compiled mostly from the church book:

At a meeting of the church held in the month of May, 1812, Deacon Purser, who was present, made the church a present of this book, it being the one in use at the present time for keeping the records of the church.

...Lattintown enjoyed years of happiness, usefulness and prosperity. Old people used to speak of the time when Elder Perkins preached in Lattintown, when the meeting-house with its capacious gallery proved too small to accommodate the congregation and those who arrived late drove up to the church and remained in their wagons at the windows and door. Elder Perkins remained with them as their pastor twelve years, during which time he baptized 160 members. In 1820 an extensive revival took place, when the records show 64 as being baptized. The largest membership during Elder Perkins' pastorate was 128. On the 20th of December, 1834, the Newburgh church, situated ten miles south of Lattintown, was constituted. The Lattintown church being in a country place, and its members scattered about the country, many of them residing nearer Newburgh than Lattintown, several such, and among them some of the officers and more prominent members, took letters and joined the Newburgh church, which greatly reduced the Lattintown church in means, strength and numbers.

The old church building is as strong and substantial as ever, and with little repairing it could be made serviceable. ...Around the old church cluster many sacred memories; the ancestors of the present generations worshipped there, and are buried in the churchyard. Their names are the representatives names in their day in the town and the names of their children and grandchildren who reside all about in the community.

Up to 1863 again—Rev. Joseph L Grimley was pastor till in the nineties; then various temporary preachers including Dr. Leighton Williams. thus church had no regular pastor but kept on with services. Williams was a Baptist minister but later an Episcopalian rector and rector of Christ Church. He filled Lattingtown pulpit for long periods.

Summer of 1931 Rev. Pietro S. Mondada of Newburgh, a Reformed Church minister, through the only living trustee, Frank Craft, got the use of the building and established Mt. Carmel Community Church, people of all Christian churches. It continues thus though he died in June 1965 after a long illness. Prior preacher is the Rev. Joseph Bock of West Nyack. Services are held regularly with the Bocks coming to Lattingtown every Sunday. Weddings are held here, vacation Bible School, many popular suppers, Sunday School, and other events.

The building is in fine shape. The cemetery has very old stones, and there are Revolutionary soldiers among others buried there. Collections are still taken on two dented and bent pewter plates, with mark on bottom, "Boardman Hart, N. York". Six brass kerosene lamps hang from iron brackets. Church is lighted by electricity but they are kept for momentos. Two rush bottom chairs, original, stand on pulpit. Lectern is very old, with hand crocheted edges and insert on covering.

From The Marlborough Record 9/8/1933

Mt. Carmel Church Plans To Observe First Birthday

Plans, are progressing for the celebration marking the first anniversary of the re-dedication of the old abandoned Church at Lattingtown under the new name of Mount Carmel Community Church.

The date for the celebration has been set for Sunday afternoon, September 24 at 3 o'clock. The committee is endeavoring to secure for this occasion some speaker of national repute, and it is in hopes to secure the Hon. Peter A. Oavicchia, a member of the United States Congress from the Eleventh District, Newark, New Jersey, who has quite a few friends in this locality.

From the House Survey

This church incorporated Jan 26, 1807. The old original wavy-clear glass twenty-four paned two sashed windows, which once were in all parts of the church, are now only on one side of the former gallery and at one end of it. The present windows have their own story. In 1965-66 they were secured from a storage room at Christ Episcopal Church, Marlboro, bought, and installed by James Poulin in place of old windows proved not repairable. Wood was skillfully cut and ornamented around the pointed tops of these windows to fit them into the oblong casings.

The story of these windows is as follows: They were in the little St. Agnes Episcopal Church at Balmville, Orange Co. right beside the Balmville Tree, the Balm of Gilead Tree to which Washington tied his horse when it (the tree) was a sapling. A few years ago this church ceased to hold services and these windows were stored in the basement of the Christ Church building Marlboro. Not long after they were given to the Lattingtown Church. They are real cut glass we are told and were put into St. Agnes some time before 1900. Some of their designs are very quaint and unusual.

Presently (2002) the Reverend David Ballou is the pastor. For a number of years Margaret Faurie has been the organist providing music on the old pump organ which has been in the church for many years.

*   *   *

METHODIST EPISCOPAL CHURCH AT LATTINGTOWN

For the record—there was at one time a Methodist Church in Lattingtown—

Woolsey

> There were two classes organized in 1786— "Lattintown class, Lattintown: Jacob Dayton class, near Lattintown." This shows that there were Methodists there at an early period, but only occasional meetings were held at the houses of the class leaders and others and at the schoolhouses, whenever preachers visited that part of the country; and afterward, some years before the church was built, they held services at the house of John Shorter, now the Odell house, and also at the Baptist meeting house. They formed a legal organization

by a certificate bearing date March 3, 1848. Isaac R. Fowler and H. S. Shorter presided at the meeting for organization, and William Mackey, Thomas S. Warren, Benjamin Harcourt, David Fowler, John D. Crook, Isaac R. Fowler, and John Shorter conveyed to the trustees the land upon which the church was built. About 1870 the church was taken down and removed to Clintondale. It never had any separate preacher, but was one of the three churches in the town which was supplied by the same preacher. Afterward the Marlborough church took charge of it.

The bell of the church was taken with the church to Clintondale and afterward purchased by the late James H. Crook and presented by him to the Milton Methodist church. It was their first bell.

*   *   *

ALL SAINTS CHURCH MILTON

From the House Survey
    Shanghai Hill, Milton
    This parish was organized as a mission of Christ Church, Marlboro, rector then Rev. Samuel Hawksley, in 1850. Cornerstone laid May 30, 1854, by Rev. Dr. Brown, Newburgh. Building completed 1856, opened for services April 12, 1857, and consecrated by Bishop Potter Oct. 1859. Cost $3000. Rector of Christ Church also took charge of All Saints.
    Services here ended about 15 years ago. Used during many summers for migrant workers' church under the auspices of national and local

Methodist, Episcopal, and Presbyterian churches and mission boards. (For four or five years has been Milton Grange Hall.)

*   *   *

MILTON PRESBYTERIAN CHURCH

The Milton Presbyterians have a history of more than 150 years of service to God and the community for which they can be rightfully proud. Formed in 1847 after splitting from the First Presbyterian Church of Marlboro, the church has been a viable force in the community continually since that date. According to the Reverend Alfred Williams, Pastor of the First Presbyterian Church Marlboro, the split occurred over the question of abolition. The Milton Presbyterians felt the Marlboro church was not taking a forceful enough stand on the issue.

They were probably influenced in their views by the strong stand of their Milton neighbors who belonged to the Quaker Church, well known for their abolitionist sentiments. They were inspired as well, perhaps, by the words of the hymn written in 1845 by the American poet James Russell Lowell:

Once to every man and nation,
Comes a moment to decide,
In the strife of truth with falsehood
For the good or evil side.

The Milton Presbyterians made the choice and sided firmly with abolition. Today they continue in that proud tradition of providing moral leadership to the community.

*   *   *

FIRST PRESBYTERIAN CHURCH MARLBOROUGH

From Cochrane—

In 1763 the following subscription was raised to found the Presbyterian Church:

"We the subscribers, for an encouragement towards building a meeting-house for the worship of God, near the Old Man's Creek, in Ulster County, to be founded in the Presbyterian foundation and government of the Kirk of Scotland, do promise for ourselves, heirs, and assigns, to pay on demand the following sums annexed to our names to those that are trustees of said building, providing the Lewis DuBois does give two acres of land to remain for that use forever." (pg. 105)

…On this land a small building, about thirty-five by twenty-five feet, was erected, and was so far completed the ensuing summer, as to be occupied for Divine worship. (pg. 107)(NB this site was on the present land of DiDonato's Funeral Home and was marked Lot #1 on the 1810 map of Lewis DuBois. This was the southernmost border of the Griggs and Graham Patent).

On the 10th day of June, the Trustees appointed Doctor Benjamin Ely (NB the Ely 1797 Map of Marlborough, also at one point town supervisor, as well as someone who gave a young slave over to the town— MLM) to secure for them the services of a clergyman for one year…"Resolved, That no Baptist or Separate Minister be allowed or admitted to preach, in the Meeting House, under any pretense whatever, without the joint and mutual consent of the trustees, or a majority of them, for the time being." (pg. 110)

From Two Hundredth Anniversary First Presbyterian Church pamphlet printed in 1964 "A brief history..." provided by Ernestine C. Wygant, Historian.—

In the mid-Seventeen Hundreds, there was no boundary line separating New Marlborough from what is now Newburgh, and all was considered a part of Ulster. This precinct included parts of what are now known as New Windsor, Middlehope, Plattekill and Milton, as well as New Paltz. Even to our hardy forefathers, the journey to "The Kirk" on Liberty Street in Newburgh was a long and difficult one; therefore, about 1750 there was formed a union for the worship of God, known as the Society for New Marlborough and conforming to the "Laws of The Kirk of Scotland."

The year 1835 found the Church wearied with changes, and embroiled in the New School-Old School controversy over Abolition consequently the members turned to their old pastor, Rev. James I. Ostrom...During his pastorate, a parsonage was built on Jagger Street (now West Street), somewhat north of the Church. (NB I had not heard of Jagger Street before).

Grave misfortune visited the Church on Sunday morning, January 12th, 1868, when over-heated stove pipes caused a fire which destroyed the church building, the pastor's library, and valuable furnishings, with the exception of the marble table which now stands in the Lecture Room, and the Pulpit Bible. All Church records were also lost in this disaster.

...and in 1888 a pipe organ was installed.

1900 saw the pastorate of Rev. Wm. Coombe started...an addition was built on the new parsonage which had been acquired in 1899; electric lighting was provided in the Church and parsonage...

May 1902 Nathaniel DuBois donated a sum of money for the preservation of Marlborough Cemetery and in June of this same year, he provided the clock which still records the hours in the Church tower.

W. J. Burrows gave a fine memorial window to the Church in 1905...

(Circa 1911)...The present Moeller organ was installed at this time, part of the cost being defrayed by a Carnegie Fund grant.

In 1916 the Methodist Church was consumed by fire. Sparks from this fire ignited and destroyed the steeple of the Presbyterian Church.

(Between 1928 and 1937) The Woman's Missionary Society and the Ladies Aid united and became the present Women's Association.

Rev. McIntosh (pastor at that time) obtained a leave of absence in December 1941 to go on active duty with the United States Army.

Rev. A. Elwood Corning served as Stated Supply...from 1941-1946....He was a noted historian and the author of "Washington at Temple Hill."

Ms. Carla Lesh
Church Street
Marlboro, NY 12542
January 1, 1995

Dear Carla,

As per your request for some history of the Marlboro Presbyterian Church organ—

Was to the library several times to read through the church minutes on microfilm there at the library. It was very frustrating as the lens on the reader is of such a magnitude that it is impossible to read a line on just one frame but must move to a second frame to catch the second part of a sentence (the move is made by the electrical switch which rarely stops just where you need it). In order to read another part of the sentence or to read the next sentence, it is necessary to move back one frame. In order to print out one page of the book, it is necessary to print four pages—then they must be taped together—often with the center missing if you want to be sure to capture the date——frustration!!!

Did find where in the minutes the discussion of the purchase of the organ began in the minutes and printed out three pages (12 pages of copy). Then called Al Williams and asked if I could read from the original books. Doris was kind enough to meet me at the church so that I could do so.

The results—

5/17/14—Meeting of session held Sunday morning May 17th. Present Rev. J. N. Kugler, Mod. Elders Bloomer, McMullen, Wygant, Carpenter and Bingham. Prayer by moderator. Elder Wygant, Com. on music reported that he had made arrangements with Mrs. Lawrence to play the organ and take charge of the choir for six months. M & S (Moved and seconded—MLM) That the report be rec'd and placed on the minutes. Carried. M & S That Elder Carpenter be a committee to request to the board of trustees that they proceed to repair the organ as it is almost impossible to use it in its present condition carried. Closing prayer by Elder Bloomer. Meeting adjourned. J. W. Bingham Clerk.

(skipped some pages)

Nov. 1, 1914 Meeting of session held Sunday morning Nov. 1st, 1914 after morning service, present Rev. J. N. Kugler Mod, Elders Bloomer, Wygant, Norton and Bingham, Absent Elders Carpenter and McMullen. Prayer by moderator. Communication recd. from Rev. Knapp of the M. E. Church, inviting the congregation of this church to join with the M. E. Church in a union service on Thanksgiving day and that Mr. Kugler preach the sermon. M & S (moved and seconded— MLM) That the invitation be accepted. Cd. (Carried—MLM). Elder Wygant as music committee reported That Mrs. Lawrence was willing to continue as organist for the balance of the year to May 1st 1915. M & S That Mrs. Lawrence be continued as organist until May 1st 1915 Carried. M & S That the clerk be appointed a committee to communicate with the chairman of the board of trustees in reference to repairing the present organ or purchasing a new one—carried. Closing prayer Elder Norton. Minutes Approved. Meeting adjourned—John W. Bingham, Clerk

Nov. 8th 1914—Meeting of session held Sunday morning Nov. 8th 1914 before morning service, Present Rev. J. N. Kugler, Mod, Elders Bloomer, Norton, Carpenter and Bingham. Opening prayer by pastor. Elder Bingham reported that he had talked with the chairman of the board of trustees and that he thought it was the duty of the session to call a meeting of the congregation to consider the matter of the organ. M & S That the report of the committee be received. Cd. M & S That a meeting of the congregation be called to be held on Tuesday afternoon Nov. 17th at 2 O'clock to consider whether to repair the old organ or purchase a new one and to take such other action as may seem necessary in reference to the matter. Carried. Prayer by moderator. Meeting adjourned. John W Bingham Clerk of session

Nov 17th 1914—Meeting of the congregation held Tuesday afternoon Nov 17th 1914 pursuant to call read at the services on two previous Sundays. Rev. J. N. Kugler, moderator, J. W. Bingham clerk. Opening prayer by moderator. Call of the meeting read by the clerk. Mr. Kugler made a statement in reference to his position in reference to the matter—that he was pastor of the whole church and that while he had preferences, the meeting should consider the whole matter and be satisfied with the conclusion. Mr. Benjamin Harcourt read a letter from Mr. Tanner saying that he would thoroughly repair the old organ and put in an electric blower for $310. Mr. Kugler read communication from the Estey organ Co. advising how to approach Mr. Carnagie, asking for assistance in purchasing a new organ.

(End of pages photocopied—the following is taken from notes and not necessarily verbatim from the records—MLM)

9/17/1914—instructed the voters to mark their ballots "old" or "new"—vote to repair—9, new—24. Committee of 3 appointed 1 from session, 1 from trustees, 1 from congregation—together with the pastor to take up matter with Mr. Carnagie and if successful in getting his help to have charge of purchasing a new organ—Cd. Mr. Crawford Harcourt representing the congregation. M & S trustees empowered to repair the old organ in case we do not succeed in getting a new one. Cd. Members of committee—Rev. J. N. Kugler, John W. Bingham, session, Elmer E Wygant, Bd of trustees, Crawford Harcourt, congregation.`

3/30/1915—The organ committee made report of progress to present time—report accepted. The committee to select an organ reported as follows—that they have rec'd a promise from Mr. Carnagie to give us $950 (Note—in the minutes there appears to be a decimal point so it reads $9.50 but I do think it is $950—MLM) towards the purchase of an organ to cost $2200, that they have received specifications from six pipe organ companies of organs to cost $2200, that they have sought information from various sources have visited several pipe organs in the surrounding country, that the specifications were submitted to a competent organ expert in New York City with all information at hand. The committee have decided to order a new organ from the M. P. Moller Co. of Hagerstown, Ind. to be ready for use on Sept. 1, 1915. The Moller Co. to take the old organ in part payment.

The organ consists of—

13 stops (Lilting tablets)
740 pipes
7 couplers 3 mechanicals
4 adjustable combinations
3 pedal movements
Tubular Pneumatic Action
Kinetic Electrical Blower

Was unable to find any other references to the organ until:

3/28/1916—M & S that a vote of thanks be given to the moderator for his efforts in having the new organ installed in the church. Cd.

12/8/1916—In reference to the tuning of the organ, it was voted that elder Wygant the music committee confer with the trustees in reference to the matter.

Read to 4/1/1917 without finding further reference to the organ.

In the town's historical collection is the 1964 "Two Hundredth Anniversary First Presbyterian Church Marlborough, New York". In it is a history of the church done by Ernestine C. Wygant, Historian with Louisa M. Gow, Editor. One paragraph states:

May 12th, 1911 Rev. J. Newton Kugler was installed as pastor, and the Church records during this term show a membership of 310 and a Sunday School membership of 163 persons. The Rotary system for selecting Elders was now in force in the Church. During this five year period the Ladies Aid provided a new carpet for the church at an approximate cost of $500.00. Normal training class was added to the Church curriculum and the Envelope system of giving was adopted. The present Moeller organ was installed at this time, part of the cost being defrayed by a Carnegie Fund grant.

In speaking with Doris Williams she advised that the organ was rebuilt in 1981-82 by A & J of Newburgh. She suggests contacting them to see exactly what services they performed. She also suggested that someone like Wendel Bloomer would possibly know if there was work done before that time. The 1981-82 records were not readily available so I was not able to check through them.

*   *   *

MARLBORO METHODIST CHURCH

Mrs. Lila Baxter
Plattekill Road
Marlboro, NY
October 8, 2000

Dear Lila,

Thank you for letting me browse through the records in your care from the Methodist Church. You had asked that I make suggestions as to which records should be kept. Please note some of them are in pretty bad shape. You had mentioned they had been in a damp basement.

Have checked them over since picked them up from Joan Partington. Have tried to straighten them out. Please note, I have put some of them in plastic bags to separate them and to try to keep similar records together. IT IS IMPORTANT THAT THEY BE TAKEN OUT OF THE PLASTIC BAGS AS THE BAGS ARE NOT GOOD STORAGE FOR THEM—they need to breathe and the bags do not allow them to do that. Have dusted off a lot of the mold, but there is still evidence of mold especially in the books. Have enclosed a sheet that explains some of the care that needs to be taken and also lists some of the supplies available. The list is an old one, but you might find it useful.

Have separated the materials into two boxes. The first one contains mostly financial records, much of which is canceled checks and old bills. As an historian, I hate to throw anything away, but, if you felt you had to discard materials, these would be the most likely suspects.

The second box, I think, is far more interesting. Here is a brief listing: (in the separate box)

1. "The Golden Treasury"—a text of songs and poems, published in 1927. While probably not too valuable from a monetary standpoint, it does have some beautiful poetry in it.

2. The Milton Epworth League—Constitution and list of members

      Book 1—starts 1897

      Book 2—1916

      Book 3—1930

      Book 4—1959

3. Records of the Ladies Aid Society—Organized 1903—minutes start 1922—contains a list of members

(outside the separate box)

4. Marlboro Methodist records

      a) Ladies Social Circle—starts 1/9/1912 to 1920

      b) Ladies Aid Society—starts 1/4/1921 to 1926

c) Ladies Aid Society—1926—1932

5. Financial Record Book—Marlboro Methodist Church 1919-1923—does have a member by member accounting

6. The newspapers from the 103rd Anniversary held in 1933. These should be open to full size. I'm pretty sure the library has a copy of that paper on microfilm. These are the recordings I copied and gave a copy to you. Usually, when it is a newspaper from that recent (from the 1900's on) they tend to disintegrate fairly quickly due to the use of wood pulp to make the paper and the resulting acidity. Be sure to take these out of the plastic bag!!! In the bag with the newspapers is a book of the guests who were present. Apparently, guests were asked to sign a memorial book. This is a neat record to keep.

These records in the second box are the ones I would try to preserve.

Again, thank you for letting me browse. I look forward to getting the last box from Joan when she is finished with it.

The Ladies Social Circle—JAN 9, 1912

(FROM MINUTES)

The Ladies Social Circle met at Mrs. Minnie Lawson on Jan 9, 1912. Meeting opened with prayer. Mrs, Knapp acting as President. Fifteen ladies were present. Secretary report read and accepted. Treasurer's report read for the past year, amount in the treasury Jan 10, 1911—$55.54—Amount received during the year 1911 $270.91—total amount of expenditure during the year $293.87—total amount $326.45. Balance on hand Jan 9, 1912 $32.58 (NB there had been $19.12 but that was crossed out and the new number placed above it).

A motion was made and carried to pay Miss Anderson when due. The Secretary read a letter from the Pastor. A motion was made that

Mrs. Hartshorn be appointed to give the Pastor a word of thanks. The following officers were elected for one year.

President—Mrs. Coutant

First Vice President—Mrs. Carhart

Second Vice President—Mrs. Hartshorn

Secretary—Mrs. C Masten

Treasurer—Mrs. Mosher

Circle A Chairman—Mrs. Purdy

Circle B Chairman—Mrs. Wright

Circle C Chairman—Mrs. Reynolds

Circle D Chairman—Mrs. Masten

Circle E Chairman—S. Haviland

Circle F Chairman—S. Baxter

A motion was made the officers and Circles meet at Mrs. Hartshorns Wed. Jan. 17 to revise the old book.

A rising note of thanks was given Mrs. Lawson—Collection $1.17.

Next Meeting—Mrs M. Masten

Mrs. Masten, Sec.

The Present Methodist Church, Built In 1918 and 1919

Sold within the last few years and completely demolished

MILTON M E CHURCH

Ladies Aid Society Organized 9/23/1903
(FROM MINUTES) (Constitution and list of members)
1922—The regular monthly meeting of the Ladies Aid Society was held
at the home of Mrs. Marion Wood on Friday afternoon April 28th.

The meeting opened by all standing and repeating the Lord's Prayer.
Roll call followed—24 members present
The minutes of the last meeting was read and approved
The assistant treasurer's report is as follows:

Cash on hand $8.52
Money in bank $17.92

It was moved and carried this report be accepted

Calling committee reported 11 calls made.

Mrs. Hyatt, Mrs. Hepworth, Mrs. Height were appointed calling committee for May.

The Sunday flower committee for May as follows: Miss Sears—Apr 30, Mrs. JR Woolsey, Jr—May 7, Mrs. HC Wood—May 14, Mrs Sarah Woolsey—May 21, Mrs. Joseph Woolsey—May 28.

Notes of appreciation were read from Mrs. J Clarke for plant sent her mother at Easter and from Mr. Stinson for flowers sent at the time of Mrs. Stinson's death—also thanks from other members sent flowers at Easter.

Motion was made and carried the secretary to insert notice of date of fair Friday July 28th in local papers.

Miss Lula Clarke was transferred from fancy table to vegetable table.

Motion was made and carried the treasurer to pay Mrs. Edith Ferguson 45¢ for new secretaries book purchased.

There being no further business the meeting adjourned until Friday May 26th. when we will meet with Mrs. S M Rutter.

Delicious refreshments were served by our hostess and a delightful afternoon was spent.

Martha H Hyatt, Secy—protem

A letter of good cheer and hopes for speedy recovery was written, signed by all present for Dr. Preston who was ill.

The Society furnished the church with 3 doz. white carnations for Mothers' Day.

MARLBORO M E CHURCH

EPWORTH LEAGUE

Marlboro, NY Jan 11, 1903

The regular monthly business meeting of the Epworth League was held on above date at the home of Harry Crook with Pres in the chair.

Opened by singing "Bringing in the Sheaves" and "Blessed Be The Name".

Led in prayer by the Pres.

Minutes of last meeting read and approved.

Report of Depts.

Mercy & Help—reports 18 social and 20 sick calls made—package of Christmas cards sent to children's hospital in New York City and fruit taken to the sick.

A letter was read from the Cor. Sect. of the Local Union which was to be held in Walden on Feb 2. Moved and seconded that the Pres. be authorized to correspond with the authorities about transportation to and from Walden and call a special meeting to ascertain the facts—Carried.

Letter was read from Rev. E. Inglehart, a missionary in Yokohoma, Japan.

The Mercy & Help Dept has received the address of a lumbermans camp and requests the Leaguers to send a box to them also to make clothing for the St. Christopher Home at Dobb's Ferry.

The name of Miss Matie Terwilliger was presented for membership, acted upon and elected an active member.

Moved and seconded that the Secretary be authorized to purchase a book for records and draw draft for money for the same—Carried.

Adjournment followed by refreshments and games.

Cora Merritt, Sec'y

*   *   *

MILTON METHODIST CHURCH

MINUTES FOR 1897

A meeting of the Epworth League was held March 11, 1897 to consider the best means of raising money for the sheds. It was decided to have a concert to be held the latter part of April in Woolsey's Hall and to ask the Appolon Banjo and Guitar Club of Po'keepsie to assist.

Admission to be 25¢.

As there was no other business the meeting was adjoined.

(NB Short and to the point!!!)

A meeting of the Epworth League was held April 29, 1897.

Amount taken in from the concert $54.45.

Motion was made and seconded that we deduct enough to pay the expenses amounting to $16.91 and that we give the balance for the sheds.

The meeting was then adjourned.

(NB there is no signature to these minutes—however, (s)he didn't waste any words).

*   *   *

ST MARY'S RC CHURCH MARLBOROUGH

The First Methodist Episcopal Church Built in Marlborough in 1930.
Used by Congregation Until 1867. Sold for $950 and Used by the
Catholics Until 925. The Building Was Made Over for Use as
A Garage La Year and is Now Owned by Olaf Sundstrom

Used by Methodists, then sold to the Catholics
Was St. Mary's church for many years
Now States Sarles Sons—9W

This church has been very active since its founding as a mission
church of Port Ewen in 1865. In 1874 the old Methodist Meeting House
was purchased. In 1882 the land for the cemetery was purchased. The
cemetery at first was called St. James. It was in 1900 that St. Mary's
Church was legally incorporated. In 1913 the Reverend James Hanley
was appointed Pastor of St. Mary's, a position he would hold for forty-
five years. In 1913 the Oddy Property, a substantial lot of land, was purchased. After spending the first years in the old Methodist Church

Building (now States Sarles Sons—9W), in 1922 the cornerstone for the new St. Mary's Church was laid. This substantial church was dedicated in 1924.

In 1948, thirty-five years after first arriving in Marlboro, Father Hanley had the privilege of burning the mortgage to St. Mary's during church services. In 1955 the Reverend John Simmons was appointed to assist Father Hanley. In 1957 Father Hanley celebrated his 50th anniversary as a priest. In 1958 the much loved shepherd passed away.

Father Simmons oversaw the building of the new Rectory and Parish Hall. After having celebrating his fortieth year as a priest in 1968, in 1975 Monsignor Simmons was retired. He was replaced by the Reverend Edward Dugan.

In 1977, still remembering the long devoted service rendered by Father Hanley, the Knights of Columbus chartered the Father Hanley Council in Marlboro.

In 1983 Father Dugan was invested as a monsignor and served eight years as Vicar of Ulster County. Additions were made to the Parish Hall in 1986. Monsignor Dugan celebrated his retirement in 1995. Much to the sorrow of the congregation, Monsignor Dugan passed away in 1995.

St. Mary's celebrated its 100th anniversary January 3, 2000. A pamphlet filled with pictures and the names and addresses of the congregation at that time was published along with a letter of commendation from the Cardinal, John O'Connor, Archbishop of New York and a brief history of the church written by Libby Manion. The current Pastor is the Reverend Alfred Pizzuto assisted by Father Joseph Xu..

USING COMPUTERS

Dear Craig—

Sorry you didn't use the last paragraph of this—thought it was the best part).

Report from the Electronics World

The Southern Ulster Pioneer is a primary source of communications between members of our community. In so many ways it is the community bulletin board. Various organizations post their upcoming events and report on their activities. The Town Board and the School Board use the Southern Ulster Pioneer as their official means of posting legal announcements.

The Marlborough Historical Society has used the Southern Ulster Pioneer as the vehicle to share stories from some of our elder residents, as a way of announcing special activities, as well as a way to reach out into the community for support. The Age of Electronics and the computer have added immensely to our ability to communicate. Mary Lou Mahan, Marlborough Historian, began the process of communication by sending typed copy to the Southern Ulster Pioneer through Judy Rappa, who both is vice-chairman of the Marlborough Historical Society and an employee of the Southern Ulster Pioneer.

Shortly, running low on time as is wont in today's times, Mary Lou started sending articles via the fax machine. The only problem with using the fax is that the article has to be typed twice—once at the point of origin, and again at the office of the Southern Ulster Pioneer. Enter the computer age—now to the great relief of all, she is sending her articles and news stories to the Southern Ulster Pioneer via computer disk. The wonders of science make this possible even though she uses a Mac computer and the Southern Ulster Pioneer uses a DOS system.

The beauty of this means of transporting data, besides the fact that it does not have to be retyped, is that the sender can include all the information necessary, can be responsible for the accuracy of the information and the correct spelling of names, places, etc. At the Southern Ulster Pioneer, the office personnel can then format the data as needed, can clip the story if necessary, and can much more quickly and efficiently add the story to that week's edition of the newspaper.

Other organizations within the community are encouraged to do the same. Lacking a computer in the home, the information can be typed and put to disk at the local library and then shipped to the newspaper. In general, it is best to save the information in a "text only" file as that allows the easiest transferal into the programs used by the Southern Ulster Pioneer.

Of course, if we can shake Craig McKinney into investing in a modem, the process would be that much easier and quicker as, just as you can presently send information via the fax, one would be able to send the information (24 hours a day) directly to the computers at the Southern Ulster Pioneer without the necessity of having someone (Judy Rappa) pick up and hand deliver the disk to the newspaper.

*   *   *

Publishing on the Web

In the attempt to learn about publishing on the Web, this is the html code for the first page that actually worked.

```
<HTML>
<TITLE> MLM'S First </TITLE>
<BODY>
```
Hi, this is my first attempt at a web page. The date is June 16, 1996.

```
<P>
```
Don't ask me why I get myself involved in this, I really don't know.
```
<IMG SRC=KYLIE01.JPG HEIGHT=100 WIDTH=150>
<P> Would you believe this is me?
</BODY>
</HTML>
```

I attempted to get input from various community leaders. Each gave me information relative to their part of the web pages.

June 24, 996
Mr. Kevin Casey
Supervisor
Town of Marlborough

Dear Kevin,

As we've discussed briefly at town board meeting—
At the last meeting of the Marlborough Town Board raised the possibility of getting a www home page for the town of Marlborough. The board blessed my researching the possibility. Have contacted James Shaugnessy at MHV.Net and Tony Pascarella, Project Director at Hudson Valley Community College. Tony indicated he could make 5 megs of computer space available free for us to put up a home page. The only stipulation is that we do the page and submit it to him ready to go. I've done research on how to set up a web page and pretty much am confident can get one up and running.
As sketched in my head, there will be the following pages:
   1) Main Page
     a) Thumbnail with link to map of the area

b) "From the Supervisor" with a thumbnail picture and link to picture and statement from Kevin Casey—perhaps list of town officials

c) "Schools" with a thumbnail picture of the high school and a link to picture of the high school and statement from Ed Sagarese—perhaps list of school board and other school officials

d) "Churches" a link to a page listing the churches, ministers and regularly scheduled church services—church listing would indicate some of the history of the churches

e) "Libraries" a link to a page listing the libraries in town (including the high school library?) indicating their hours of operation, a short message about their collections from the library directors

f) "Local Businesses"—with a link to a page listing various businesses in the town

g) "Local History" with a thumbnail and a link to a page with a brief history of the town and links to:

(1) Census of 1790

(2) Old Houses

(3) "Marlborough from Memory"—several of the interviews done

As you may imagine, the possibilities for the future are limitless. Within the limitation of the 5 megs of computer space we might:

1) have a community calendar

2) have a student page

3) have the minutes of the town board, etc. etc.

If you are willing to participate in this project, I am asking that you formulate a statement to go on your particular page. I won't promise, but with your cooperation, it might be possible to have the page in place by July 4th. of this year. I'd appreciate your sending me your statement by this Friday, June 28th. You can e/mail me your statement or fax it (please call me first so I can set up my equipment, I only have one telephone line). My e/mail address is MLMahan@Compuserve.com or MLMahan2@pipeline.com. My home phone number is 236-7363. Feel free to call should you have any questions or suggestions. Note this is just to get us started, changes are always possible at almost any time they are desired. I do plan a preview of the page(s) prior to getting them on line. You, naturally would be invited to the preview.

If you choose not to participate, it is also important for me to know as early as possible so that alternative plans can be formulated.

Hope you are as intrigued by this possibility as am I.

PS Would also need a picture of you—Wednesday?
Fax also sent to Ed Sagarese,
   Libby Manion
   Pat Russo

_____

Then came the difficult task of taking the pictures and setting up the code for the pages. The code for the first page looked thusly—

```
<HTML>
<BODY>
<HEAD>
<TITLE> THE MARLBOROUGH, NY HOMEPAGE </TITLE>
</HEAD>
<BODY BGCOLOR=#6FFFFF TEXT=#000000 LINK=#724765>
<H1> <P ALIGN=CENTER> The Marlborough, NY Home Page
</P></H1>
<H2><P ALIGN=CENTER>
Welcome to the Town of Marlborough Home Page.
```

```
</P>
</H2>
<P>
<H3 ALIGN=CENTER>
```
The town of Marlborough is made up of the villages of Marlboro and
Milton and the smaller hamlet of Lattingtown. We are located on the
`<BR>`
west bank of the Hudson River almost half-way between New York
`<BR>`
City and Albany in the southeast corner of Ulster County. `<BR>`
We are centered in the Hudson Valley fruit growing region. `<BR>`
`<P>`
 COME VISIT!
`</H3>`
`<P>`
`<IMG SRC=THCKLIN.GIF>`
`<P>`
`<H4 ALIGN=CENTER>`
Written by people who are unabashedly fond of their neighbors and proud of their
community!
`</H4>`
`<P>`
`<IMG SRC=THCKLIN.GIF>`
`<P>`
`<UL>`
`<A   HREF=TnINTRO.HTML><IMG   ALIGN=TOP   WIDTH=72` HEIGHT=48 SRC=TNTown.JPG
ALT=Town Hall>
`<L1> Town Government </A>`
`<P>`

<A   HREF=HstINTR.HTML><IMG   ALIGN=TOP   WIDTH=72
HEIGHT=48 SRC=TNMcC.JPG
ALT=McCourt>
<L2> Town History </A>
<P>
<A   HREF=SchINTR.HTML><IMG   ALIGN=TOP   WIDTH=72
HEIGHT=48 SRC=TNSch.JPG
ALT=Marlborough Schools>
<L3> Marlborough Schools </A>
<P>
<A   HREF=LibINTR.HTML><IMG   ALIGN=TOP   WIDTH=72
HEIGHT=48 SRC=TNLib.JPG
ALT=Marlboro Free Library>
<L4> Marlboro Free Library </A>
<P>
<A   HREF=SHHINTR.HTML><IMG   ALIGN=TOP   WIDTH=72
HEIGHT=48 SRC=TNSHH.JPG
ALT=Sarah Hull Hallock Free Library>
<L5> Sarah Hull Hallock Free Library </A>
<P>
</UL>
<H2 ALIGN=CENT><EM><P ALIGN=CENTER> In the Heart of the
Hudson Valley </P></EM></H2>
<P>
<IMG SRC=THCKLIN.GIF>
<P>
<ADDRESS> Mary Lou Mahan e/mail MLMahan2@Pipeline.com
</ADDRESS>
<P>
<P>
Mary Lou Mahan
18 Gobbler's Knob

```
Marlboro, NY 12542 <BR>
(914) 236-7363 <BR>
<HL>
</BODY>
<HL>
</HTML>
```

The first Web page ready for the internet looked something like the following when viewed through a browser. Note this is almost as it would appear on the net. Be aware that it is not in color, is missing some of the small graffics, and missing some pictures. It is also not as complete as the original. Left some pages out.

The Marlborough, NY Home Page

Welcome to the Town of Marlborough Home Page.

The town of Marlborough is made up of the villages of Marlboro and Milton and the smaller hamlet of Lattingtown. We are located on the west bank of the Hudson River almost half-way between New York City and Albany in the southeast corner of Ulster County. We are centered in the Hudson Valley fruit growing region.

COME VISIT!

Written by people who are unabashedly fond of their neighbors and proud of their community!

(picture)   Town Government

(picture)   Town History

(picture)   Marlborough Schools

(picture)   Marlboro Free Library

(picture)   Sarah Hull Hallock Free Library

In the Heart of the Hudson Valley

Mary Lou Mahan e/mail MLMahan2@Pipeline.com

Mary Lou Mahan
18 Gobbler's Knob
Marlboro, NY 12542
(914) 236-7363

The Town of MARLBOROUGH
Fax #795-2031

Town Officials

Supervisor   Kevin Casey

From our Supervisor

TOWN BOARD

Councilman	Eric Affuso
Councilman	Anthony Andola
Councilman	Thomas Coupart
Councilman	Pete Neckles

OTHER TOWN OFFICIALS

Deputy Supervisor	Michael J. Canosa
Town Justice	Carl DiDonato
Town Justice	Eleanor Gallagher
Town Clerk	Natalie Felicello
Town Attorney	George Rusk, Jr.
Town Attorney	Michael Kraiza
Highway Superintendent	Carmelo Alonge
Water Superintendent.	G. Calvin Cosman
Assessor	Ken Herman
Planning Board	Paul Faurie (CHRM)
Zoning Board	Keith Festa (CHRM)
Building Inspector	Egnazio N. Colletta
Fire Inspector	Tom Dubetsky
Chief of Police	Richard P. Wenz
Town Historian	Mary Lou Mahan
Recreation Director	Pierre Ferguson
Park Superintendent	Keith Stohr

Support Staff

Secretary to Supervisor	Jeanne T. Galioto
Bookkeeper	Cherie Martin
Deputy Town Clerk	Linda Brooks
1st Assistant Water Superintendent	Michael Logue
Sewer Plant Operator	Tony Falco
Assessment Assistant	Cindy Hilbert
Assistant Building Inspector	George Salinovich
Secretary to the Building Inspector	Deane Beck
Landfill	George Graziosi
Dog Warden	James Meyer
Custodian	Vincent Casabura
Voting Machine Custodian	Ralph Walters
Voting Machine Custodian	Salvatore Scilla

LOCAL CIVIC SERVICES

Marlboro Hose Co. #1
Milton Engine Co. #1
Marlborough Volunteer Ambulance Corps
Marlboro Free Library
Sara Hull Hallock Library
Cluett Schantz Memorial Park
The Marlborough Historical Society

CHURCHES

Lattingtown Baptist Church
Chapel Hill Bible Church
Christ's Church Episcopal
First Presbyterian Church Marlboro

St. James' Roman Catholic Church
St. Mary's Roman Catholic Church
Milton & Marlboro United Methodist Church
Milton Presbyterian Church

From the TOWN OF MARLBOROUGH SUPERVISOR

The Town of Marlborough is very pleased to be a part of the World Wide Web and welcomes travellers to explore this exciting overview of our Town and Hamlets. After perusing the pages ahead I am sure that you will be as impressed with our unique community as I am.

Our community of 7500 residents is dotted with picturesque fruit farms where visitors are offered the opportunity to pick their own fruit at a very reasonable cost. We are also home to various wineries which offer the finest in New York State Wines. A visit to the tasting rooms will prove the outstanding quality.

Our Town borders the beautiful Hudson River and also is readily accessible via the nearby New York State Thruway and U. S. Route 84. There is ample space, both pre built and building sites, for businesses and industry to locate in our very affordable Town. We offer the convenience and beauty of a small town atmosphere, while at the same time being located within 10 miles of major roadways and Stewart International Airport.

We invite you to discover our "sleeping beauty on the Hudson" on the World Wide Web and look forward to you visiting our town to experience our very special way of life.

Kevin Casey, Town of Marlborough Supervisor

Marlborough History

Town of MARLBOROUGH

(Author unknown—Date circa late 1930's)

A trip around the Town of Marlborough, the southeastern corner of Ulster County, covers old Indian trails, passing flats where corn and pumpkins were grown, meat and other produce were brought to the docks in Milton for shipment and grains to the numerous mills for grinding. The roads, now macadam, (Marlborough has a large percentage of hard- surfaced roads) pass houses some of which ante-date the Revolution and many of which were built before 1830.

The fruit growing region was settled for the most part by English people from Long Island and Westchester Counties. Many of the family names in the town now are the names of the early inhabitants of Revolutionary days—for example Carpenter, DuBois, Mackey, Woolsey,

Terpening, Frazer, Wygant, Purdy, Berrian, Quick, Perkins, Valentine, Caverly, Plumstead, St. John, Bloomer, Lockwood, Polhemus, Kent, Pembroke, Young, Baker, Harcourt, Tuthill, Quimby, Hallock, Fowler, Canniff, Conklin, Warren. From the time of the earliest known settler, Dennis Relyea, who came to live on Capt. John Evans' patent, 1694, at Old Man's Kill, on what is now Marlboro Mills, and of Captain Bond who settled on the grant given him in 1710, an increasing number of settlers came to this section particularly from 1750-1830. The population has remained almost constant. In the period 1913-1923 a large number of Italian people, attracted by the terraced hills of grapes reminiscent of their native Italy and by favorable prices for fruit, bought property here.

Persons whose activities are known beyond the Town confines are Frederick Gowdy, famous designer of type, who lives on Jew's Creek; James Scott, artist, and his wife Kirsten Scott, pianist; Grace Taber Hallock, author of books for children; Mrs. Edward Young, Sr., former president of the New York State Home Bureau Federation; Walter Clarke, former president of the New York State Horticultural Society; Tony Canzoneri, former lightweight champion. Several citizens in years passed have served as assemblymen and other posts of honor, among them Edward Young, Sr. A distinguished citizen was C. Meech Woolsey to whom the town owes a debt for a carefully compiled "History of the Town of Marlborough."

The general farming of the early days has been replaced by the more specialized fruit growing. Apple seedlings had been planted on the Old Hall place as early as 1760. Tourists have always been attracted to this section by the beautiful views of the Hudson and the hills. Wulfers Roost, Elm Grove, and Shady Brook have been known to city people for years. Today the Italian boarders as well greatly increase the town's summer population. The First National Bank of Marlboro and The First National Bank of Milton, The Hudson River Fruit Exchange, the Italian-Cooperative as well as others, the Hudson Valley Press, the Shell

Corporation, the Marlborough Manufacturing and Supply Company furnish the necessities for carrying on the main businesses of this section, fruit-growing and inn-keeping.

The Marlborough Presbyterian Church, the first of the town's eleven churches dates from 1764. This was followed by the Milton Methodist and the Lattintown Baptist Churches. The Quaker meeting from an early date, the Catholic Churches Missions in 1865, the Episcopal churches and Amity Chapel have all had part in the community.

The two new school buildings, the Marlboro Central High School and the Milton Grade School, built as a result of centralization are modern in every way, offering opportunity to all the children of all the people. These school and the Lattintown School are the descendants of the two early schools, the Lattintown and the Turnpike schools, built before 1795. Several other schools both public and private have paved the way for a modern school system of which the town may well be proud.

Marlborough named after the Duke of Marlborough, was once part of the territory bought from the Indians by Governor Dongan in 1684. This land was granted by patent (afterwards annulled) to Capt. John Evans, September 12, 1694. Marlborough, Plattekill, Newburgh, and New Windsor formed the Highland precinct of Ulster County in 1743, but in 1772 the New Marlborough precinct was formed from the Marlborough and Plattekill portion and was first called "Town" in 1788. Lewis DuBois, whose home was the house on 9-W north of Marlboro where John Rusk, Sr., now lives was a high-commissioner of this Highland precinct as well as (later) of the New Marlborough precinct, chosen at a meeting held at the home of Henry Deyo in Lattintown, April 7, 1772. In 1800 the boundaries of the Town of Marlborough were defined as at present. The territory of the Town of Marlborough had been granted in patents to John Barbarie (1709); to Captain William Bond (1710) who settled south of Milton, and built the stone house on 9-W south of Indian Road; to Griggs and Graham (1712); to Lewis

Morris (1714) also Augustus Graham, Lyman Clarke, Henry Wileman, William Bond, Henry Rainier, Alexander Griggs; to Archibald Kennedy (1715); to George Harrison (1750). These original lands were divided and sold to settlers, many of whose homes may still be seen on your trip. The Elizah Lewis house on 9-W at the Indian Road and the Anning Smith house on the Milton Road north of Milton, the mill house at Jew's creek south of Marlboro are pre-Revolutionary houses as well as those previously mentioned.

1790 CENSUS
TOWN OF MARLBOROUGH
A-M

1790 CENSUS
TOWN OF MARLBOROUGH
N-Z

(NB these are now available on our web page and I have not copied them here—MLM)

McCourt House

The McCourts bought the house from John Bingham. In early histories it is listed as "the brick house". On an 1810 map of the village commissioned by Lewis DuBois, it appears as "Village Lot #6". There are some old panes in the windows and some original hardware. The house was restored in 1920 keeping as many of the original features as was possible.

There is a fan window on south side, 9 over 6 panes in windows on middle floor. At an early time there was a private school in the smaller part of the house. According to "Schools of the Town of Marlborough," PTA of Marlborough, 1937, "Another of the earliest schools of which we have any record was a boarding and day school kept about 1840 in the old Hepworth brick house, now owned by C.S.McCourt, by a gentleman named Northrip."

The pamphlet continues—"About 1860-1862 John Burroughs, the great Naturalist of West Park, conducted a private school where C.S. McCourt's house now stands. Later, it is thought, Mr. Burroughs taught in the old building on Main Street. This great Naturalist, a teacher in our village at the beginning of his literary career, spent his early morning hours and holidays prowling around the creeks and brooks or exploring the hills and dales of our vicinity in order to become better acquainted with Mother Nature and to make her secrets his own. It was while he was teaching in Marlborough that his essay, 'Expression', was accepted by the "Atlantic Monthly", and he received a check for thirty dollars in payment for the same".

It is believed the small wing was built about 1750—the larger part about 1815.

The Colonel Lewis DuBois House

"In 1757, Colonel Lewis DuBois...built himself a commodious house on the second rise from the river not far from the King's Highway. It was stoutly framed of heavy timbers and encased with clapboards, the first clapboarded house to be erected in Ulster County."

"The pitch roof was truncated at the ends, jerkin-head wise, a fashion of roof that seems to have found favour amongst the colonists of this part of the Hudson....Maple Grove presents substantially the same appearance as it did when the doughty Colonel inhabited it, surrounded by his family and a retinue of black slaves."

"The mode of life maintained by Colonel DuBois was not only patriarchally ample and comfortable, but elegant as well, according to the standards of the time, for Maple Grove enjoyed the distinction of being the first house in the neighbourhood where a china dinner service was used, and curious housewives from the country round about came journeying thither to gaze with interest on the unwonted piece of luxury."

"Colonel DuBois being a personage of prominence in the vicinity, and his anti-British sentiments and activities being well known, when the British forces ascended the river in October, 1777, on their way to burn Kingston, under General Vaughan, Maple Grove, which could be plainly seen from the river, became the object of marked attention from the gunners on the men-of-war who fired red hot cannon balls at it in hopes of setting it a-fire. They failed of their purpose, but the cannon balls were preserved and, for years afterward, the children of the household, when they went into the attic to play on rainy days, used to roll them back and forth along the floor to simulate thunder."

"In this house was held the meeting of the Masonic lodge when Benedict Arnold's name was deleted from the rolls."

The above taken from "The Manors and Historic Homes of the Hudson Valley", Harold Donaldson Eberlein, 1924

Raccoon Saloon

The oldest hotel still in existence in Marlborough, the Raccoon Saloon, got its name from the family of raccoons that once lived there—coming up through an opening in the wall and being fed by the enthusiastic patrons. This was primarily during the ownership of Gus Mondello. Prior to Mondello, the Riverview Hotel was owned by two generations of Moses McMullenses.

According to the "Commemorative Biographical Record of Ulster County" printed by Beers, Moses McMullen was born September 18, 1822 in Plattekill. In 1854 he went to the village of New Paltz and took the management of the "Put Corners Hotel". In 1857 he moved to Marlboro and leased the hotel which at that time was owned by Robert Spence. In 1862 he purchased the property.

Moses McMullen, the second was the popular landlord of the "Pleasant River Hotel" which was the name back then. He was born in 1852 in Modena. Moses the second had leased the "Eagle Hotel" in Wappingers Falls prior to returning to Marlboro where he kept saloon.

"He took charge of the hotel when it was all run down, and two years later bought the property, added to the building, and made such valuable improvements that it is now one of the best in the county, and a very popular place of resort for travelers." (Commemorative Biographical Record 1896)

Records indicate that Robert Moses bought the property from Robert B. Mapes and it was occupied by him (Mapes) as a public house or tavern.

The present owner is Rita Truesdale who has done much to preserve the nineteenth century ambiance. Sit at one of the window seats and, besides getting a beautiful view of the activity on the river, one can take in a lovely waterfalls which flows into the "sucker hole" and various small pools. The Raccoon has an extensive and tempting menu that goes far beyond the burgers which have claim to be "the best in the valley".

WELCOME TO
THE MARLBOROUGH CENTRAL SCHOOL DISTRICT

ADDRESSES

Administration—50 Cross Road Marlboro, NY 12542
Marlboro High School—50 Cross Road Marlboro, NY 12542
Marlboro Middle School—1375 Route 9W Marlboro, NY 12542
Marlboro Elementary School—1380 Route 9W Marlboro, NY 12542
Middle Hope Elementary School—13 Overlook Dr. Newburgh, NY 12550
Milton Elementary School—PO Box 813 Milton, NY 12547

GRADES: K-12

PHONE NUMBERS:

Superintendent of Schools	236-5802
Marlboro High School	236-5810
Marlboro Middle School	236-5840
Marlboro Elementary School	236-5830
Middle Hope Elementary School	565-9620
Milton Elementary School	795-2730

REGISTRATION INFORMATION:

Contact the Guidance Department at the High School (236-5809) and Middle School (236-5844)or the Main Office at the Elementary Schools.

STARTING DATE:

School starts Sept. 4

HOURS:

High School and Middle School: 7:40 am—2:40 pm
Elementary Schools: 8:20 am—3: 30 pm

ADMINISTRATION:

Edward Sagarese, Superintendent of Schools	236-5802
Kathryn Rohe, Pupil Personnel Services	236-5820
John J. Staiger Jr., Business Administrator	236-5803
Paul Hughes, High School Principal	236-5807
Kenneth Mitchell, Middle School Principal and Director of Secondary Education	236-5842
Susan Spinelli, Marlboro Elementary Principal	236-5833
Richard Cooper, Middle Hope Elementary Principal and Director of Elementary Education	565-9623
Thomas DeAngelo, Milton Elementary Principal	795-2731

SCHOOL BOARD:

David Conn.   President
Edward Pross.   Vice President
Stephen Adamshick
Kenneth Brooks
Estelle Festa
Ellen Healy
Dominick Tomanelli

Meetings held each month in the media center at Marlboro High School   TIME AND DAY TBA

ENROLLMENT:

1988-89	1,901
1989-90	1,948
1990-91	1,987
1991-92	2,033

1992-93	2,037
1993-94	2,037
1994-95	2,030
1995-96	2,015

SCHEDULED CLOSINGS:

Oct. 14	Columbus Day
Nov. 11	Veterans Day
Nov. 28-29	Thanksgiving
Dec. 23—Jan. 1	Winter Recess
Jan. 20	Martin Luther King Day
Feb. 14-17	Mid-Winter Recess
Mar. 27—31	Easter Recess
Apr. 21-25	Spring Recess
May 26	Memorial Day
June 24	Last Day of School

BUS INFORMATION:

Contact John J. Staiger Jr.- Business Manager   236-5803

WELCOME TO THE MARLBORO FREE LIBRARY

(picture)   Library Information

(picture)   History of the Library

(picture)   Library Goals

(picture)   FastCard

THE MARLBORO FREE LIBRARY
1252 Route 9W
P. O. Box 780
Marlboro, New York 12542-0780
Telephone: 914/236-7272
Fax: 914/236-7635

Library Hours Monday   9:30AM-8:30PM
Tuesday   9:30AM-8:30PM
Wednesday   9:30AM-8:30PM

Thursday	9:30AM-8:30PM
Friday	9:30AM-5:00PM
Saturday	11:00AM-5:00PM
Sunday*	1:00PM-5:00PM

*Closed Sunday during July and August

*   *   *

Renewal by Telephone

*   *   *

No Fines

*   *   *

Monthly Newsletter

*   *   *

Notary Public

*   *   *

Community Room Meeting Space

LIBRARY HISTORY

1911 The Marlborough Free Library was granted a provisional charter by the Board of Regents of the State of New York on December 9th.

1912 Library begins service in a school located at the corner of Grand and Church Streets.

1913 Certificate of Registration issued by the State of New York on February 20th showed that the Library had met certain standards and was eligible to receive tax moneys.

1914 Library moved to Methodist Church.

1915 Fire completely destroyed the Methodist Church forcing the Library to return to the school on the corner of Grand and Church Streets. Library received its absolute charter on December 2nd.

1916 The Library moved to a store location in the Village.

1921 Money raised through the efforts of the Association purchased a site on the point of land where King Street and Route 9W meet and the doors of the new Library opened on November 19th.

1937 Town awarded the Library its first monetary tax support in the amount of a $500.00 grant.

1959 Marlborough Free Library joined the newly formed Mid-Hudson Library System, a cooperative library system developed to assist local libraries in upgrading service.

1965 The constitution and by-laws were amended in April to include the entire town of Marlborough, and the areas of Plattekill and the Town of Newburgh which lie within the local school district.

1970 Flossie Linsig retires as Librarian of the Marlborough Free Library after 20 years of service to the community. Citizens committee is formed by the Board of Trustees to promote and plan for a new larger Library facility.

1971 Fund Drive Committee Chair Michael J. Canosa launches money raising campaign.

1972 Library changed its status from an association to a school district public library by a vote of the taxpayers of the Marlboro Central School District on June 27th. And approved a budget in the amount of $21,058.21. An organizational meeting of the newly created school district library (hereinafter to be called the Marlboro Free Library) was held on July 13. A Provisional Charter was issued to the Marlboro Free Library by the Board of Regents of the State of New York on September 28.

1977 Board of Trustees contracts with Milton Chazen Associates to design a new library of 3600 square feet to be built on the property on the corner of Route 9W & Bloom Street, which was donated to the Marlboro Free Library specifically for construction of a new library.

Bids for construction of a new library and sale of the King Street building were published in the SOUTHERN ULSTER PIONEER and THE
EVENING NEWS on May 11th. Bids were opened on May 27th and
contracts awarded on July 11, 1977. Mr. John Alessi was the successful
bidder for the King Street library.

1978 May 21st marked the dedication of the library building on the
corner of Route 9W & Bloom Street.

1986 Peter R. Hoffmann of Hudson Bluff Drive, Marlboro, New York
was hired as architect of record to develop plans for an expansion of the
library building on Route 9W & Bloom Street. Moneys to construct the
new addition were received from:

    Power Authority of the State of N. Y.—$28,310.00

    Federal LSCA Title II Funds—$89,753.00

    N. Y. S. Public Library Construction Funds—$29,750.00

    Marlboro Free Library Building Fund—$158,615.25

The positive vote of school district taxpayers on December 18th
assured funds in the amount of $249,000.00 for the library building
expansion completion.

1987 Formal construction bids for the Library expansion were
opened on February 6th and awarded on March 23rd. Groundbreaking
ceremonies took place on March 25th.

1988 Dedication ceremonies for the Marlboro Free Library addition
take place exactly 10 years to the day from the original dedication on the
site, May 21st.

1991 Plastic bar-coded FASTCARDS were issued to all Marlboro Free
Library patrons beginning March 1 of this year. This card replaces all
cards including Universal Borrower Cards and will be used at any
library in the Mid-Hudson Library System. Automated circulation
began at the Marlboro Free Library on Wednesday, June 12. The
Marlboro Free Library was the recipient of a bequest from the estate of
ALICE PIERCE MILLS of Amherst, Erie County, New York to be used
for the benefit of the Library.

1993 The Library purchased adjacent property with the proceeds of the MILLS ESTATE and a $50,000.00 LSCA (Library Services and Construction Act) Title II Grant from the State of New York. Formal bids for the construction of additional parking space, the conversion of dwellings existing on the property to storage purposes, and the installation of expanded and redesigned handicapped accessible entrances to the Library were opened on May 27, 1993, and awarded on June 7, 1993. The Public Access Catalog (PAC) component of our automated Circulation System became functional.

1994 Access to technology for patrons was enhanced by the creation of a local area network (LAN) providing multiple user access to software selections. Three on-line databases were made available to patrons completing Marlboro Library's entry through the "Electronic Doorway." To enhance stewardship over the Library's multifaceted collection a CHECKPOINT security system was installed in the summer of 1994. The detection system serves as an effective deterrent against unauthorized removal of library materials. Dedication of the West Street Parking Lot and adjacent property took place at special ceremonies held on Sunday, November 13, 1994, the week after the Library's 83rd birthday.

LIBRARY GOALS

ROLE INDEPENDENT LIFELONG LEARNING AND COMMUNITY INFORMATION CENTER

GOAL

The Marlboro Free Library will serve to:

1. Provide library users with information needed for daily living and decision-making.
2. Function as an information center for individuals of all ages who are pursuing self-determined study on one or a variety of subjects.
3. Provide a center for community programming emphasizing cultural, historical and educational activities.
4. Make Community Room meeting space available to groups and organizations.

WELCOME TO THE SARAH HULL HALLOCK LIBRARY

Milton, NY

Library Information

Current hours are:
Mondays and Thursdays—10 a.m. to 8 p.m.

Saturdays—10 a.m. to 5 p.m.
In September 1996 the library will open also on Wednesdays from 2
p.m. to 6 p.m.

The library offers a local history collection with emphasis on the
Hallock Family. Many children's programs are offered, including story
hours from tiny tots through second grade, and special interest groups
such as writing workshops and
American Girls clubs.

SARAH HULL HALLOCK FREE LIBRARY
58 Main Street, P. O. Box 802
Milton, New York 12547
Phone: 914-795-2200
Fax: 914-795-2200
Director: Patricia Russo
Program Director: Michele LaCoste

*   *   *

We were finally ready to have the last review prior to publishing on
the web:

August 13, 1996
Mr. Craig McKinney
Southern Ulster Pioneer

Dear Craig,

As per our phone conversation last night—here's the write-up of the
presentation of the Marlborough Home Page on the www. Hope your
pictures turned out well. If not, let me know.

An Historic Event

At the last Marlborough Town Board meeting, Mary Lou Mahan, Town Historian unveiled for the first time in public the "Town of Marlborough Home Page." Plans are to launch the page on the World Wide Web (the Internet) shortly. The Home Page had links into pages describing town government, town history, the school system and the two local libraries. The town government page lists various town officials, civic organizations and local churches as well as linking to a page of "Greetings" from Kevin Casey, our town supervisor.

The town history page had links into pages giving a brief history of our town, the federal census for the year 1790 for the town (which at that point also included Plattekill), and several of the old houses in town. The school page listed the various administrators for the schools, the school board, addresses and phone numbers, a school calendar for the 1996-1997 school year and enrollment figures for the last 10 years. The Marlboro Free Library page had links to pages on the library goals, the history of the library, and the benefits of the library "FastCard." The Sarah Hull Hallock page listed information regarding the times of operations and the programs available at this library.

Of course, the beauty of the web is the possibility of using graphics. There were pictures of town hall, several of the old houses in town, the Marlborough High School, the Marlboro Free Library and the Sarah Hull Hallock Library. The pictures are clear, bright, and show the buildings in a favorable light.

Mary Lou thanked those who had helped with the setting up of the page—Natalie Fillicello, Town Clerk; Ed Sagarese, School Superintendent; Libby Manion of the Marlboro Free Library and Pat Russo of the Sarah Hull Hallock Library who provided the information for the various pages; Harold Herbert, the CyberSlave who helped proof the page and ensure its portability; Jackie Samselski who provided technical assistance as well as proofing; Jason Giaconne from "Your

Computer Connection" who helped set up the equipment to show the page; and Bruce Latorre, owner of "Your Computer Connection" who provided Jason, the equipment as well as will provide space on a server to get the page on the Web.

There will be a second public viewing of The Marlborough Home Page on Tuesday, August 27th at 1:00 p.m. at "The Internet Coffee Bar—Your Computer Connection" on 9W north of the village of Marlboro. That showing will be a part of the regular meeting of The Marlborough Historical Society. The meeting, as are all meetings of the Society, is open to the public.

Shortly we will be publishing the address of the Marlborough Home Page so that all those "surfers" out there will be able to view it. We think you'll enjoy!

AND FINALLY, WE ARE THERE!!!

Craig McKinney
SUP
Highland, NY

Please Post

September 30, 1996 9:24 p.m.

To All:

We're Up!!!
The Marlborough Home Page URL is:

http://ourworld.compuserve.com/homepages/mlmahan/marlhp.html

Any questions, give me a call.
Enjoy!!!

Didn't have a counter set up on the web page so never did know how many visitors we had. Do know I got quite a bit of e/mail. Following are some samples:

April 3, 2000
Letters to the Editor
Southern Ulster Pioneer
Attn: Craig McKinney

Dear Craig

Received the following e/mail from Gloria Defelici after she had visited the Marlborough Web Page that was set up a few years ago. From her note you can see she is interested in re-establishing contacts with her friends from Marlborough. Please publish this so that her friends know how to contact her.

"From: AMCHANGLO@aol.com
Subject: Marlboro, old friends
To: mlmahan2@pipeline.com

Hi, I just found the Marlboro home page. I lived there, graduated in 1950 and understand they are having a reunion in Sept this year. Just wanted to say hello, love your history. Those were good years, would like to get in touch with anyone from Marlboro, especially from the school class of "50". I do keep contact with F. Mahusky (Fran Rizzo) and my sister Marie Graziosi still lives there. I am now in California, retired and just got a computer.

It is a great thing this machine. I do miss the small town atmosphere, there is nothing like it. Bye for now, if you know any contacts from that era, maybe you can pass my email along. Thanks
Mickey, formerly Gloria Defelici."

and

Hello my name is Kevin Darlington, and I am a student intern at a company called Bank Capital Services in Pittston Pensylvania. I am interested in learning the value of an internet homepage for cities such as yours. I would greatly appreciate it if you could answer a few breif questions for me.

1. Why did you decide to make a Homepage for your city
2. Do you feel that creating a Homepage was a good decision?
3. Has having this homepage made any noticeable impact on your administration?
4. If so, in what way?
5. On a scale of 1-5 (1 being most negative, and 5 being most positive), how would you rate the decision to create a Homepage? How would you rate this decision to create a homepage for other municipalities?

Thank You Very Much

and

Dear Mary Lou,

My name is Victor Chimera & I want you to know I enjoyed your info on the Raccoon Saloon. Gus Mondello was a distant relative of mine. Gus's mom, Catherine was my grandmother, Pauline Chimera's aunt.

Back in the 1930's my grandmother owned a home at 70 Hudson Terrace in Marlboro which she used as a bed & breakfast for vacationers. Gus' son, Lukey as far as I know, owns the Marina in Marlboro not far from the Saloon. He also has a sister, Carol Bushnell & a sister, Rita Perretta living there.

Like I said, we are distant relatives, & I haven't seen them in years.

Thanks for the Memories.

Sincerely,
Victor Chimera
2785 Cedar Ave.
Ronkonkoma, N.Y.

PLACES

Marlborough House on National Register

It was Shakespeare who said, the good that men do "is often interred with their bones." Thank goodness, in this case it is not so.

The James Birdsall House

In 1976 Frank J. Taylor and his wife first saw and fell in love with "The James Birdsall House" on Bingham Road. Frank, a graduate architect from the Rhode Island School of Design saw in the house what few others could conceive.

The house had not been lived in for several years. There was no indoor plumbing; water was obtained from the well in front of the house. There was no central heating; several fireplaces and a kerosene stove in the living room provided the only heat. The house had never been a mansion; the first inhabitants were simple Quaker farmers. The paint was peeling and the exterior and interior gave evidence of needing extensive repair. The house had not, in 1976 been touched by the twentieth century.

What others saw as a liability, Frank saw as an opportunity. Since the house had never had extensive repairs, much of the eighteenth century wood, trim and design were still intact. And so, the Taylors bought the house and spent twenty years in restoration. Frank's wife, Sandra, who lives on Ridge Road indicated the work was a "labor of love."

The lintels, under the front of the house were rotted and had to be jacked up and repaired. The shutters were taken down, stripped, (in some cases two good halves of shutters were put together to make one good shutter) and replaced. Mrs. Taylor said the most difficult task was restoring the inside trim. The trim had many coats of paint and they had to use a torch to burn off the old paint, then sand and refinish. This was done on every inch of trim in the house! Frank insisted the house should not be vinyl sided and thus resided the house with clapboard. The Taylors worked on one room in the house at a time.

While still in the process of restoring the house, Frank also took upon himself the arduous chore of getting the house on the National Register. He spent countless hours in Kingston and elsewhere researching the beginnings and the history of the house. He worked on the project for five years! After all the paperwork was submitted, there was the wait to learn the results.

Frank J. Taylor died in December of 1996 just a few short months before the word came through that the house had qualified for the National Registry. With the notification came a bronze plaque to be placed on the house that reads:

"James Birdsall House has been placed on the NATIONAL REGISTER OF HISTORIC PLACES by the United States Department of the Interior—Built 1797"

The house was recently purchased from the Taylor family by Steve and Laura Bianco. Imagine how pleased they were when Sandra Taylor presented them with the plaque as well as all the documentation that Frank Taylor had collected in order to qualify the house for the National Register.

Now, the good work that Frank Taylor did lives on in the beautifully restored Birdsall House and the entire Marlborough community can take pride in the fact that we have our first listing on the National Register.

     *   *   *

From the House Survey
Samuel Hallock House (Kent Property)   Milton

The old house begun in the 1760's overlooks the Hudson. When Vaughan's expedition went up the Hudson to burn Kingston in 1777, some shots were fired at this area. Tradition has it that Samuel Hallock rowed out into the river and berated a British officer for firing at "this peaceful Quaker settlement."

Edgar M Clarke House   Old Indian Rd, Milton

Built approximately 1750. Residence of Dr. Gedney. The house bought by EM Clarke, Jr had an addition that was used by Dr. Gedney for his office. This was torn down by Mr. Clarke. House and farm bought from Emma Harcourt Estate, Townsend H Sherman and Stephen G Guernsey, executors on March 28, 1888 by EM Clarke.

Edgar M Clarke and his wife Bertie Jones Clarke who owned this house and its farm till after Mr. Clarke's death in 1967 were both very active in the move in the twenties and early thirties to centralize all the seven school districts then in the town. The central district now includes others from the Town of Newburgh also. Mrs. Clarke served as tax expert in all preliminary negotiations and immediately after centralization in 1935 and was consulted by the state education department people in Albany.

Mr. Clarke, who had headed the trustees of the Lattingtown school district was the first president of the first Central School District No. 1 board of Education and participated in all negotiations to get the first new school buildings, and in their actual building, in the district. These were the high school, now the Middle School, and the Milton elementary school.

Mr. Clarke raised prize dahlias on this place; he headed the Milton Grange and county Grange groups; he was a Farm Bureau officer and leader; conservation (state) officer, etc.

Crowell House—Hewitt—Crook   Dock Rd, Milton

Only a few years ago this former hotel was restorable but has since fallen apart. In the twenties a lady of Modena or Wallkill, then in her eighties, told this reporter, Mrs. Plank, that when she was 8, 9, 10, and 11, she went every year with her grandparents on a wagon or walking, and an ox team, to the Milton dock with honey to sell along the way and at Milton. They camped along the Turnpike, which was their route, but stayed a few days at this house. Every night families sang together and children loved to go.

One of the Crook families once lived here and had a blacksmith shop here. In the twenties owned and occupied by Grace Crowell Hewitt and her nephew, Ralph Crowell, of the Central Hudson Steamship lines, who was killed backing his car out from in front of this house. Mrs. Crowell had an auction of notable antiques.

When the West Shore was being built in the '80s workmen roomed and boarded here with the Crooks.

This is a spot of sunshine in Milton—the house that seemed to be destined to be destroyed has recently been restored due to the hard work and TLC of its present owners.

Jesse Lyons now Winifred Driscoll Manion   9W, Milton

Built before 1858. Jesse Lyons original owner used as homestead. Original owner wed four times—had 21 children. Only section beside porch remodeled was for a small office for Dr. James Manion located in basement with outside entrance in 1964. Original floor boards and ceiling beams in cellar. Winifred Driscoll Manion owned, formerly Jeremiah Driscoll, her father.

*   *   *

Flat Iron Building

The FLATIRON Building—pictured circa 1915

It stood on the corner of King Street and Main Street until 1921 when it was torn down to make room for the then, new library.

On the Lewis DuBois Map of 1764 the triangle bounded by King Street, Main Street and Western Avenue was called, "The Reservation Lot". In later years it was called, "The Park Lot".

*   *   *

ANNING SMITH HOUSE

This home is of great historical significance. It is an early colonial farm house with gables added later. It is brick lined covered with siding;

post construction with brick infill and scalloped shingles over doors. It has 10 rooms plus attic; one fireplace which the present owner says is doubtful as to originality; ceilings under 8 feet; floorboards in attic are wide and believed to be original, others covered; ceiling beams heavy but covered. There is some original hardware on a few old doors. Gabled dormers cutting into roof are not original but are old. The house has been remodeled many times and enlarged over many decades.

Historical Significance: Leonard Smith built part of the present house. His son was Anning Smith who was a first Lieutenant in the New Marlborough militia during the Revolutionary War. Vaughan's expedition on the way to burn Kingston fired at the Smith house trying to burn it. After the Revolution, Anning Smith was a leader and industrialist of his time. He gave the bell still in the Highland Presbyterian Church. The house remained in the Smith family from 1760 to 1929. It has been listed as one of three oldest in the town. One wall of the Smith Mill still stands. Smith Mill had stores and was a commercial center in the early 1800's.

The cemetery on the property was originally Indian, then both Indian and Settler's used it. Peaceable Indians intermarried with both white settlers and slaves. Some such are buried here. The burial ground has been long neglected. Recent owners cleared away trees and uncovered stones. Now some fifty stones can be seen. The earliest stone is for Hannah Smith born 1697 who lived to be over 100 years old.
(From the 1968 House Survey)

2002—much has been done by the present owner not only to restore the Anning Smith house but also the extensive grounds.

*   *   *

The Kramer House

The home of Frances and Ralph Kramer was built in the mid 1700s and, like many buildings in this area of the Hudson Valley, reflected the style of home that was indigenous to the Long Island from which a number of Marlborough residents had come.

Beams were hand-hewn: probably from selected trees cleared from the surrounding land; the sturdy durable timber was shaped to interlock. Carved pegs secured the construction of the original home and hand-made nails used in a subsequent addition. Most homes were, as is the Kramer house, 1 1/2 stories. Some of the newer walls of the house were made of or lined with brick. It is assumed these may have been obtained from early Marlborough attempts at brick making.

The Ely-Livingston map of 1797 does not clearly pinpoint the home of Joseph Morey but the histories definitely show him to have been a key figure in the story of the Lattingtown section of Marlborough. Joseph Morey (or Mory) was a Commissioner of Highways in the newly formed Precinct of New Marlborough in 1772. He is also listed as an Overseer of the Poor. He signed the Articles of Association supporting the American cause in the Revolution, was a member of the Committee of Safety and served as sergeant in the war. A Joseph Morey may be found in most of the early area records of Precinct and Township. Through county recordings it appears that this was where he resided.

It is easy to envision members of the Committee of Safety, who did meet at his home, approaching the house under cover of the surrounding wooded area and entering the home via the then "back door" that opened almost directly on the steep high-stepped stairway leading to the upper 1/2 story—no interference with family routines was required. It is a room in this upper section that has a chair-rail that has protected the wall over many years of history. Because of the "rounded" corner that joins wall and ceiling it has been suggested that this room may have served for church meetings at some time; or perhaps, a school room.

Wide boards give evidence of much use. In later years it served as bedroom for young Kramers and even now has a crib for small visitors.

After the property was sold in 1815, it went through a number of owners. Richard Smith is mentioned and later Guernesy Smith. Since the town historian indicates that a gentleman of the same name went west for a time, later returned to marry and then settled permanently in Iowa, it is possible that the house may have been unoccupied for a while. Ownership is traced thereafter through Daniel Wygant, Thomas Warren (and possibly some co-owners), Charles Harcourt, James Wygant, Phoebe Decker, Samuel and/or Isaac Penny. In the 1897 Directory of the West Shore and New York Central Railroads I. R. Penny is a fruit grower on Lattintown Road. Since earlier land transactions secure the produce of then growing fields of flax and grain products, it is assumed that several kinds of farming have been done on the land.

John Kramer purchased the house in 1908 and it has since been in the Kramer family.

It is now a cozy home reflecting the kindness and sincerity of its present owners.

Visitors will note that straw still helps to bind the original mixture used to construct the cellar walls. They may give their opinion as to the purpose of the "mystery base" in the cellar. Of note also is the main entrance of the house for it was designed in earlier times.

(NB the above taken from a newspaper story regarding the Heritage House Tour—courtesy of Frances Kramer)

*   *   *

HALLOCK MILL
Historic Hallock Mill Clean-Up

The attached photo shows Ben Shor, chairman of the Historic Hallock Mill Clean-Up Day, scheduled for May 6 1:30—4:30 p.m. (Rain date May 7). Ben is holding an old photo of the Hallock Mill House which was on the site of the proposed clean-up.

The committee thought a short history of the site would pique interest in the clean-up. History buffs will forgive our digressing to fill in the background.

According to Cochrane (History of the Town of Marlborough, 1887), "Edward Hallock, the first of the name to settle within the precinct of Marlborough, was a descendant of Peter Hallock, one of the flock of Pilgrims who located with Rev. John Young in Connecticut in 1640." According to Theodora M. Carrell (Our Quaker Forbears), "It is true the name Peter Hallock is not found on lists of passengers coming to

New England, but he may have had a reason for assuming a name temporarily, since King Charles forbade captains of British vessels to accept for passage Puritans headed for the new world."

Cochrane continues, "Edward Hallock was a sea-faring man and owned several vessels, all but one of which were destroyed by French cruisers in the struggles between that nation and the English. He then brought his family from Long Island, and December 31, 1760, came to Milton- then New Marlborough. The party landed on a rock, which today is known as "Forefather's Rock," and bears the inscription "E. Hallock, 1760." The old landmark stands on land now owned by Christopher Champlin, on the line of the West Shore R. R." ("Forefather's Rock" may have been standing in 1887 when Cochrane wrote his book, but it is believed to be since buried under the rock that was brought in to form the base for the railroad tracks.)

Edward and his family traveled to Milton in 1760 in an open boat. Carrell writes, "In his account of the arrival of our branch of the Hallocks at Milton on the Hudson in 1762, Nathaniel Hallock gives some particulars…They were able to use a boat on Long Island Sound and the Hudson River, but they met the usual hardships of pioneers of that period, although Uncle Nathaniel makes little of that fact. Try to imagine the vast forests of the time, still merely nibbled at where settlements existed, the settlements often far apart, and miles counting so much more than in our day." Nathaniel Hallock, of whom she writes was the son of James Hallock, son of Edward Hallock. Edward lived to be 97 years old and his grandson Nathaniel remembered him well. The first Nathaniel "moved from Setauket, Long Island, with their ten daughters and two sons, my father (refers to James Hallock son of Nathaniel), an infant. My grandfather had owned and sailed a vessel to the West Indies during the war between the English and the French and the Indians, before the Revolution. His vessel was captured by a French privateers man and confiscated. His father had given him a place a Setauket, on which was a mill, but being of a roving disposition as sailors generally are, and in debt, with a wife and twelve children to provide for, it was not strange that he should look to better his condition, if possible. I remember no stories of the leave-taking or embarkation, but (was told) that in his early life.. having owned and commanded a trading vessel, and still living by the sea, he could not live without a water craft of some kind. We next find him, strange to say, landed with his family at a low point of rocks, regarded by his children and known to this day as Forefather's Rock, in Milton, then a part of Marlborough."

"What was considered most remarkable was that they should have embarked so late in the season. Grandfather said it was between Christmas and New Year's, 1760. They had sailed at the commencement of winter, in a little open schooner, on an almost unknown river, trusting I suppose, 'to Him that tempers the wind to the shorn lamb'….Anyone who ever saw this wild and peculiarly romantic scenery with lofty hills and rocks looking out over the greatest river in the world, before it was disfigured by the West Shore Railroad, can better imagine the feelings of this helpless family of migrants than I could describe.."

Next episode—The original homestead in Milton.

Meanwhile—Keep in mind the Clean-Up date and please register your participation by calling: Ben Shor 236-4291 or Kathleen Murphy 236-3221

Historic Hallock Mill Site Clean-Up

The Historic Hallock Mill Site Clean-Up Committee invites members of the Marlborough community to a Clean-Up day May 6 1:30-4:30 p.m. (Rain date May 7) at the Hallock Mill Site, part of the Cluett Schantz Town Park. In order to stimulate interest in the site and the

Clean-Up, we are giving some of the background of the site and the family that lived there.

Original Young House

The attached photo shows the original Young House lived in by Edward Hallock and his family during the winter of 1760. The second photo shows what was remaining of the house in the 1950's. The house is since completely gone.

Remains of Young House in 1950's

Edward Hallock and his family of wife, nine daughters and two sons sailed in an open boat from Long Island to Milton in 1760. They arrived in Milton between Christmas and New Year's 1760. When they arrived they moved into the house of Edward's Son-in-law, John Young. According to Theodora M Carrell (Our Quaker Forebears) "There was a little stone house built about a half-mile back from the river by John Young, who was a son-in-law of grandfather. In this little house, one story and attic high, not more than fifteen or twenty feet square, these fifteen persons spent the first winter in an almost unbroken forest."

After that first winter in the John Young house, Edward began his building.

Next episodes—the paper trail on the land and the history of the Mill and Mill House.

EXCERPTS FROM "A VICTORIAN GENTLEWOMAN IN THE FAR WEST"

The Reminiscences of Mary Hallock Foote
(Henry E Huntington Library, 1972, San Marino, CA)
(NB Mary Hallock Foote was a direct descendent of Peter Hallock—she
was born in 1847—MLM)
Voyage up the Hudson

These old farms owned by the Hallock brothers were settled by
Edward Hallock in 1762….Edward had been in the coasting trade with
the West Indies, but lost his larger craft by privateers (there was always
trouble enough in those waters) and having made a deal with an uncle,
Foster Hallock, for some wild land up the Hudson, he loaded his goods
and his wife and eleven children in a little sloop, the last of his sail, and
landed them safely—"the river being mercifully clear of ice"—on the
usual rock, the stepping stone of so many hazards of new fortunes in the
wilderness. He seems to have done a good deal for a ruined man between
the date of his landing and the Revolutionary War. He had built the mill,
which ground flour for both armies, and a good stone house. Our father
remembered the burning of that house and the family's removal to the
Mill House, the home of one of his married brothers.

The Mill place fell by inheritance to Uncle Townsend . (NB The New
York Anti-slavery Society was organized at a convention held in Utica in
1835 with Townsend Hallock, as one of the vice-presidents. The object
was the "entire Abolition of Slavery in the United States"—MLM) He
became involved in the affairs of a beguiling stepson, a member of the
"great race" of borrowers, and the old place would have had to go if our
father had not bought it in to keep a home for the aged couple. They
ended their days in the Mill House peacefully, if somewhat querulously,
in an atmosphere of shut-in warmth in winter, with sunshine through

the south windows and the droning of the mill out side. I recall the pang it gave us to see that room and the whole place change its character after the Crosbys moved in, Mrs. Crosby being a very different class of house-keeper from Aunt Rachel. The mill suffered a loss too when the ancient overshot wheel had to go, with its dripping buckets that plunged and rose with a dashing spray out of the cool, thunderous wheel pit. Its work was done by a marvelous new invention called a turbine wheel, no big-ger than the seat of father's armchair—wonders of efficiency replacing the joys of the beautiful past.

But the milldams were the same that Edward Hallock stoned up before the Revolution. They stood wedged fast between the hills, and the reservoirs they guarded had been settled so many years on their native mud they might have been mistaken, with their bordering woods and paths among old willows, for natural lakes; Long Pond, Old Pond and the Mill Head—linked by streams noisy or silent as the headgates were open or shut. The lane past the Mill House went up between old pastures to the Long Pond woods and that was our road to Arcady. That way we went for the first wild flowers in spring and the first skating in winter; we took our visitors up there, when we were girls, to stroll in the June moonlight—the young poets and artists of those lyric summers when sonnets were born overnight like the roses in the garden. You turned off from the hedgerows perfumed with wild-grape blossoms that lined the lane, crossed the upper dam by one of those old footpaths hid in willows, and directly you were in the perfect woods.

Excerpts from a diary

Written by Theodora M Carrell and published in 1949 as part of *Our Quaker Forebears*. Theodora was great granddaughter to Nicholas Hallock who was grandson to Edward Hallock who landed in Milton in 1760. My calculations with respect to her chronology are as follows:

1869—Born
1884—First visit to Milton at age 15
1889—2nd visit at age 20
1891—visit 2 years later at age 22
        Start of her matriculation at Vassar College
1948—last visit to Milton at age 79
1949—Our Quaker Forebears written at age 80

Milton the Place and the People

1884   The summer I was fifteen Aunt Hannah and I went from Buffalo to New York to visit Aunt Mary Allen and her husband, Uncle William who had lived in New York many decades. We were on our way to Cromwell [?] and my anticipations of both visits were high. Moreover, it was decided that we should go to Milton, and after the upstate young girl had been dazzled by New York, she was overwhelmed by the Hudson River trip on the "Mary Powell" [a famous ship that ran from New York City north and stopped at the Milton docks—MLM], the charming village and the Quaker homes. Although mother and visiting relatives had in part prepared me for the atmosphere of Milton and the generations of relatives, perhaps the distinctive quality and the loveliness of the Hudson country could not be wholly imparted. I lived those enchanted days in a new yet old world. Five generations must have been represented, the eldest by Uncle Nathaniel Hallock [the author of a manuscript on Milton] and his sister Aunt Martha Ketcham [the mother of the Ketcham brothers who died in the Civil War]. That they were uncle and aunt to my grandfather made them venerable to me, and indeed they were venerable in themselves. Aunt Martha wore the garb of the Friends to the last, and both had impressive personalities. That very year Uncle Nathaniel wrote his account of the early days at Milton which forms part of this family record....At Quaker meeting on

Sunday, or First Day in Friends' speech, everybody present was related by blood or marriage, and once married into a Quaker family one was accepted fully as in-laws are in the South. The elders of the family, Uncle Nathaniel and Aunt Martha, sat in front, facing the congregation, the place of honor.

1889   Five years later, in 1889, Sue and I met at Milton, and my delight in the place and people was equally felt by her...the old mill and mill house, with the well and well-sweep in the lane—oh, well and well-sweep most of all—cast a spell upon us, made a background vivid yet. Never have I heard such a morning chorus of bird songs....near the mill and mill house and the great willow which gave its name to the corner, was full of charm....Of course, Charlotte, Sue and I went to meeting in 1889, and I noted in my diary that Aunt Martha [mother of the Civil War Ketcham brothers] had a rocking-chair up front, a concession to her advanced age....After supper Cousin Phil, Nannie, Burling, Sue and I walked down to the river to see the night boats come in. "The City of Kingston", a very large and fine boat, came first and took a load of fruit for New York, says Diary, and goes on, "Before the Kingston went, the 'Baldwin', a still prettier boat, but smaller, came and went. Then the 'Kingston' moved away, taking all the life and light with her, leaving the river cold and gray.

The graveyard was a sweet, well-shaded, sloping, grassy and peaceful place back of Cousin Henry's house. It somehow made me think of the lines about an English burying-place:

> "Between the river flowing
> And the fair green trees a-growing
> Do the dead lie at their rest."

Before Sue and I ended our visit Charlotte took us through the woods to the ponds, a beautiful walk. Woods and ponds were to become, in the nine years I lived at Poughkeepsie, at college and teaching, very dear to me, as Milton did as a whole, with the changing personnel through the years. Long after, some of my love for Milton found partial expression:

> There are bird songs with certain cadences
> That reach beyond the ear and joy of sense;
> There are in woodsy places fragrances
> That stir in me a passion for our Mother Earth.
> Against a sky of fading orange light
> The ever-new surprise of crescent moon
> Can deeper go than merely mortal sight.
> A drift of bloodroot blossoms on a rock of gray
> Silvery white and seen long years ago,
> May speak a word that never dies away.

Before further delay let me mention that Quakers in general and ours certainly, with the connections by marriage, were advanced in their views of slavery, women's rights, suffrage, education and improvement in every way. Many stations on the "Underground Railway" were in the homes of Friends, whether any at Milton I do not know. But at Milton they received Frederick Douglass gladly, proud to have him come. One heard considerable talk about women suffrage...

1891   Quite suddenly, two years after my second visit to Milton, I decided to enter Vassar. That was in 1891, and my college years and the teaching years in Poughkeepsie High School gave me many opportunities to go to Milton. Indeed, the place and the people became part of my whole future life, the very warp and woof of my mind. In the two years losses had come, Aunt Martha Ketcham at ninety-one.... Uncle Nathaniel's son Thomas [father of Mary Hallock Foote, writer and artist] and his family had moved into the mill-house, so that I became acquainted with its quaintness and that branch of the family. It was about a hundred and thirty years old then, and is still (1949) occupied, but by strangers.

1948   Last spring I was at Vassar for a class reunion, and wrote Sarah Hallock Bailey that I should like to go to Milton. She set a day and was characteristically hospitable. I went across from Sarah's house, in the old days Cousin Phebe's, her grandmother, to the lane [on the south side of Long Pond], but found it so choked with weeds and bushes that I made little headway. Mill and well were gone, and the mill house so buried in saplings and shrubbery that I turned away. A state road had been put through in such a way that had I not asked the bus driver to stop at Willow Tree Corner I should have gone by without recognizing it....The old Milton is gone, and I knew that I was making my last visit.

*   *   *

TOWN PRESERVATION COMMITTEE

I attempted to get the Town Board to create a Preservation Committee in order to protect and preserve some of our community treasures.

Southern Ulster Pioneer
108 Vineyard Ave.
Highland, N. Y. 12528
Fax 691-8601
Attention Judy Rappa

News Release

Preservation Board

The Marlborough Town Board will hold a hearing on Monday evening September 23rd regarding the setting up of a Preservation Board for the town. The concept for such a preservation board was first raised at a recent meeting of the Marlborough Town Board when Percy Gazlay and Eleanor Rosencrantz, from the town of Rochester Preservation Board, explained the purpose for setting up such a board. They explained that a preservation board usually must first make a survey of what historically significant buildings or places are located within the town's borders. This survey often takes several years to be completed.

The Preservation Board can be established so that it is solely an advisory board. It is meant to provide information to the community and to individual home owners regarding various means of preserving buildings.

Marlborough is an unique community. There are a number of fine old homes and buildings within the community that give it its own character. There has been concern expressed regarding the number of old buildings that have either been demolished or disfigured during the last few years that has changed the appearance and the character of the community. There was an "Historic House Survey" made in 1968 by members of the community—a copy is available at the library or from Mary Lou Mahan, Town Historian. One cannot help be concerned when one sees the number of buildings that were on that survey and that are now gone.

Members of the community who would like to see the town more carefully guard its historic treasures are urged to attend the meeting and make their opinions known. If the Town Board does decide to establish such an advisory board, there is the need for individuals to serve on the board. If you are interested, please consider attending the meeting and making known your views and your availability to serve.

Unfortunately, the Town Board wasn't yet ready to establish such a board.

*   *   *

The Polizzi Home

From notes taken during a phone conversation with Tom Polizzi
1/12/95

Tom has materials from the architect (NYC) with a materials list—by brand—but it is not dated

The owner (Kramer) reserved the right to fire anyone working on the project—on the spot—with no reasons needed to be given

$2,500 to build house including the cost of the land

Owner was a merchant in NYC and used house as a summer home

Occupants used to sit up on the bay window—the captain of the Hudson River boat would shine a light up towards the house as a signal the grandfather was aboard and the horses should be hitched in preparation of picking him up at the Marlboro dock

The owner was the great grandfather of Eddie Kramer who lives in Milton—Tom was given the information by Eddie's uncle, Henry, who lived in Kingston

The house was built in the early 1890's—the house is not on the 1890 map but 1/6 of the barn is—the front of the barn has a full cellar

Florence William's father worked on the farm—(she's in nursing home in Highland now)—Florence caught the measles as a young girl and Mrs. Cole took her in to nurse her

Mrs. Bob Cole was the nurse for the first Mrs. Cole—Tom bought the house from Mrs. Cole. Mr. Cole had made his money in the fish market (NYC?) The first Mrs. Cole's father was a banker in NYC therefore she was quite wealthy

Robert Cole was a member of the Presbyterian Church
Owners—Kramer—?—Cole—Polizzi

Notes from tour of the house by Bernadette Polizzi after Historical
Committee Meeting 1/18/95

A spirit?, ghost?, apparition whom the Polizzi's have fondly named
"George" has been seen on numerous occasions. He is a young man
dressed in Edwardian clothes. He is usually seen either going in or out
of the barn. The barn appears to have been a tenant house with a cellar
prior to the building of the main house. "George" seems to be looking
for something. Bernie reports, "We could 'feel' somebody every once in
a while—but not a scary feeling".

Every once in a while there appear to be noises "people talking
and/or music".

These visions have been seen by people one would normally consider
"non-believers" in ghosts.

During the tour of the building we viewed the lovely high ceilings,
the beautiful library doors (2 sets) that glide into the adjacent walls, and
the beautiful woodwork in the home.

*   *   *

SHADY BROOK FARM

(from Happy 200th Birthday to the Town of Marlborough March 7,
1788—March 7, 1988 A Growing Community—newspaper supple-
ment)

Mildred Erceg Markonic "moved to Marlborough at four years old. We
lived down on the Old Post Road, opposite the Meckes' Shady Brook

Farm, in the middle of Buckley's Hill (that was the old Rt 9W at that time.) She went to the Union Free School (located at the present site of the Marlborough Firehouse.) She remembers the boarding house at Shady Brook Farm as a place where there was always activity, "and interesting people..."

Memories of the Boarding House at Shady Brook Farm
By Margaret Meckes Conrow

The summer boarding house that my mother ran at Shady Brook Farm on the Old Post Road in Marlboro from about 1930 to the early 1950's was such an important part of my childhood that when someone told me that the summer months were only a quarter of the year, I found this fact to be completely irreconcilable with my experience. (I believe that at one time we had boarders all the year round, but I only remember one or two when I was very little.) Most of my memories are of the war years. During this time, when I was 6 to 10, the "business," as my parents called it, expanded greatly, so much so that they were able to give most of it up in 1948, when they converted the bedroom cottages to apartments, and took many fewer boarders only in the main house.

The main house had 8 bedrooms for boarders, and cottages had 8 bedrooms apiece—four on each floor. Most rooms were doubles, so we could accommodate nearly 50 people. In the years I remember all rooms were often filled. We also had 3 bungalows—little wooden structures on short stilts, with only screens and shutters instead of windows. These were occupied by the waitresses, or sometimes the boarder's older children. I slept in them often, and recall with pleasure their dampness and the night noises—animals, birds, occasional people taking late night walks, the sound of the brook below the bank, and of course the suddenly rising winds before a thunderstorm, which meant getting up to close the shutters. We used the bathroom on the back of the nearby South Cottage, as did the boarders in the North Cottage, a converted barn that had no bathrooms at one time. The South Cottage was a real house, with a cellar, an attic, and indoor plumbing. All guests shared bathrooms, even in the main house, which had a full bath (with a tub—there were no showers anywhere) and two half baths on the second floor, and a full bath on the third floor. In the main house the family had two rooms and a full bath in a separate wing.

(NB there is more to this—MLM)

       *   *   *

(Off the Record by Liz Plank 2/8/1968)

Mr. & Mrs. James Appler—This charming little house on the Old Highway at Milton still has an old Dutch oven, which, when uncovered by the present owners in the 1940's, had an original crane and one andiron intact. There are home made pegs fastening the house together, many original panes in windows, doors of "honey pine" with some of the original eighteenth century hardware, a tree with its bark intact holding up the ridgepole, and other features that tell the history of the house and its "do-it-yourself" builders. It is thought to have been built by the Jansens, early settlers, and has belonged to Ed Garvey, who bought it from a later Jansen in the 1920's. The Applers bought it from the Garveys in 1946 and love and cherish it.

Pieter Jansen owned this land and more around it in 1718, tax rolls for "New Marlborough" that year show. Perhaps he built this house. It is included in the "old house survey" now in progress, and anyone with additional information on it can notify Mr. or Mrs. Appler, or the Town Historian, Mrs. Plank, her assistant Mrs. George Spagnola, or the official photographer, John Matthews. The County Planning Board and the U. S. Department of the Interior sponsor the survey.

       *   *   *

Jan. 17, 2000
Mr. Glen Clarke
Chairman
Milton Railroad Station Committee
Milton, NY 12547

Dear Glen,

You had asked that I share some of my thoughts about possible uses of the restored Milton Railroad Station. You know I would love to see it used, in part, as a local history museum.

1) Marlborough has over the years lost many of its artifacts due to lack of a suitable place to house them.

    a) the original Bond Patent from Queen Anne 1710 is presently stored at the Senate House in Kingston and can be viewed only after making prior arrangements to see it,

    b) the original town map done by Benjamin Ely in 1793 is stored at the State Archives in Albany (last time I contacted them, they could not find it, but did send me a copy of a copy they had),

    c) diaries from Milton in the 1860s are presently located at the Farmer's Museum in Cooperstown,

    d) Will Plank's memorabilia has found its way to the West Point museum,

    e) the clock from an early store in Milton is at Monroe Village, and

    f) the early church book from the Lattingtown Baptist Church is in New Paltz.

These are but a few of the artifacts from the town that have been found at other sites. If we cannot have the originals because of the need for archival storage, we should at least have reasonable copies for display.

2) A number of residents in the town with artifacts are willing to donate them to the town, but they want to know they will be secure and available. Marlborough's residents on the whole, have been very generous in giving of their treasures.

3) When I started in my position as Town Historian, I was promised a space to display some historical artifacts and documents. The town budget has been hard pressed these past few years and that has not come to pass. Originally I had a file cabinet at the town hall, but that was moved out. Now I have no space other than a mailbox. I do entertain researchers and genealogists at my home, and I don't mind doing so, but it would be better to have a town museum and research center more readily available.

4) The Milton Railroad Station is an ideal building and the site awesome with the possibility of access to the river. The town has no public access to the river at this time and it seems a tragedy that the people should be cut off from this, one of the towns most beautiful assets. The building is virtually untouched from the time it was in service and is a handsome and well constructed facility.

5) Our school children could profit greatly from a place to make class trips that would encourage them to become more interested in and familiar with their community's history. Indeed, as a working museum, it would be most advantageous to all concerned to have students help in the functioning of the museum.

6) Marlborough has a rich historical past, a viable present and the possibility of a thriving future. We need to be able to share our historical

and agricultural traditions with others. Other towns, much smaller and with a shorter recorded history (i.e. the midwest) have local historical museums and the pride that people have in their communities is reflected in the fine museums they have to show visitors and tourists. Marlborough can do no less.

*   *   *

COFFEE ANYONE?

If you went to the Marlborough Schools in the 40's and 50's you can't forget this old treasure. It was situated where Amodeo's gas station is now.

At one time the Lyons' Diner and at a later date Jim Woodward ran it.

BITS AND PIECES

Southern Ulster Pioneer
108 Vineyard Ave.
Highland, N. Y. 12528
Fax 691-8601
Attention Judy Rappa

News Release

Catching the spirit of cleaning up and beautifying the town, Pam Kelly from the Raccoon Saloon recently contacted the Town Historian. Pam, pleased with the attractiveness that the flower barrels placed by the Marlborough Historical Society have added to the town, offered to pay to have the railing on the corner of 9W and Western Avenue painted if someone would pay for the paint. Seems no one, town, county or local businesses "claimed" the railing as belonging to them. The result has been that for a good number of years, the railing has rusted and been an eyesore.

Robert Kronner, owner of the Marlboro Hardware store was prompt in rising to the task. Recently, Toney Calguohoun and Tony Lawrence spent a lovely fall day painting the railing. As a result of these efforts, the whole town has benefited.

*   *   *

Southern Ulster Pioneer
108 Vineyard Ave.
Highland, N. Y. 12528
Fax 691-8601
Attention Judy Rappa

Letters to the Editor

On behalf of the community, the Marlborough Historical Society would like to express our appreciation to the Marlboro-Milton Lions Club for the lovely new Christmas decorations in town. It is recognized the decorations took money, time and talent to set up. They add a very special attractiveness to our community. We encourage other organizations to follow the example the Lions have set. We look forward to enjoying this gift from the Lions for many years.

*   *   *

From Plank

A wheelbarrow factory was started (near the pin factory dock) there in 1844 but burned in 1852. New and larger buildings were constructed near what became the West Shore station in Milton after the founder, Sumner Colman sold to John Newman of Newbury port, Mass., in 1861. The New York Gazatteer published in 1860 says that the plant was turning out 40,000 wheelbarrows a year at that time. The business grew in importance until the factory again burned in 1870. Rebuilt again the factory was operated by Newman & Son until the death of the latter in 1885 when H. H. Bell & Sons bought the property and operated a plush factory there.

Bells Had Big Business

Henry H. Bell and two sons. Winslow and Arthur moved to Milton from Long Island in 1880 and started a plush and glove lining plant in the former pin factory. The business prospered and six years later the owners bought the wheelbarrow plant located on the present site of the Milton cold storage and altered it for their use. The sons took over the business which became a stock company, and enlarged the building into a four story structure with 17,000 square feet of floor space. Here eiderdown blankets and woolen cloth were made on a big scale. Employment was provided many local men and women until 1904 when the firm went into bankruptcy.

Building Housed Milton Woolen Mills and Printing Business

The Milton Woolen Mills operated for years afterwards in the building until a new modern factory type plant was built for it in the late 1920's. Here it operated as the Institutional Supply Co.. under the management of Walter McMichael until it, too, gave up the ghost. Altered, the building became the home of the Hudson Valley Press where for 18 years Will Plank published the Marlborough. Milton. Highland. Wallkill and New Paltz papers until the property was sold to Louis Schwartz. a New York magazine publisher, who improved it for use as a larger printing plant and bindery. The building burned in the middle 1950's throwing a large number of employees out of work. The big four-story frame structure used by the Bells was razed to make room for the larger concrete block cold storage.

Few people of the town have ever stopped to consider the importance of the cold storage industry even though we are in the heart of the great fruit growing area. There are at present 35 modern plants in the town, ranging in capacity from 5,000 to 320,000 bushels. This means that there are more plants for the preservation of fruit here than in any township of its size in the United States. In Ulster county there are a total of 94 plants. The county leads the world in this respect. Most of the plants are common storages maintaining a termperature of 32 degrees, but a large number are modified air plants with accommodations for a million bushels of fruit. Other plants are freezers or have much of their space available for this service. So great has been the increase in modified air plants recently in this area it is reported that Ulster county had more last year than all other sections combined.

Although many local fruit growers had storage plants on their farms using ice, salt and sawdust for as far back as the last part of the nineteenth century, it was not until recently that modern cold storage plants came into use on farms. J. M. Hepworth was the pioneer in this field, having built the original plant in 1924. J. Walter Clarke followed with his plant in 1925 and Westervelt Clarke opened his in 1926. Velies built their plant in 1927 and the Milton Cold Storage completed its big commercial plant in 1928.

*   *   *

MARLBOROUGH HOSE CO.

(NB think the following was taken from a pamphlet put out by the Hose Company as part of their celebration)

Marlborough Hose Co. Active About 65 Years

The Marlborough Hose Company, which for nearly three quarters of a century has been one of the most useful and active organizations in the town, has repeatedly demonstrated its zeal in the protection of property. It is now larger, better equipped and a greater asset to our community than ever. Hundreds of conflagrations which might have caused untold damage have been quelled by the firemen in the long history of the company.

Some of the worst fires which have been combated by the local 'vamps" include that of the Whitney Basket Factory in 1898, the blaze which destroyed the Methodist church in 1913, the fire in the three-story Carpenter Block in 1925, the Main Street fire which destroyed business houses, and that of the Drago market and adjacent buildings more recently. Another fire in buildings adjoining the last named is remembered by older firemen. It was in 1896 or '97 when the Exchange Hotel property then owned by Dory Kniffin caught fire in early evening and for most of the night threatened the rest of the village. Local firemen did all they could with the limited equipment they had but feared the worst and called Newburgh for help. A fire engine was sent here by rail, loaded on a flatcar, taken off at the depot and rushed to the scene of the blaze which was quenched by combined effort.

The fire which consumed the Methodist church was one of the most spectacular known here. The frame structure had a high steeple and the burning shingles and embers were carried high in the air for a great distance. Not only was the steeple of the nearby Presbyterian church set afire and destroyed, but roofs of houses on Main Street caught fire.

By an odd coincidence the new LaFrance pumper ordered for the fire company arrived here just a few hours before the bad fire in the Carpenter block started early Christmas morning in 1925. It was used to excellent advantage in quelling the blaze. which was discovered, unfortunately, too late to save Mrs. Lisa Coutant from suffocating from the smoke.

The original hose company dates back to the nineties. It was incorporated in 1897, Apparently no records have been kept of the early days of the organization but it is remembered that Alonso Kniffin was fire chief for years. J. C. and Elting Merritt. John Kramer, Ed Covert, LeGrand Haviland, Elbert Berean. Joe Greaves were officers and older members in addition to D. S. Hutchins, Pat Gallagher, Ralph Young and Edward Wyms. The later was treasurer for years.

In 1908 Frank Horton was president; Will McConnell, first vice president; Theodore Covert, second; Bert Clark, recording secretary; George Suiter, financial secretary; E. B. Dexter, treasurer; and

M.V.B.Morgan,Jr., foreman. M. McMullen. Jr was first and Win. Brown, second assistant foreman.

A picture of be old hose company's quarters in the building opposite the hardware store on Main street taken in 1900, shows the old hand-drawn hose cart with its 150 feet or more of hose at the entrance, ready for a quick run to a fire. Members had recreation rooms adjacent and nearby were the quarters of the Marlborough Athletic Club where boxing matches and other entertainment was offered.

The original hose company had to provide for itself to a large extent. When the boys wanted something more serviceable in the line of fire fighting equipment they raised money by dances and other entertainment. For the purchase of a Ford truck in 1916. Louis Steinbach built a body for it suitable for their needs. It was effective if not the kind of equipment a community like this should have, and served for years.

In 1924 the hose company was reorganized. With the formation of a fire district with the power to vote money for modern equipment the newly elected commissioners were quick to provide it. The old Ford was used as an auxiliary for the big pumper for years but was sold when a second modern fire truck was added. Public money was provided to build a fine building to take the place of the limited quarters occupied for so long. The firemen took on the task of providing a new flagpole for the village and now additional property has been purchased to make the firehouse more convenient and attractive.

No longer do the firemen have to depend upon someone dashing out to hammer on the old steel rim to spread the fire alarm. For years past we have a modem fire siren to turn the trick, and, just in case said siren might be out of order when needed the most, a second siren has been installed. Both of them have the power to set every dog in the fire district howling like a banshee.

(NB 1997 the Marlboro Hose Company celebrated 100 years of faithful service to the community)

Craig McKinney, Southern Ulster Pioneer

Dear Craig,

Attached find some documents from the original incorporation of the Marlborough Hose Company #1. With the Firemen's Parade coming up this weekend, thought you'd be interested in publishing typed copies of these hundred year old documents.

Incorporation of the Marlborough Hose Company #1

We the undersigned, citizens of the Village of Marlborough, Town of Marlborough, County of Ulster and State of New York, do hereby certify that we have associated together as a corporation pursuant to section 65, of article IV of Chapter 559, of the laws of 1895 of the State of New York for the purpose of extinguishing fires and preventing injury to persons and property by reason of fires in the unincorporated village of Marlborough, Town of Marlborough, Ulster County, New York; that the name of said corporation is "The Marlborough Hose Company No.1 of Marlborough, N. Y.;" that the number of directors of said corporation is ten, and that the following are the names of its directors who will manage its concerns for the first year, to wit: Joseph Greaves, W. J. Staples, John Suitor, E. V. Covert, Moses McMullen, F. W. Vradenburgh, C. E. Westervelt, C. J. Purdy, P. E. Merritt and E. Dayton, all of whom reside in the Village of Marlborough, Town of Marlborough, Ulster County, New York.

                    (signed by the 10 people listed above)

This is to certify that Nathaniel T Kniffin of the Village and Town of Marlborough has been duly elected an active member of Marlborough Hose Company No 1 of Marlborough, N. Y. and is now acting as such.

And I further certify that said Hose Company is duly organized under the laws of the State of New York.

(signed Joseph Greaves, Foreman)
June 12th '97 (1897 that is)

Resolved, that we, the undersigned, town officers of the town of Marlborough constituting the Town Board of said town, do hereby consent to the incorporation of the proposed Hose Company, known as "The Marlborough Hose Company No. 1 of Marlborough, N. Y." in the Village of Marlborough, Town of Marlborough, Ulster County N.Y.

Dated, Marlborough, N. Y. March 3d 1897
(signed)
E. F. Patten, Supervisor
E. E. Berean, Town Clerk
John Rusk Jr., Fred H. Smith, C. S. Northrip, Clarence Bingham—Justices of the Peace

I, the undersigned, one of the Justices of the Supreme Court, in and for the second Judicial Department of the State of New York, do hereby approve of the incorporation of the Hose Company known as "The Marlborough Hose Company No. 1 of Marlborough, N. Y.," in the Village of Marlborough, Ulster County, N. Y., pursuant to section 65 of article IV of Chapter 559 of the Laws of 1895 of the State of New York.

Dated, Poughkeepsie, N. Y. this 15 day of March 1897.
(signed J. F. Barnard, Justice Supreme Court)

To William T Brodhead, Clerk of the County of Ulster:

You will please take notice that the following is an inventory of the property now owned by the Marlborough Hose Company, No. 1 of Marlborough, N. Y. taken this 13th day of January, 1898, pursuant to statute in such case made and provided, and also a list of the officers of said company elected on the 4th day of January, 1898.

Inventory of Property

1 Hose Carriage	valued at		$65.00
700 feet of hose, and 4 nozzles	"	"	225.00
1 Hook & Ladder Truck "	"		310.00
3 Red Lanterns "	"		1.50
1 Roll top desk	"	"	14.00
3 Stoves "	"		25.00
3 Lamps & Chandelier	"	"	10.00
50 feet garden hose "	"		5.00
Lumber bunting & Flags	"	"	25.00
Carpet and Linoleum "	"		47.00
3 doz. chairs "	"		30.00
1 chair "	"		2.50
4 Tables "	"		10.00
1 Ballot box and contents	"	"	3.00
Cash on hand			60.95
Total			$846.95

The following are the officers now in office as dated Jan 4th 1898: Directors—E. Dayton, J. W. Suitor, E. C. Westervelt, F. W. Vradenburgh, C. J. Purdy, W. J. Staples, P. E. Merritt, M. McMullen, Joseph Graves, E. V. Covert

W. J. Staples, President
E. Dayton, 1st Vice President
N. T. Kniffin, 2d Vice President
J. W. Suitor, Secretary
Geo. Suitor, Financial Secretary,
C. A. Hartshorn, Treasurer,

Joseph Greaves, Foreman
C. E. Westervelt, 1st Ass't. Foreman
Geo. A. Badner, 2d Ass't. Foreman

Marlborough Record 1911
Firemen's Annual Meeting

The annual meeting of Marlboro Hose Company was held Tuesday evening. A goodly representation of members were present and the best of feeling prevailed. There was only a little strife for the officers. The following were elected for the ensueing year: President, John Alexander; 1st Vice President, CE Westervelt; 2nd Vice President, Frank McConnell, Jr.; Secretary, DE Berean; Financial Secretary, Geo. Suter; Treasurer, CA Hartshorn; Foreman, JC Merritt; 1st Assistant Forman, Jesse R. Masten; 2nd Assistant Forman, FM Covert.

The report of the treasurer showed that the company is in quite a satisfactory condition. A committee was appointed to procure a pool table to be placed in the company's parlor for use of the members.

In 1923 the stone on the corner of King Street and 9-W was dedicated as a memorial to the World War One veterans. A capsule was buried. In the capsule, the Marlborough Hose Company #1 was recorded thusly:

Marlborough Hose Company No 1
   Walter Raymond, President, 1st Vice President Lester Mackey,
   Foreman Edward McGowan, 1st Asst Foreman John Baxter
   Sixty-five members

Old (but not oldest) Marlborough firehouse
on Western Avenue

*   *   *

Blizzard of '88

As one reads through journals and certain accounting books, especially farmers' journals, one is impressed with the number of people who record the daily weather. These reports never impressed me as being terribly significant, until….until I read in the Hallock Genealogy about the total eclipse of the sun that had happened in 1804. Now, that impressed me! To be able to recapture that experience and the emotions elicited by the natural phenomenon almost 200 years after the event, really had impact for me.

Shortly after the interview of Joe Conroy had been published, Joe called me to tell me he had more stories to tell. Especially eager at the possibility of being published again, he shared more of his remembrances. One that struck a responsive chord, was his telling of the Blizzard of '88. This sat in the back of my mind for quite some time—until one evening there was a bad snow storm...and I joined those who document the weather in hopes that many years later, someone will feel a connection.

Southern Ulster Pioneer
108 Vineyard Ave.
Highland, N. Y. 12528
Fax 691-8601
Attn: Craig McKinney—(Letters to the Editor?) (If you want to use this, I can send it in on a disk with Judy Rappa—let me know—236-7363

Dear Craig,

It's Friday, March 8, 1996. The ground is covered with a soft blanket of snow. It has been snowing steadily for over 24 hours. Haven't ventured out physically, but from the comforts of my home last evening sat at my computer and entered the world of cyberspace. Picked up the following article on the "Blizzard of 1888." Reading it brought back a flood of memories. No, I don't have personal memories of the blizzard, but do have a wonderful set of mental pictures my grandmother painted for me. My grandmother, Louisa (from whence comes the Lou in Mary Lou) Jones was 20 years old at the time of the blizzard, living in New York City and was one of those faithful working girls mentioned in the article. The Blizzard of '88 (1888, that is) is still on record as being one of the most significant in the last few hundred years.

My grandmother told me of the hardships endured during and after the blizzard—they had to use ten horses to pull the trolley cars through the drifts, people tunneled from their front doors to the streets or used second story windows as egress as the snow was so deep in some spots, there were many deaths of people and animals who succumbed to the wrath of the storm, and fire was a dreaded threat to the block after block of tenements. And yes, the firemen, the policemen, the postmen, the merchant were the unsung heroes of the day. There was a special bonding between neighbors and even strangers brought about by the shared hardships endured. People smiled and greeted each other with a warmth unusual even for that period that ushered in the "Gay '90s."

Joe Conroy, in an interview, also reported on stories that had been handed down to him by his father, Thomas. During the storm of '88 in Milton, transportation was also at a standstill. The only indications of roads were the straight lines of trees that bordered them. Farmers, fearful that their animals would freeze or starve, made their ways to their barns by walking atop stone walls. At the conclusion of the storm, neighbor helped neighbor—to dig out wood piles, to clear the path for the doctor, by sharing even non-bountiful larders.

Embedded in these stories is a superb accounting of the American character.

There are personal memories of the "Year of the ice". During that winter (in the 1960's) we had had snow and then a freezing rain. The trees in the orchards were covered with a silky looking ice that shimmered in the sunlight and in the moonlight. Orchard and wood became fairylands. The ground had a heavy covering of ice. Walking was very difficult as there was not a safe spot to plant one's feet. There were a number of falls and broken bones. The weather was sub freezing for quite some time. The ice coating remained on the ground. The world became a giant skating rink. One could ice-skate in parking lots, on lawns, in orchards. Should one not care to skate, it was possible to sit on almost anything and "go for a ride"—beer trays, cafeteria trays, cardboard boxes, tarps all became wonderful sleds. Since the ice was everywhere, there was little friction to stop the sleds, thus they went on for long distances sailing over the ground giving those riding a speedy, bumpy and thoroughly exhilarating ride!

A PERSONAL REPORT ON THE BLIZZARD OF 1888 IN NEW YORK

Cuban hero Jose Marti was a fine writer, a journalist who came to New York in 1880,…Marti was in New York City in mid-March 1888, when the city was paralyzed by a great blizzard and he reported on his observations in print the following day. Since this weekend's great blizzard of '93 occurred on the 105th anniversary of the blizzard '88, I thought some might be interested in Marti's personal observation of New York under the Snow…

Enjoy.   Charlie Bowen

Excerpts from
New York Under the Snow
By Jose Marti

…The first straw hats had made their appearance, and the streets of New York were gay with Easter attire, when, on opening its eyes after the hurricane had spent its force, the city found itself silent, deserted, shrouded, buried under the snow….

At no time in this century has New York experienced a storm like that of March 13….

The streetcars attempted one trip, and the horses plunged and reared, defending themselves with their hoofs from the suffocating storm. The elevated train took on a load of passengers, and ground to a halt half-way through the trip, paralyzed by the snow; after six hours of waiting, the men and women climbed down by ladder…

Families trapped in the roofless houses sought madly and in vain to find a way out through the snow-banked doors. When water hydrants lay buried under five feet of snow, a raging fire broke out, lighting up the snowy landscape like the Northern Lights, and swiftly burned three apartment houses to the ground. The fire wagons arrived! The firemen dug with their hands and found the hydrant.…Although the water they played against the flames was hurled back in their faces in stinging pellets by the fury of the wind, although the tongues of crimson flame leaped higher than the cross on the church steeple, although the wind-tossed columns of smoke bearing golden sparks singed their beards, there, without giving an inch, the firemen fought the fire with the snow at their breasts, brought it under control, and vanquished it. And then, with their arms, they opened a path for the engine through the snow.

Without milk, without coal, without mail, without newspapers, without streetcars, without telephone, without telegraph, the city arose today.…

In the hour of stress, the virtues that work heightens completely overshadowed those which selfishness withers.…Those who unfeelingly push and jostle one another all the rest of the year, smile on each other today, tell of the dangers they escaped, exchanged addresses, and walk along with new friends. The squares are mountains of snow, over which the icy lacework clinging like filigree to the branches of the trees glitters in the morning sun.

The city digs out, buries its dead, and with men, horses, and machines all working together, clears away the snow with streams of boiling water, with shovels, plows and bonfires. But one is touched by a sense of great humility and a sudden rush of kindness, as though the dread hand had touched the shoulders of all men.

*   *   *

A HITCHING POST IS A HITCHING POST IS A HITCHING POST

Several months ago LeRoy Christopherson after hitch hiking to a town board meeting, reminded the Marlborough Town Board of the need to repair the HITCHING POST that stands in the center of the village of Marlboro—towered over by the flagpole and with the village water trough as a backdrop. Apparently the hitching post had been sheared off at the base during the snow removal processes last winter. LeRoy implored that the hitching post be repaired as, being a concerned citizen, he did not want to see it lost to the town.

LeRoy thinks he knows the last time the hitching post was ever used for its intended purpose—to hold the reins of a "parked" horse. He remembers seeing the horse of Walter Walker tied there. Walker was a local character—also known as "one ear". That's a whole 'nother story (check with Paul Faurie). Walker worked at Shantz's mill in Marlboro and lived at the top of Mt. Zion Road.

We were Walker's nearest neighbors and I recall how my mother, Freda Hennekens, was so impressed with the courtesy displayed by Walker. Each night as he passed our house, in his horse-drawn wagon, he would tip his hat in greeting.

Seems he was sweeping up the floors at Shantz's mill after the day's work and was bringing the sweepings home with him where he used it to make "home-brew". Little did we know, until the Troopers raided the place, that he was selling this home-brew throughout the community.

On a much smaller scale, but with similarities to our recent marijuana growing.

It is not known whether or not Jeff "Booney" Baxter used it when he was driving his mule and wagon around town.

According to Joe McCourt, there were several hitching posts in town at one time. Farmers taking their produce down to the docks for shipment, and in some cases picking up the manure brought up from New York City when that city still had police horses, needed a break for their horses after the long haul from the river. It is believed the hitching post that still exists came from in front of Bart Kniffen's and later Deed Badner's meat market. The post is made of stone with a hole at the top through which the driver could tie the horse's reins.

Known users were a black haired woman who lived in the Marlboro Mountains and drove a one seat surrey and "Old Lady" Miller—an elderly gent who worked on the Baker farm on Mt. Zion.

Town legend has it the local farmers got together and decided to put in a watering trough. Each farmer brought a field stone from his farm for inclusion in the trough.

This in color is very attractive

In the picture notice how lovely the watering trough looks. It was Memorial Day Week-end, we were due to have the parade that day, when one spotted Kitty Graziosi and her daughter in law, Rosalie, putting the plantings in the trough. Rosalie is the owner of Jesse James Beauty Salon which is right near the trough.

No one had the foresight to recognize there was a need to do this. For many years Jim Graziosi had planted and tended the trough. In his quiet way, he brought floral beauty to the town for all to enjoy while not making a fuss about it. As a result, most townspeople tended to thinks it "just happened". We were unprepared when Jim passed away, to think of how this would be done and who would do it.

We are indeed indebted to LeRoy, to Kitty and to Rosalie for caring enough about their community to do something about it.

*   *   *

OLD HOME WEEK

OLD HOME WEEK A BIG SUCCESS DESPITE RAIN
(Friday, Oct. 6, 1911—Marlborough Record)

Parade Held Saturday Was a Revelation to Visitors and Natives

SUNDAY SERVICE LARGELY ATTENDED

Mile Long Parade, Athletic Events, Afternoon and Evening Entertainments and Band Concerts Help to Make Days Enjoyable

Although the rain of last Friday, which continued throughout the greater portion of the day, made it necessary to postpone the Old Home Week parade until Saturday and to curtail the program some-what, the celebration was a success. At about nine o'clock Friday morning the committee saw that it would be impossible to go on with the day's program, and notice of the postponement was sent or telephoned to the out of town speakers and organizations that were to take part. The Marlborough Hose Company telephoned to Walden in an attempt to stop the Walden Drum Corps from starting for Marlborough, but the message was received too late. They arrived in town on the 9:50 train and spent the day in the hose rooms, where a fine dinner was served at noon. After dinner they rendered several selections and gave a short parade on Western Avenue. The hose company tried to secure music for the parade on Saturday, but none could be had on such short notice and as a consequence the boys were compelled to turn out on Saturday without music.

Late in the afternoon, the rain ceased and Advance Lodge Band got together and gave a concert which livened things up a bit and in the evening another concert was given on McGowan's hotel porch.

Saturday dawned clear and bright. Early in the morning, visitors began arriving and, by the time scheduled for the parade to start, the streets were thronged with people. The formation of the parade was practically the same as published last week, but on account of the postponement, it was not quite as long as was at first planned. The line was about a mile in length and as it moved through the streets of the village visitors and natives alike began to wonder if they really were in Marlborough.

Village officer William Yeaple, in full police uniform, and J. J. Ennist rode at the head of the column. Then came the town officials in William Wardell's automobile; the village officials in C. R. Buckley's handsome car and the village clergy in H. S. Tuthill's car. J. C. Merritt, grand marshall and aides came next followed by a well drilled troop of horsemen under the command of James Frazier, assisted by Chester Gaede, who escorted Harrison Dawes dressed to represent Marlborough. After the horsemen came the parade proper, headed by Advance Lodge Band, in the following order; Uniform Band, K. of P., K. of P. float, school children, Highland Drum Corps, Milton Fire Engine Company,

Marlborough Hose Company, orders and floats representing "The Year of Fruits," carriages, wagons, and decorated automobiles.

On arrival at the park the paraders were formed in a half circle and photographed, and an opportunity was given to inspect the various floats. All of the floats were exceedingly well gotten up. "Blossom Time" the public school float, is deserving of special mention, although all the others were very beautiful and brought forth much favorable comment.

After the paraders had been photographed the afternoon program was given. Some of the speakers who expected to be with us on Friday were unable to come on Saturday but the committee was fortunate in being able to secure good substitutes. Dr. James M. Taylor, president of Vassar College, was the principal speaker. In his boyhood days he lived in Marlborough and his reminiscences of those days were most interesting. Among the other speakers were the Rev. Dr. Leighton Williams and the Rev. J. H. Lincoln of Middle Hope. A scarf drill by eighteen girls drilled by Miss Louise Jackson was another pleasing feature. Alexander Johnston was master of ceremonies.

*　　　*　　　*

AMERICAN LEGION

VIEBY SUTTON POST

Viebey Post Named After Sailor Lost at Sea.

Many Milton men joined the Charles W. Viebey post, 124 which was organized July 19, 1919 and is one of the older posts of the state. It bears the name of Marlborough's first sacrifice in our nation's service. Young Viebey was in the navy, a firemen on the transport Mt. Vernon when it was torpedoed in the English channel in 1918.

More than the required fifteen ex-service men were on hand to become charter members as Walter Betts was elected commander. He served two terms and was succeeded by Alfred Shortt, who, as a member of the 77th Division had been captured on the river Vesle in the summer of '18 and spent the rest of the war in a German prison camp. Shortt, who was killed some years ago when struck by a car in Newburgh, served two terms, He was succeeded by Walter H. Baxter, who served as a corporal in the same division and was commander five years. He was also vice commander of the county organization. The post had around 50 members and was later commanded by Curtis Northrip of Milton, Dr. W. B. Harris, Allen Purdy, Ingham Grimley, Jas. Santaniello and others. After the end of World War II the post received new life from the number of young service men who helped improve and pay for the building that serves as the Legion home. The membership has greatly increased and the post is more active than ever. Since its organization the post has taken over the task of decorating the graves of war dead, as was done for so many years before by the Ketcham Post of the G. A. R. (From Post archives)

Veterans of 4 Wars
W.W.I, W.W.II, Korea, Vietnam

VETERANS' GRAVES

April 20, 1994
These are names from slips of papers found in the town history collection—They are the names of (some of) Veteran's whose graves are decorated at Memorial Day.

River view Cemetery
    Charles W. Vieby
    Warren L. Bigelow
    Edward J. Hulge
    Charles A. Bailey
    James Pembrook
    Victor Baxter
    Abram Masten
    Theodore Simpson
    Charles C. Wygant
    Wilson Wygant
    Charles Wygant
    John Valentine
    Jacob Berean
    Col. Lewis DuBois
    (on back—John Baxter)
Hillside Quakers Cemetery—Milton
    Henry F. Wilkie
    Sidney M. Taber
    (on bottom)
    Alfred Short
Christ Church Cemetery
      Matice
    Mary Berkery
Milton Methodist Cemetery

Isaac F. Williams
Henry B. Growell
Lester W. Davis
Peter V. Purdy
John W. Williams
W. Greatsinger
William H. Roe
George H. Miller
K.E. Dahlgreen
      Perkins
Friends of Progress Cemetery—Milton
Edward Ketcham
John Ketcham
Nehemiah Hallock
Jud Mackey
N. Hallock
Lattintown Cemetery
Thomas Conway
John G. Hectus
Battista Visconti
Dora Lyons (crossed out marked AUX)
Charles E. Ryan
Patrick Pape
Joseph Thoran
Carmen Inbernodo
Patrick Conway
Eugene Colombo
Anthony F. Cutillo
James Wym
John F. Casey
Wilbur Casey
Edward Gaffney

Kenney
Matt McCourt
Todd Conway
Downs
Mike Conroy
Tom Prizzia
Corcoran
Sciortino

Vinnie Russo decorating the graves of the Ketcham Brothers
Friends Cemetery Milton

To The Editor
Southern Ulster Pioneer
108 Vineyard Avenue
P.O. Box 458
Highland, NY 12528
June 6, 1994

Dear Sir,

From the early morning hours on this date many million Americans have been riveted to their t.v.s watching the beautifully touching ceremonies marking "D Day +50". I trust most were impressed as I was, not only by the speeches and activities, but by the sheer beauty of the final resting places of those Americans who gave their lives for liberty on that fateful day 50 years ago today. How difficult to be a casualty for the protection of your country and laid to rest in foreign soil. Yet, much to their credit, and because they recognize the debt owed to those many Americans, the French have done a remarkable job of erecting memorials and maintaining the cemetaries. It is my understanding, flowers were kept in the cemetaries by ordinary French people remembering the sacrifices made.

It was a truly touching experience for me this year as I joined several of the local American Legion members as they placed flags on the graves of their gone comrades. To see men and women, mostly in their 60's and 70's, paying honor to the veterans who have gone before them—from all the wars fought by the United States—helps one appreciate the efforts to remember that have taken place for longer than any of us can remember. The American Legion, in this act, is representing all of the American People in saying "Thank You for your sacrifices".

There are concerns. Not all of the cemetaries are well maintained. In some cases the head stones are fallen, broken, or not existing. At one cemetary, there are graves of Civil War Veterans that cannot be reached because they are on the downhill side which is quite overgrown and almost impossible to get to. Each year the Grim Reaper takes his toll of those remaining veterans willing and able to decorate the graves. Who will pick up the torch when they can no longer carry it?

My intent is not to criticize those who care for the cemetaries. To do a formidable task without financial and physical help is quite impossible. I would hope to raise community awareness so that, as a community, we can chose. We can decide to ignore the conditions of our veteran's gravesites (and many of our founding fathers also), or we can choose to remember our history and pay homage to those whose sacrifices made our liberties possible.

Memorial Day Parade

The American Legion has for many years sponsored the Memorial Day activities to pay honor to those who gave the supreme sacrifice.

An important part of the day is set aside for THE parade. The Milton and Marlboro Hose Companies, Boy Scouts, Girl Scouts, Church groups, Lions Club, local politicians, classes from the Marlborough schools, the Jr. and Sr. High School Bands, community sports groups, antique car affectionados, horse back riders—as well as dignitaries from the town board and the American Legion—all take part. Indeed there are often so many involved, it is difficult to round-up a large audience, though there is always an enthusiastic applause for the steadfast marchers.

Troop 72 Boy Scouts

Ambulance Corp Float

With a sense of humor, with a community spirit, and with immeas-
urable creativity, one of the favorite participants has been Frank

Troncillito. Each year is different, and each year seems better than the last. Thank you Frank.

*   *   *

THE NICKLIN LETTERS

John Nicklin was kind enough to allow me to copy the following letters which were sent from William Nicklin in Marlborough to his parents living in Minnesota.

Marlboro Ulster Co NY
Sunday Sept. 29 (1872)

Dear Father and Mother:

We have waited to hear from you. Nothing having arrived I sit down to pen you a line. I hope you have your arrangements nearly completed for your contemplated trip and all works well with you. I suppose 4 more weeks you will be here. All hands are busy getting ready, cleaning house, drying apples, gathering chestnuts, hickory and other choice things from the woods, 50 quart jars ready put up of fruits, tomatoes cooked and cooking for sauce. Hog getting fat. Nell and Will experimented to fat him quick one afternoon unknown to us—so gave him about 10 gallons of buttermilk then a dose of 1/2 bushel apples and a finisher of about a peck of corn. Well I went to the pen and was surprised as the poor hog was laying down with a belly like a balloon and blowing like a porpoise. I thought him sick, called my wife, she thought him sick to. I thought he might die, felt bad about it. Well Nell and Will came laughting up and said they wanted to see how much he could eat and drink and make him fat quick; they had used up everything, enough to keep him nearly a week—all gone clean, but he is OK again now and making good pork. I have sent off my grapes, got 2 cts per lb. over best price. Westerns selling 3 to 5 cts per lb. I got 8 cts. Sent off 300 lbs just nearly. 2 more seasons can send 2000 to 3000 lbs. My strawberry patches still hold on A1. All hands conceded them to be splendid. I am yet busy weeding and thus save Spring work; wet days I work in the house. I have been lucky in a small way with my bees and hope in a year or two to make them profitable. I am learning fast about them. Shall winter 2 hives for a start. We are fixing house so that it will be tenable for all hands this winter without incurring outlay of cash and give you time to satisfy yourselves of our part of country and modes of fruit growing. Some of my young trees have shown their first fruit and they are lovely. One apple is like a mammoth peach—none like it in the country or any account in agricultural works of it. I have 3 trees—may probably make something on those bye and bye. Will save specimen for you to see—it's lovely, lovely. If you were here now we could give you an occasional small feed of strawberries just picked. Fruit this season is overabundant, best apples $1.25 per barrel in NY—cider 6 cts per gal. When you come if you like, we'll invest in a barrel. My late potatoes, peach blows are ripening and will dig good, I think. So that so far as grub is concerned for winter prospects look favorable. If you have any choice kinds of seeds, bring a few, also Felaver (?) seeds. If you can get mink skins, wolf, otter, beaver, etc. you have a cash market in NY at high prices. Get all you possibly can of them—they are sure to pay you well. But leave heavy farm tools. I think you had better, instead of getting off train at Poughkeepsie, go to next station New Hamburg—7 miles nearer and nearly opposite Marlboro landing on the west side of the river. Ask anyone for the ferryman or mailman, John Harbison, he will row you over. He will tell Millard Bros. Marlboro dock to get your freight and bring over in their boat to Marlboro. Then I can get a horse and haul it up for you. I tell you this in case I should accidently miss you which is unlikely if you name the day you will be on hand here. Don't forget the alteration of place of getting off, the river will surely be open and you get off train some nearer to us. Don't confound Newburgh 7 miles south of us and reached by Erie RR with New Hamburg opposite Marlboro 7 miles below Poughkeepsie on the Hudson River RR. Below is the relative positions on the river. I will close up having to shave, wash etc.

> **Love to both.**
> **Affectionately,**
> **William**

PS Had any frost yet up your way. None here yet but the leaves are leaving the trees. I send you this week's paper S2271—I vote for Greeley- Please send one of yours (Map)

I love how distinctly he pictures his life on a small family farm in Marlboro. The number of fruit is commendable. I am also impressed with how one could get to Marlboro from the railroad on the other side of the river. One tends to forget the barrier the river was to those in earlier days before bridges.

*   *   *

Marlborough Record 1911
Annual Meeting
The annual meeting of the stockholders of the Marlborough Water Works Co. will be held in the village of Marlboro on Tuesday Jan. 29, 1901, at 2 p.m., at the office of E Dayton, secy. Dated Marlboro Jan 4, 1901

A Good Article
Is always to be chosen over something that is not at all satisfactory. We pride ourselves in keeping only standard groceries and giving full measure at prices that are always the lowest.

We have a complete line of all the canned goods, and everything that goes over our counter is with a guarantee that compels customers to recognize our fair dealings.

Give us an opportunity to supply your demands.
Elbert Warren Carpenter's Block   Marlborough NY

Chas. I. Purdy, Undertaker Marlborough, NY. Black and white hearses, also Coach for infants. Prices in accord with goods furnished. Telephone connection in all directions. A few Lots in a prominent cemetery at low rates.

Building Materials, and Lumber. Millard Lumber Co. Marlborough, NY. We keep everything needed to construct a house from a nail to the largest piece of timber. Estimates cheerfully furnished. Our coal is the best, always clean and well screened.

Inventory Sale Big Mark Down in Every Department.

Mens' fleece lined shirts and drawers	$.37 1-2
Mens' all wool red shirts and drawers	.49
Blankets, double blankets	.63
Ladies' Cambric wrappers	.75
Comfortables, comfortables	.89
Boys' (12 years) Ulsters	1.98
Mens' heavy peajackets and vests	3.98

Winter goods must go to make room for Spring stock
Dexter's Popular Dry Goods Store and Mens' Furnisher.
Main Street, Marlborough, NY

*   *   *

FIRST POLICEWOMAN

Daisy Helen Pascale

To my knowledge, the first policewoman in Marlborough was Daisy Pascale. She took her responsibilities seriously and was respected for her commitment to the community.

*   *   *

THE FUGITIVE KIND

How exciting it was in the 1960's when Milton was chosen as the setting for the film version of Tennessee Williams' "Orpheus Descending". The stars were in our eyes as we watched Marlon Brando, Joanne Woodward and Anna Magnani play out their roles. Several members of the community were given the opportunity to appear in the film. We were all pleased that Howard Quimby (and his mule) had "important" roles in "The Fugitive Kind". Each day there was a crowd of people watching the filming fascinated by the transformation given to Main Street in Milton. I suspect most of the town went to see the movie when it was released.

An informal picture
Faces identifiable are Rocky Benevento, Anna Magnani and Jimmy Dirago

*   *   *

From The Marlborough Record 9/8/1933

As We Heard it

Marlborough Girl Scouts will hold their first meeting on September 20.

Cluett Schantz and Olof Sundstrom are on a motor trip in Canada.

Mrs. Cornelius Eckerson's school and kindergarten will not open until October first.

---

350 Bushels of Pears Shipped to London

The last of the Bartletts bought in this section by J. Edward McGowan for export to Europe, were loaded on a liner in New York last Friday night. The last shipment about three hundred and fifty bushels, was sent to London

Bartletts brought here for export were only the finest and largest which could be found on local farms Shipments were made to Liverpool, London and Glasco.

This ends the exports of fruit from this section by Mr. McGowan until later in the season when he will start exporting apples.

*   *   *

Marlboro Country of the Mid-Hudson

By John Matthews

"Tomvac" is the Town of Marlboro Volunteer Ambulance Corps, with a building located on 9W between Marlboro and Milton.

A doctor's office was erected and paid for by popular subscription within the past few years. This is also located on 9W between Milton and Marlboro.

In earlier days of this century, the Rosoffs bought a Haviland property on the river bank just north of Marlboro. They conducted a sand and gravel business for a long time.

The Central Hudson Steamboat, Benjamen B. Odell burned at the dock on this property in the 1930's.

*   *   *

The Marlborough News
Friday December 1, 1922

HARVESTING NEW BEDS

Tucker & Strong, whose great mushroom beds north of town have been yielding exceptionally good during the last "breaks" are now gathering the high priced table delicacy from their new beds, that are coming into bearing for the first time. Although their caverns have been a source of great expense to them until they were able to get them producing, they are now repaying them well for their outlay, and when all of their beds are planted and bearing, as they contemplate having them, they will be veritable caverns of wealth.

*   *   *

BIG CELEBRATIONS

Marlborough does like to celebrate!!! The US Bicentennial in 1976 and Marlborough's own Bicentennial in 1988 were both occasions for extended activities. Parades, plays, balls, sports, picnics, speeches galore had all segments of the community, young and young at heart, involved. There was the printing of the "As We Are, As We Were" picture history of Marlborough.

Spirit of the Times

More to come....

0-595-65509-2

CPSIA information can be obtained at www.ICGtesting.com
Printed in the USA
BVOW020417130712

295087BV00002BB/5/A

$ 33.95